About Island Press

Since 1984, the nonprofit organization Island Press has been stimulating, shaping, and communicating ideas that are essential for solving environmental problems worldwide. With more than 1,000 titles in print and some 30 new releases each year, we are the nation's leading publisher on environmental issues. We identify innovative thinkers and emerging trends in the environmental field. We work with world-renowned experts and authors to develop cross-disciplinary solutions to environmental challenges.

Island Press designs and executes educational campaigns, in conjunction with our authors, to communicate their critical messages in print, in person, and online using the latest technologies, innovative programs, and the media. Our goal is to reach targeted audiences—scientists, policy makers, environmental advocates, urban planners, the media, and concerned citizens—with information that can be used to create the framework for long-term ecological health and human well-being.

Island Press gratefully acknowledges major support from The Bobolink Foundation, Caldera Foundation, The Curtis and Edith Munson Foundation, The Forrest C. and Frances H. Lattner Foundation, The JPB Foundation, The Kresge Foundation, The Summit Charitable Foundation, Inc., and many other generous organizations and individuals.

The opinions expressed in this book are those of the author(s) and do not necessarily reflect the views of our supporters.

The Bird-Friendly City

The Bird-Friendly City

Creating Safe
Urban Habitats

Timothy Beatley

◐ **ISLAND**PRESS | Washington | Covelo

Generous support for the publication of this book was provided by
Margot and John Ernst.

Library of Congress Control Number: 2020936538

All Island Press books are printed on environmentally responsible materials.

Manufactured in the United States of America
10 9 8 7 6 5 4 3 2 1

Keywords: Audubon; Beeliar Wetlands; Boreal forest; Boreal Songbird
Initiative; Burrowing Owl; Catio; Chicago; Chimney Swift; Climate
change; Common Swift; Cornell Lab of Ornithology; eBird;
Fatal Flight Awareness Program; Global Big Day; Habitat loss;
Habitat restoration; Juniper Titmouse; Lights Out; London;
Migratory flyway; New York; Oriental Pied Hornbill; Perth;
Pesticides; Phoenix; Portland; Predation; Rachel Carson;
San Francisco; Singapore; Silent Spring; Swift Conservation;
Toronto; Vancouver; Vulture; Wild At Heart

To Anneke, Carolina, and Jadie

Contents

Preface

Design of *The Bird-Friendly City*

Few aspects of the natural world touch us as deeply as our interactions with birds. Watching birds is therapeutic and entertaining, as birds behave and move and fly in ways that delight and astound us. And for many people in cities, they create daily moments of awe and wonder.

For me, it's the songs of the American Wood Thrush that calm me and make me profoundly happy, embed me in the place I live, and immediately return me to my childhood days of time spent outside exploring and camping in the backyard tent. Research shows that it's not just me who feels this way. Birdsong is therapeutic music to our human ears. Taking advantage of this, a pediatric hospital in the United Kingdom records birdsong and plays it during stressful times for patients, such as right before going into surgery.

Part of what compelled me to work on this book was the realization that birds are the backdrop to my life, as they are to most of our human lives. I had the pleasure and great privilege of growing up in a house surrounded by trees in the middle of a city. There were birds always, and my parents always had bird feeders near the house. My mom especially was a keen lover of birds; whatever I learned in the way of identifying and appreciating birds likely came from her.

I tend to recall places by the birds I experienced in them. I have fond memories of time spent on the coast in North Carolina (where I am said to have walked for the first time) to the Gulf Coast of Florida—places that were always filled with birds. The wondrous frolics of Brown Pelicans, sailing and surfing just inches above the crest of waves and maintaining tight flight formations, mesmerized me.

When I was in my early teens, my dad and I took a momentous trip through Alaska. We began with a boat trip up the inland passageway, and I recall excitedly seeing my very first American Bald Eagle. The species was, at that time in the early 1970s, not doing very well. I kept a careful running tally of the Bald Eagles I saw (a remarkable number) over the course of those several weeks, and I will always associate these majestic birds with the time I spent with my father, exploring a place so exotic to both of us.

My household itself was a flying one. My father was a captain for United Airlines, piloting stretch DC-8's to West Coast cities and Hawaii. My aspiration was always to be a pilot as well, a compelling interest for me from a young age, fueled undoubtedly by pride in what my dad did. I obtained my pilot's license at age seventeen, learning to fly in the family's single-engine Cherokee 140. Even before flying power planes, I cut my flying teeth on gliders (or sailplanes), later earning a commercial sailplane license and for a short time giving glider rides.

Sailplanes offered an experience about as close as possible to being a real bird. And I felt a special kinship with the Turkey Vultures with which I shared the skies of Piedmont Virginia. I marveled at their ability to bank, glide, and circle endlessly and effortlessly, rarely needing to flap their wings. My fondness for Vultures predates my sailplane flying, but we glider enthusiasts had a special fascination with them, and we knew to try to head in their direction and catch the thermals they were using to stay aloft. To me, a soaring Vulture was always the epitome of beauty and grace in action. They seemed to defy physics.

My adult life has also been marked to a large degree by contact with birds. When my wife and family and I lived in Leiden, Netherlands, a dense, ancient city, we spent many happy hours watching the birdlife of the city's canals, including newly hatched Swan families and the Coot, one of our favorite birds. Without the presence of these birds, our experience of this beautiful, historic city would have been much reduced. About a decade later, we found ourselves living in Australia and in turn defining daily life by the birds, quite exotic to us, that we heard and saw. As we moved into a new apartment in the Sydney beach suburb of Coogee, we were greeted on the balcony by a group of cheeky Sulphur-crested Cockatoos, which were interested in who these new occupants were and whether they might be generous with food. We enjoyed those birds and many others in Australia. We later lived in Fremantle, Western Australia, and fondly returned a number of times to be greeted by the magical sounds of Australian Ravens and the flute-like serenades of Magpies. I came to consider these Magpies my friends and co-residents, and I remember interacting with them fondly.

Figure 0-1 Birds deliver an immediate dose of magic and are ever-optimistic companions co-sharing our spaces and lives. Here, a Catbird perches on the author's deck in Charlottesville, Virginia. Photo credit: Tim Beatley

Even on shorter visits to other parts of the world, the result of my long career of research aimed at understanding cities and innovative approaches to managing urbanism, birds have always made remarkable appearances. I treasure my memories of a spectacular Doctor Bird in Kingston, Jamaica, the country's official bird, and a beautiful Long-tailed Hummingbird.

For most of my life I have been aware of the ways that built environments kill or harm birds. For more than thirty years, I have seen the result of bird strikes on the glass facades of the University of Virginia School of Architecture, where I teach. I have transported an injured Snipe to the Wildlife Center of Virginia and recorded other bird fatalities. What to do about preventing these bird strikes has been an ongoing source of discussion over the years. For a time, there were silhouettes on the larger windows, though for some reason they were eventually taken down. I feel guilty for not having done more to push for bird-friendly glass or facade treatments; this book is my small effort to compensate for that failure. But the circumstance of this very educated school is indicative of the challenge of elevating concern for birds where we live and work. We need to overcome a potent mix of complacency and unawareness.

Fast-forward forty years and I find myself rediscovering birds, realizing, really, how important they have always been: a constant and steadying presence in my life, creatures I have always enjoyed and always looked forward to seeing and hearing.

As I researched this book, I began to hope that maybe the tide is turning for birds in cities. I am hopeful that planners and designers are beginning to recognize the need to *include* birds, not just to reduce the negative impacts of the buildings we construct. I hope this book inspires readers to do what they can to actively enhance cities as bird habitat, as essential homes for birds—for our own good and in the interest of birds.

It is encouraging to see cities such as San Francisco take the lead in adopting mandatory bird-safe building standards and to see many other cities, from New York to Chicago, following suit. It's also encouraging to see how we are designing sports facilities, such as Milwaukee's new basketball arena, with bird safety in mind. There is much more to do, many questions to answer about which design and planning strategies will best ensure a city with abundant and healthy populations of birds, but as awareness of the scale of the threats grows, we are beginning to head in the right direction. These are daunting times, though, when many species are in decline and facing a terrible combination of dramatic habitat degradation and loss and the severe effects of a changing climate. There are also many things that lovers of birds must do that involve conservation and change beyond the boundaries of cities. But cities can be a driving force for change, with powerful beneficial impacts.

A few preliminaries about the stories told in the following chapters. First, there are many heroes to thank and exemplary conservation stories to note. Audubon groups in major cities were especially helpful in the writing of this book, including the remarkable bird-committed staffs in Portland, Oregon; San Francisco; New York; Phoenix, Arizona; and Pittsburgh, Pennsylvania. Where possible, I conducted interviews in the cities where these stories unfolded, and in some cases a short documentary film was prepared in the process (with a full-length film to be made from these compelling pieces; in the meantime, the short films can be found at https://www.BiophilicCities.org). Often, however, interviews were conducted by phone, with dates and other details as noted in the endnotes.

Many different species of birds are described and mentioned in the pages to follow. For the most part, I have used popular names for birds and have not provided scientific names, in hope of making the text more readable. I have also capitalized all bird names, a practice that reflects my commitment to the inherent moral worth of all living things.

This book reflects my perspective as an urbanist and urban planner: cities are good, and they can and must be better for birds. We want birds around us; our lives are profoundly enhanced by living near to birds and seeing and hearing them every day, if not every hour.

As we work to keep our planet livable for humans and all other creatures, we need to increasingly view cities as places of nature. Birds fit into this emerging vision of biophilic cities, or *natureful* cities, which seek to maximize connection with the natural world and which put nature at the center of their design and planning. This book will help us expand those efforts and give cities some practical guidance and inspiring examples about how to make cities profoundly more hospitable for birds. The vision of biophilic cities is one of coexistence and of sharing space with other forms of life, especially including birds, and this, I believe, is an ethical imperative in our new model of global urbanism.

Acknowledgments

Many heartfelt thanks to the many individuals and organizations working on behalf of birds around the world.

Thanks especially to those many individuals who spent time hosting site visits or being interviewed for this book, including Robyn Bailey, Nikki Belmonte, Adam Betuel, Roxanne Bogart, Jim Bonner, Justine Bowe, Brian Brisbin, Lena Chan, Greg Clark, Cam Collyer, Charles Daugherty, Chip DeGrace, Kim Dravnieks, Alan Duncan, Susan Elbin, Carl Elefante, Mary Elfner, Katie Fallon, Moe Flannery, Gerrit Gerritsen, Marison Guciano, Lonnie Howard, Ivelin Ivanov, Kate Kelly, Walter Kehm, Daniel Klem, Matthew Knittel, Susan Krajnc, Karen Kraus, Drew Lanham, Nina-Marie Lister, John Marzluff, Edward Mayer, Michael Mesure, Noel Nannup, Peter Newman, Tim Park, Dustin Partridge, Andrew Perry, Judy Pollock, AnMarie Rodgers, John Rowden, Lawrence Rubey, Clark Rushing, Bob Sallinger, Vicki Sando, Carl Schwartz, Paul Spehen, Wong Mun Summ, Rumiyana Surcheva, Ron Sutherland, Deborah Tabart, Doug Tallamy, Adrian Thomas, Laura Thompson, Noreen Weeden, Jeff Wells, Jane Weninger, Nikkie West, Don Wilson, and Cathy Wise.

Thanks especially to Courtney Lix of Island Press for her wonderful editing and her creative ideas about how to organize the content of the book, Annie Byrnes for additional editorial assistance, and the entire Island Press team, whom I've had the pleasure of working with on many books.

During the research and writing of this book, we managed to produce several short films. Special thanks to the organizations and people who helped with the making of these films and, especially, to the talented filmmakers. These include films produced and edited by Antony Cooper, *Burrowing Owls: Building Habitat in Phoenix, AZ*; *Catio Tour, Portland, Oregon*; and *Swift Roost at Chapman Elementary School, Portland, Oregon*. Laura Asherman produced and edited *Making Atlanta a Bird-Friendly City*, which includes the story of the new Swift tower at Piedmont Park. These and other short films can be viewed at the Biophilic Cities website, https://www.BiophilicCities.org.

Chapter 1

The Benefits of Birds in a World Shaped by Humans

To listen to Curlews on a bright, clear April day, with the
fullness of spring still in anticipation, is one of the best
experiences that a lover of birds can have.
—Viscount Grey of Fallodon[1]

B irds are remarkable because of the many benefits they bring
to our world. From their roles as ecological linchpins in ecosystems around the world to the joy felt by a solitary person
watching them hop on the ground near a park bench, there are myriad
reasons to work hard to ensure a safe environment for birds. Fascinating studies reveal the contributions birds make to our emotional well-
being, their ability to boost economies at both local and global scales,
and their ecological importance. There are also compelling ethical
arguments for preventing hazards to birds because of their inherent
worth as living creatures.

Birds and Human Emotions

Our attraction to birds runs deep. The pleasure and joy we feel when
they are around are undeniable, and for many of us their presence is

a key aspect of our innate affiliation with and love of nature and of living systems. This connection is called "biophilia," a love of life and living things. There are many who speak of the power of birds and the importance they play in their lives.

We want and need birdsong in urban areas. Cities are more enjoyable and more livable, and we lead more meaningful lives, when we hear them around us. We see it in the earnest song playing of a Northern Mockingbird, the family antics of Cardinals, the curiosity of an American Crow. I have often believed that the hours spent by Turkey Vultures thermaling in the air—yes, looking and smelling for the next meal—could also be explained in another way: that they are engaged in a joyful activity, biological but also deeply enjoyable to them. And it is certainly something joyful for earthbound humans to watch.

Viscount Grey of Fallodon's 1927 book *The Charm of Birds* is an eloquent treatise on the many reasons we are drawn to birds. There is an entire chapter titled "Joy Flights and Joy Sounds."[2] The sight and sounds of Curlews in spring, to him, suggested "peace, rest, healing, joy, an assurance of happiness past, present and to come."[3]

There is sheer joy and joyfulness in seeing the flights and hearing the sounds of birds, and, just as important, they seem to be engaged in feeling joy as well. "The main purpose served by flight is utilitarian," Grey said, "to enable birds to reach feeding-places, to escape from enemies, to change their climate; but they also use flight to express blissful well-being; by this as well as by song they are gifted beyond all other creatures to convey to the mind of man the existence in Nature of happiness and joy."[4]

Rachel Carson, author of *Silent Spring*, wrote eloquently about the importance of awe and wonder in our lives and of the need to impart this especially to our children as they grow up. From an early age, she wandered the hills of her childhood home in Pennsylvania in search of the wonder of birds and other animals, a love she carried throughout her life. In an early (1956) essay published in the *Woman's Home Companion*, she wrote:

> If I had influence with the good fairy who is supposed to preside over the christening of all children, I should ask that her gift to each child in the world be a sense of wonder so indestructible that

Figure 1-1 Few birds are as wondrous and surprising as Hummingbirds. Here, a Ruby-throated visits a feeder at the author's home. Photo credit: Tim Beatley

it would last throughout life, as an unfailing antidote against the boredom and disenchantments of later years, the sterile preoccupation with things that are artificial, the alienation from the sources of our strength.[5]

In a recent visit to the Cool Spring Nature Preserve, a thirty-two-acre preserve and birding center in West Virginia owned by the Potomac Valley Audubon Society, I spoke with avid birder Nancy Kirschbaum, who told me she has been birding since the age of twelve. "I was a kid who loved animals. You can't see lions in your backyard, but you can see birds in your backyard," she told me. "The rest is history and a lifetime of birding."

In discussing the more recently developed technology that lets us dissect the nuances of birdsong, British sound expert Julian Treasure said, "Over hundreds of thousands of years we've found that when the birds are singing things are safe. It's when they stop you need to be worried."[6]

For the experienced listener there are many unique sounds to hear: the drumming of Woodpeckers and Snipes, the yodeling of Redshanks, the churring of Nightjars.

For me, birdsong has delivered doses of hope and optimism and pleasure. Some of my earliest memories involve birds and listening to their songs and calls. My favorite is the flute-like melody of the Eastern Wood Thrush, a song I look forward to hearing every spring and that immediately takes me back to my childhood in Virginia.

A recent essay in the *New York Times* by a doctor specializing in palliative care makes the point well. Dr. Rachel Clarke, with the United Kingdom's National Health Service, wrote of her experience with patients in hospice care, at the end of their lives, and the "intense solace some patients find in the natural world." She related the words and thoughts of one patient, Diane Finch, who had terminal breast cancer and was grappling with how to preserve herself in the face of death:

> Somehow, when I listened to the song of a blackbird in the garden, I found it incredibly calming. It seemed to allay that fear that everything was going to disappear, to be lost forever, because I thought, "Well, there will be other blackbirds. Their songs will be pretty similar and it will all be fine." And in the same way, there were other people before me with my diagnosis. Other people will have died in the same way I will die. And it's natural. It's a natural progression. Cancer is a part of nature too, and that is something I have to accept, and learn to live and die with.[7]

Clarke related the experience of another patient who wanted to keep the windows open and to "keep on feeling the breeze on my face and listening to that blackbird outside."

Clarke ended her essay by noting the immediacy of nature and the value that it has to patients nearing the end of life. "What dominates my work is not proximity to death but the best bits of living. Nowness is everywhere. Nature provides it."

And birds deliver a powerful dose of the nowness of life. Their energy, animation, and constant purposeful movement embody life itself and vitality itself.

I think it is difficult to overstate the poetic pleasure and joy of seeing or hearing a bird in the course of an otherwise routine day. That we are drawn to the beauty of birds has been demonstrated recently by the way an errant Mandarin Duck has fascinated the entire city of

New York, it seems. Residents and tourists (and lots of media) clamor to Central Park to see him. The remarkable beauty of this creature is undeniable, even if his origin remains unclear.[8] More recently, the arrival of a European Robin in Beijing, China, was met with similar throngs of birders and casual watchers.[9]

There is a beckoning otherness that birds exude—an invitation to take a moment to look around, to enjoy a daring movement or a melodious song, to slow down and to be deeply mindful of time and place.

Birds uplift us in so many ways. They are common kin, co-occupying the spaces of homes and cities, and at the same time impossibly beautiful, exotic, otherwordly. A glimpse of the color of a Cardinal, the screech of a Blue Jay, or the knowing gaze of an American Crow gives us a jolt of energy and optimism and sheer happiness. It is interesting to consider the hidden public health benefits of birds. There are countless moments during a typical day when we experience an uplift from a bird sighting or sound, not to mention the times when individuals intentionally set out to watch and listen to birds. The stress-reducing and mental health benefits of birds in cities are immense and uncounted, though no less real.

Economic Benefits and Ecosystem Values

We value the presence of birds, and we benefit from them in ways that can be translated into the language of economists: they generate extensive consumer surplus for us; we value seeing and hearing them far beyond what little we are asked to pay in the market economy. We know that a house in a leafy neighborhood sells for a much higher price than a similar house in a neighborhood without trees and, thus, without birds and birdsong. The Chimney Swifts that migrate through the Cool Spring Preserve, where I spoke with birder Nancy Kirschbaum, eat a lot of insects, including mosquitoes: each Swift consumes some six thousand insects per day.

A series of essays in the book *Why Birds Matter: Avian Ecological Function and Ecosystem Services*[10] make a strong case for the value of birds beyond our enjoyment in seeing them and hearing them. They perform many important ecological functions, including pollination, seed dispersal, and nutrient cycling. Swifts and Swallows consume a large number of mosquitoes, and in many agricultural areas there are sizable economic benefits associated with control of crop-eating insects.

The ecological benefits of the waste management and community sanitation services provided by Vultures contribute significant economic value. We ignore the ecological functions of birds at our own peril. There has been a dramatic decline in the numbers of Vultures in South Asia, especially in India, where they are despised and have been poisoned with diclofenac, an antibiotic and anti-inflammatory medication used by veterinarians. The result has been a health crisis and a rise in the number of human deaths from rabies—as Vulture populations have declined, feral dog populations have risen, and so, in turn, have the numbers of rabies cases.[11]

For communities and cities, events that take advantage of growing ecotourism and bird-watching can generate sizable amounts of income, employment, and tax revenue.[12] As the Cornell Lab of Ornithology points out, "birding stands out as a powerhouse in the outdoors economy."[13]

A large percentage of the human population enjoys watching birds. According to the 2016 National Survey of Fishing, Hunting, and Wildlife-Associated Recreation, the most recent survey by the US Fish and Wildlife Service, some forty-five million Americans engage in watching birds. The vast majority of this bird-watching happens around the home, according to this survey. This total figure of bird-watchers is a high figure, to be sure, but it actually seems too low.

It is estimated that American consumers spend $1.8 billion on birding equipment (e.g., binoculars and spotting scopes) and $4 billion on bird food. These are just a few of the ways we spend money on birds.

Because They Exist

Jeffrey Gordon, president of the American Birding Association, implores us, in his foreword to the book *Why Birds Matter*, not to lose sight of the intrinsic value of birds, their inherent worth, irrespective of the value humans place on them: "Apart from all these human-assigned, instrumental values, there is the intrinsic value of the [birds]

Figure 1-2 Birds deliver many benefits. Some are economic, such as substantial income and employment generated from bird-watching. Photo credit: Tim Beatley

themselves: sentient, social beings amazingly adapted to some truly challenging conditions."[14]

The fact that these are creatures that evolved millions of years ago from dinosaurs might suggest that they have a special right of existence. We humans are certainly not free to cause extinction of their species or inflict undue harm on their populations and individuals.

I like very much the ideas of the late eco-feminist Val Plumwood, who many years ago advocated for a more agency-based moral theory of animals and nature. The "others," including birds, with whom we co-occupy the planet are not simply extras on a human stage set; they are species and individuals that exert creative agency. Plumwood argued for the need to overcome the sense of separateness and otherness of the natural world, and she encouraged us to see the agency, wisdom, and intelligence of the non-human world.[15]

Birds help us do this to an unusual degree. They are natural ambassadors between the limited sentient world we have defined as human and the large natural world beyond: it is our world as well, we are a part of this community of life, and birds tug at us to join in: to see ourselves, to paraphrase Aldo Leopold, as a plain member of this community of kin. And when we adopt this view of birdsong, it changes our outlook profoundly. It shifts from sound to voice.

Living Poetry in the City

Birds are a living form of poetry.

From Shelley's "To a Skylark" to Keats's "Ode to a Nightingale," birds have found their way into the literary and poetic world. Birds figure in important ways in the poetry of more contemporary writers, such as Mary Oliver, who wrote frequently about the red bird and the remarkable things she would do and her depth of resonance.

In the attention and care we give to the birds around us, in their ability to induce us to break free from narrow self-absorption, birds expand our horizons and help us to see a world we would perhaps otherwise neglect.

We will need all of these arguments—economic, ecological, ethical—on behalf of saving birds. As Jeffrey Gordon put it, "We need as many arrows in our quivers as we can get."[16]

Birds Allow Us All to Be Conservationists: The Key Role of Cities

Cities have historically formed on rivers and shorelines and harbors, places that facilitate commerce and transportation, but these are precisely the places that are essential habitat and migration corridors for birds. Jim Bonner, executive director of the Audubon Society of Western Pennsylvania, told me, "Birds are still coming through urban areas because they were doing it before they were urban areas. Just because we've built a lot of buildings and suburbs around it, that doesn't change their migratory paths."[17]

So cities must play an important part in the future of birds, and, as this book will explain, many cities are beginning to take aggressive steps to make room for birds. Many cities, such as San Francisco, Chicago, New York, and Toronto, Ontario, lie on important bird migration routes, with millions of birds passing through these urban

Figure 1-3 Birds deliver moments of wonder and delight throughout the day. As we watch them soar and fly, we do as well. Photo credit: Tim Beatley

environments. Cities have important opportunities to modify the design of buildings and glass facades, which kill almost a billion birds each year, and to modify and control the lights that confuse and kill. Cities can work to enhance bird habitat in important ways by planting trees and retrofitting rooftops planted with bird-friendly vegetation. Urban residents can take steps to reduce predation by domestic and feral cats, which likely cause the deaths of as many as four billion birds each year in North America alone.

We sometimes (usually) forget that cities are home to many different kinds of birds. A city such as New York contains a variety of different and often essential habitats for birds. Susan Elbin, director of conservation and science for New York City Audubon, spoke to me of the organization's long-term monitoring and research regarding wading birds.[18] The Harbor Herons project monitors long-legged waders on seventeen islands in and around New York Harbor, from Jamaica Bay to the Verrazzano-Narrows Bridge. This busy environment is home to Black-crowned Night-Herons, Great Egrets, Double-crested Cormorants, and Herring Gulls. New York City, perhaps surprisingly to some, is home to 80 percent of the state's population of Black-crowned Night-Herons. There is a small colony of Common Terns on Governors Island (directly across from Lower Manhattan, monitored by a small webcam) and many species of shorebirds, including Sandpipers and more than fifty pairs of nesting Oystercatchers. As New York and many other coastal cities rediscover and begin to celebrate their inherent connection to water, perhaps there will be a rediscovery of the waterbirds with which we share these shorelines and waterways.

It is often a "delicate dance," Elbin told me, working to protect and foster appreciation for birdlife in a bustling city that often has other priorities in mind. She told me about the Gulls she is studying on the roof of the Rikers Island prison, just a few hundred feet from the end of one of the runways at LaGuardia Airport (a population the New York State Department of Health seeks to actively control), and about New Yorkers laying their beach towels a few feet from Piping Plovers. But at the end of the day, there is an understanding that even a megacity such as New York is bird habitat and that the quality of life in such places is enhanced immeasurably when we find ways to accommodate this birdlife. "'Oh my goodness, I never realized!'" is how Elbin described the reactions of New Yorkers when they hear about some of the bird diversity living around them. "Once people realize they're here [the birds, that is], it's like looking at one of those magic eye pictures," she said.[19] It changes their perception of the city and perhaps of their own position in the busy urban tableau.

It is impressive to hear from Elbin how much attention and deference birds are afforded in New York. Many cities over the past couple of decades have developed new programs and efforts to help birds, both terrestrial and aquatic. There has been special and growing appreciation for the ways that urban lights and buildings represent clear dangers to birds living in cities or migrating through cities by the millions.

These new efforts include lights-out programs, in cities such as Chicago and Toronto, designed to reduce the disorientation and mortality of birds during peak migration periods, as well as new bird-friendly design guidelines designed to reduce window and building strikes. Cities including San Francisco and Portland, Oregon, now mandate bird-friendly building facades, and a number of other cities are following suit. The political support for protecting birds seems to be changing in a hopeful way as legislation to enact bird-friendly design requirements has been introduced at state and federal levels, with a real prospect of passage of these measures.

Remarkable organizations are working on behalf of birds. Toronto's Fatal Light Awareness Program (FLAP) is a citizen-led force conducting daily collision monitoring in that city and raising awareness of the urban dangers to birds. Citizens in Phoenix, Arizona, are working to enhance habitat for Burrowing Owls; a developer in the United Kingdom is installing Swift boxes in new homes; and in a neighborhood near Santa Fe, New Mexico, residents are working together to monitor, celebrate, and make room for the threatened Juniper Titmouse.

This is a hopeful book that tells the stories of cities—and the people, organizations, and leaders in these cities—and the powerful work they are engaged in to protect, preserve, and celebrate the birds with which we share our urban spaces.

Chapter 2

Birds in a Changing World

I pray to the birds because they remind me of what I love
rather than what I fear. And at the end of my prayers,
they teach me how to listen.
—Terry Tempest Williams[1]

In 2012, approaching the fiftieth anniversary of the publication of Rachel Carson's monumentally important book *Silent Spring*, a group of us at the University of Virginia School of Architecture had the idea of preparing an exhibit to honor her work. It led to considerable research and writing, and we reached out to the Rachel Carson Council (now called the Rachel Carson Landmark Alliance), which owns the suburban Maryland home where Carson wrote *Silent Spring* over the course of five years.

As I entered the house, the first thing that caught my eye was the beautiful window in the living room looking out to the back garden. Carson worked in every room of the house, but it was in this living room that she did most of her writing. The garden still has hanging bird feeders, and on the day I visited there was abundant birdlife. I could picture Carson there watching the birds, being inspired by them but also motivated by a sense of concern. It was for me a sacred kind of space and an opportunity to feel closer to Carson and her life's work.

Although *Silent Spring* did much to transform people's awareness of threats to birds and other species, many bird species have continued to face growing threats in the decades since it was published. The most shocking recent study of the conditions of birds in North America was published in the journal *Science*.[2] Utilizing data from annual bird surveys, researchers at the Cornell Lab of Ornithology found a remarkable 30 percent reduction in bird numbers—some three billion birds—since 1970. The lead author, Kenneth Rosenberg, called the finding "staggering," and indeed it has been a sharp gut check for many of us who care about and love birds.[3]

The threats and challenges facing birds today might be best appreciated by putting ourselves, if ever so briefly and tenuously, in the body of a migratory bird traveling from its wintering ground to its nesting site, traveling, as we have seen, sometimes thousands of miles. Looking down as that bird travels, we see fewer natural sites for stopover, more roadways and buildings to navigate around, more power lines to avoid. Land relied upon as a place to stop, rest, and refuel the previous year, whether a shoreline wetland or a suburban tree lot, may no longer exist this year.

BirdLife International's most recent "State of the World's Birds" report concluded that 40 percent of the world's ten thousand bird species are in decline.[4] That is a remarkable and disturbing finding, indicative of the multifaceted threats that exist. For example, car-dependent urban sprawl is energy- and carbon-intensive, and it is a significant part of the reasons why our planet is warming. Deforestation, whether in the tropics or the boreal forest, takes habitat away from birds and exacerbates climate change. In essence, these land use changes and consumption patterns are compounding and multiplicative; they are destructive to bird and human habitat alike.

The good news is that the reverse is also true—that steps taken to preserve birds and bird habitat will also have other important positive effects, for instance, sequestering carbon and moderating climate change. From pesticides to deadly glass to urban lighting to domestic cats, there are many important threats faced by birds living in and passing through cities. It is important to understand the scale and diversity

Figure 2-1 Birds today face many hazards, including building facades and glass, which they have difficulty seeing. Estimates suggest that perhaps a billion birds die each year in North America as a result of window strikes. This Golden-crowned Kinglet died after hitting the clear glass of the University of Virginia School of Architecture. Photo credit: Tim Beatley

of these threats, to better understand how to address them. Much of what follows in this book is more detailed exploration of these threats and the many things planners, designers, and others can do to reduce these risks.

Modern cities have evolved, in an era of cheap energy, to love windows, yet birds have difficulty perceiving glass as a barrier. Brightly lit buildings, especially during migration periods, confuse and disorient

Figure 2-2 Groups such as FLAP (Fatal Light Awareness Program) in Toronto send volunteers to find and rescue injured birds during peak migration periods. Here, a FLAP volunteer carefully rescues an injured and traumatized bird. Photo credit: 2018 FC Layton Meaghan Hunryn, FLAP Canada

Figure 2-3 Birds have difficulty seeing windows as barriers, and modern buildings are designed with expanses of glass that reflect clouds and greenery, which disorients passing birds. The skyline of Downtown Atlanta, Georgia, as with many other cities, shows the dominance of glass in building design. Photo credit: Tim Beatley

birds, putting them at risk of fatal building strikes. As many as a billion birds die in North America each year from building strikes, but the tide may be changing, with cities such as Toronto, San Francisco, and most recently New York adopting mandatory bird-safe design standards. Addressing the threat of domestic and feral cats may be harder still, but there are new and creative approaches here as well.

Pesticides and Light

Silent Spring did much to galvanize action for phasing out use of DDT, but myriad other pesticides have been developed, and we are only now discovering their direct and indirect impacts on bird populations. Particularly troubling has been the growing evidence of pesticides' role in the decline of insect populations around the world and the implications for insectivorous bird species, such as the Golden-crowned Kinglet.

A study of flying insect populations in sixty-three protected nature areas in Germany found a shocking 76 percent decline in biomass (rising to 82 percent in summer) between 1989 and 2016.[5] The authors stated that these effects "must have cascading effects across trophic levels and numerous other ecosystem effects." A long-term study of arthropods in Puerto Rico's El Yunque National Forest came to similar dire conclusions, finding that they had declined sixtyfold since 1970, with definite cascading effects on other species such as anole lizards.[6] Causes are unclear, but the authors of the German study speculate that intensification of agriculture and pesticide use are possible explanations.

A more recent survey of evidence and systematic analysis of drivers, authored by Francisco Sánchez-Bayo and Kris A. G. Wyckhuys and published in the journal *Biological Conservation* in 2019, is equally alarming, predicting decline that "may lead to the extinction of 40% of the world's insect species over the next few decades." Four drivers were identified: habitat loss, from conversion of land to agriculture and urbanization; pollution, from use of synthetic pesticides and fertilizers; biological factors such as pathogens and invasive species; and climate change. The authors pointed a special finger at agricultural practices:

Habitat change and pollution are the main drivers of such declines. In particular, the intensification of agriculture over the past six decades stands as the root cause of the problem, and within it the widespread, relentless use of synthetic pesticides is a major driver of insect losses in recent times. Given that these factors apply to all countries in the world, insects are not expected to fare differently in tropical and developing countries. The conclusion is clear: unless we change our ways of producing food, insects as a whole will go down the path of extinction in a few decades.[7]

Some of the insect declines were seen in species occupying specific ecological niches, but many were among generalists and common species. Sánchez-Bayo and Wyckhuys found this especially troubling. And these declines, in flying insects especially, bode ill for birds. Reshaping and reforming our agricultural consumption and production systems is an urgent task that is essential for protection and conservation of birdlife on this planet.

At least some of the loss must be attributable to the rise in the use, beginning in the 1990s, of new classes of chemical insecticides, especially the neonicotinoids, commonly referred to as "neonics." A recent study of toxicity loadings published in the journal *PLoS ONE* concluded that we have witnessed a fundamental shift in the direction of neonics, which are "considerably more toxic to insects and generally persist longer in the environment."[8] Perversely, today many common agricultural seeds are coated with neonics, leaving significant toxic residues in the soil and water. A very high percentage of corn seeds (80 percent or more) are coated with neonics, even though they are not needed. According to the Center for Food Safety, most farmers don't even have the option of buying seeds without the coating.[9] Neonics are also found in the local garden store and in common lawn care products, though it is unlikely that most homeowners understand the toxicity and the damage done.

Increasingly, the crash of flying insects is also understood as an outcome of light pollution and indiscriminate use of outdoor lighting in urban and suburban environments. In a comprehensive review of 150 studies, Avalon C. S. Owens and colleagues concluded that lighting is a significant "driver of insect declines."[10] Lighting interferes with a host of biological functions of insects, including reproduction, predation, and foraging. And it is not just lighting associated with buildings: a

Figure 2-4 Light pollution created by cities and built environments creates both direct and indirect dangers for birds. Exterior lights such as this one are increasingly believed to be a major driver in the loss of flying insects, in turn reducing an important food source for birds. Photo credit: http://www cgpgrey.com

German study estimated losses from vehicle headlights at one hundred billion in just a summer's time.

University of Delaware ecologist Douglas Tallamy, a passionate advocate for native trees and plants, pointed out in a recent interview the importance of taking steps to reduce outside lighting. "You don't have a thriving population of moths for those birds [and the caterpillars that are a key food source for raising bird chicks] when you have the lights on all the time," he told me.[11] We have literally left the lights on for decades. Much of the public understands the problem of no longer being able to see the night sky, but most don't understand the impact on birds. "Not being able to see the stars is one thing, but wiping out our birds is something else."

Challenge of Urban Coexistence

Cars, roads, and driving have huge impacts on biodiversity and urban wildlife in other ways as well, including serious direct impacts on birds, even though we think birds might be able to avoid impacts because most of them can fly. In Florida in recent years, for example, cars have killed or injured many Sandhill Cranes, which are slow-moving and low to the ground. Many species, including Owls and other birds of prey, fall victim to collisions with tractor trailers and automobiles.

Bird deaths that result from vehicle strikes are more serious than often thought. My personal experiences of very nearly colliding with low-flying birds, even on small roads where cars are moving relatively slowly, in combination with seeing the carnage on major highways, convince me that this is a serious threat and a serious design and planning issue. One estimate puts the annual loss of birds in the United States to vehicle collisions at between 89 million and 340 million, but clearly the number is high.[12] Much positive work has emerged on designing roads to allow safe crossing of wildlife, through wildlife passages of various kinds and sizes, but it remains unclear what, if anything, can be done to reduce the threat to birds.

For species such as the Canada Goose, coexistence has been more about managing the perceived nuisances associated with these birds, which were once migratory but have become year-round residents in many communities. Near airports, there are understandable worries about aircraft collisions, sometimes leading to extreme bird control responses that have little tolerance for the presence of birds, even birds that are some distance away from runways and flight paths and are not likely be a danger.

Turkey Vultures roosting in trees in large numbers, often during winter, are viewed negatively by communities, which in turn leads to efforts to disperse them. This has been done by means of sound cannons and even through use of what seem barbarian techniques of killing Vultures and hanging them upside down, which does seem to dissuade other Vultures. However, little damage is done by Vulture roosts. In some places they are viewed positively, and in some communities celebrations are even held! (More on that in chapter 7.)

The proliferation of light in urban and suburban areas represents a challenge of coexistence, but so also is the way we plant and landscape the public spaces in our cities and the private spaces around our urban and suburban homes. Worrisome is the predominant use of non-native plants and trees, many of them considered invasive, that provide little habitat for insects and berries needed by birds to raise their young and to sustain them during migration.

Climate Change: A Threat Like No Other

Few threats to birds are as significant or as serious as climate change. We have already experienced an increase of approximately 1 degree Celsius (1.8 degrees Fahrenheit) in average global temperature since the beginning of the industrial revolution. The summer of 2019 in North America and Europe was the hottest on record (and the period 2015–19 the hottest five-year period on record), with significant negative impacts on all wildlife, including birds, foreshadowing heat-wave events.

The National Audubon Society published in 2014 a groundbreaking study of the likely effects of climate change on North American birds. With changes in habitat projected for several time frames, including to the year 2080, the results are alarming. Of 588 species of birds, more than half (314) are predicted to lose more than half of their current range. As habitat shifts in response to climate change, there is the potential for birds to shift as well and to colonize new areas, but the study identifies 126 species of birds for which range expansion will not be possible.[13] More than half of these North American birds, then, are found to be climate threatened and endangered, even under the scenario of low emissions of greenhouse gases. This is on top of the variety of serious threats these birds already face.

As a case in point, one of the birds I love, the Wood Thrush, is classified as climate threatened and projected to lose, in this study, 82 percent of its current summer range by the year 2080, extending its new range into Canada's boreal forest. Burrowing Owls, another species of special concern to me, will lose 77 percent of their current breeding range, and 67 percent of their winter range will be classified as disturbed by 2080.

The year 2080 seems quite far away, but of course these habitat shifts caused by changing climate are already underway, and they will get worse in the decades ahead. Many bird species will be able to adapt, but many will not. And in places such as my home in Virginia, the mix of species will change, and I will mourn the increasing scarcity of Wood Thrushes and the loss of their flute-like song, which for me is so closely connected to my home place and landscape.

Other modeling studies have come to similar conclusions, including an influential study of the effects of climate change on the boreal forest, again predicting that bird habitats will shrink and shift in serious ways.[14] Jeff Wells of the Boreal Songbird Initiative, which prepared the study, told me about the impact of climate change on the billions of songbirds that depend on that part of the world for at least a part of their life cycle. The boreal forest, that expanse of largely intact northern woodlands, sees as many as three billion nesting birds each year—Wells calls it the nursery for North American songbirds—so it is hard to overstate the importance of this ecosystem. He estimates that the habitat "exports" these billions of birds "as new young hatch and begin migrating to populate their wintering ranges, from southern Canada and the US and south through Mexico, the Caribbean, Central America, and South America."[15]

Wells modeled business-as-usual climate change scenarios to see what would happen to the boreal forest over time, looking specifically at how fifty-three boreal bird species would be affected. His study concluded that this incredibly important boreal biome "could shift northward and shrink in size by an astonishing 25%." By 2040, twenty-one of these species would see a decline in suitable habitat, and the number would rise to twenty-nine species by 2100.[16]

Five years after releasing its groundbreaking climate impacts study, Audubon released, in 2019, an updated and expanded analysis of the climate change threat by looking at the likely impacts of an increase of 3 degrees Celsius (a 5.4-degree increase in Fahrenheit) in global temperatures. The new study, titled "Survival by Degrees,"[17] focused on 604 North American bird species. It came to similar conclusions, but the findings are even more alarming (if that is possible). It concluded that some two-thirds of these species (389) were threatened by climate change.

The popular news coverage of this important report understandably focused on the shocking outcome that in a number of states the official state bird would no longer be a summer visitor.[18] No more Brown Thrashers in Georgia, Common Loons in Minnesota, or Goldfinches in New Jersey, each a state bird that would no longer likely be a summer resident.

There is good news, of course, and there are important conservation stories to tell. Much of the boreal forest remains forested and ecologically intact, for example. But that may not be the case in the future as timber harvesting, mining, and oil and gas development continue to threaten the region. Protection will be essential for these large landscapes, especially the "climate refugia"—those areas that will likely not change much in response to climate change. And as habitat shifts farther north, there will be a need to create movement corridors to allow birds and other species to make use of the new habitat.

As Wells's 2018 report states,

> Canada has a special responsibility to conserve the Boreal Forest in the face of climate change. The boreal is the largest intact forest left on the planet and the nursing grounds for billions of birds that migrate throughout the Western Hemisphere. Ensuring birds thrive in the forest will help preserve biodiversity across vast areas.[19]

The Canadian government has committed to protecting a minimum of 17 percent of the land by 2020, and more protection must happen soon. Wells is encouraged by the efforts of a number of First Nations peoples who are moving forward to develop and propose new protected areas within the boreal. And some positive work is being done to certify forests through the Forest Stewardship Council (FSC) and in this way steer consumer dollars in the direction of protection of songbird habitat. But much more will need to be done, and the first order of business is taking the strongest possible steps to reduce carbon emissions.

As the climate continues to heat up, birds will be affected in many other ways. Heat stress for birds will be a major issue, and already studies are showing sharp reductions in bird species inhabiting places such as the Mojave Desert. Work by Eric Riddell and colleagues from the University of California to retrace earlier bird surveys found a 43 percent decline in bird species over a hundred-year period (something they describe as a "community collapse"), likely the result of heat stress and rising temperatures.[20] As many parts of the world become hotter

Figure 2-5 Birds today face a highly altered human landscape. Birds reliant on coastal habitats confront an increasingly inhospitable shoreline of seawalls and homes and shrinking coastal marshes. This aerial view of the Miami, Florida, oceanfront tells the story well. Photo credit: Tim Beatley

and drier, birds will suffer. The cooling demands for many birds will rise sharply because they will need more water, and will need to consume more insects and seeds, to keep hydrated and cool.[21] A world of more frequent heat waves, droughts, and wildfires will take its toll on birds.

Climate change is also affecting coastal habitats. Ongoing and future sea-level rise is a remarkable threat to the world's coastal nesting birds. Recent evidence from ice sheet melting has led to adjusted estimates of the increased and accelerating global sea-level rise. In a study published in 2019, Jonathan L. Bamber and colleagues concluded there is a high probability that we will experience a global sea-level rise of 2 meters (6.56 feet) by 2100.[22] Many coastal birds will be negatively affected, directly and indirectly. Researchers are finding that species such as the Eurasian Oystercatcher and the Saltmarsh Sparrow (native to the coastal regions of the eastern United States) do not appear to be adapting well to sea-level rise and are literally running out of room to nest, reproduce, and fledge their young as tides and tidal flooding extend ever farther landward. There is increasingly little space between areas of beach and surf and the roads, houses, and other developments that characterize much of the modern coastline. Coastal habitats in many places are changing even in advance of inundation. Saltwater intrusion along the North Carolina coast, for instance, is leading to so-called ghost forests as closed-canopy coastal forests gradually shift to more understory vegetation and, eventually, coastal marshes.

Some bird species will benefit and others will lose habitat, but in the context of highly human-altered coastlines (including the construction of seawalls and other shore-hardening structures), room for birds will diminish.

Some environmental challenges, including climate change, seem beyond the control of individuals and can cause a feeling of paralysis. But actions on behalf of birds offer the possibility that tangible steps can be taken that will make a difference. And there are many things that cities, city planners, designers, architects, and citizens can do to help birds, as we shall see.

Chapter 3

Protecting the Birds around Us
How Cities Such as Portland Are Nurturing Unlikely Alliances of Bird and Cat Lovers

As we sat there, the house finches began to descend,
springing lightly from branch to branch, until they collected at
the seed feeder hanging a few feet from us. The pounding of
their tiny hearts, the nervous flurry of hunger and joy as they
cast their caution aside, was palpable. My son, hypnotized,
inched forward on his seat to meet the birds.
—Kyo Maclear[1]

The birds we see at our feeders and in our yards often seem ubiquitous, a steady flow: we relish what seems an animated, carefree life. Yet each day (each hour and minute) they face dangers, and they are, necessarily, constantly on their guard. Birds, as well as lizards and small mammals, are subject to a remarkable amount of predation by free-roaming cats especially, both those with owners and those that are feral. As loving as they are toward their human owners, their instincts to hunt and kill are not far below the surface. This is another somewhat hidden and remarkably underappreciated threat to birds. Thanks to new tracking technology and use of cat cams, we know that many cats are far-ranging. And birds are at risk everywhere they travel. (It is also important to note that in some parts of the world, notably Brazil and New Zealand, where flightless and land-oriented birds have evolved without the existence of such predators, off-leash domestic dogs also represent a serious threat to birds.)

Yet pet owners are notoriously clueless, it seems, about the extent of the impact of their cats when they are outside the home and the extent of their travels. A New Zealand study called "Cat Tracker" has provided fresh and startling insight into the daily travels and home ranges of domestic cats.[2] In a kind of citizen science project run by Victoria University of Wellington, researchers placed Global Positioning System (GPS) tracking collars on 209 cats. From this they were able to see the cats' daily and weekly travels and to calculate and map their "home ranges." The home ranges varied in size, but many were quite large. The average home range size was 3.28 hectares (more than 11 acres), but because there was quite a spread, the authors determined that a better measure would be median home range, and that was 1.3 hectares (about 4.5 acres). One cat became referred to as SuperCat because she had an astounding home range of 214 hectares, about 529 acres! Many cats clearly had modest home ranges, but many (and the tracking maps show this vividly) were traveling a considerable distance and covering a lot of ground over the course of a typical day.

American researchers Scott R. Loss, Tom Will, and Peter P. Marra put numbers to the extent of cat predation in the United States in a systematic review of data in a 2013 article published in *Nature Communications*. The range of bird mortality per year is unsettling: they estimate that in the continental United States alone, cats are responsible for 1.3 billion to 4 billion bird deaths each year. They conclude, "This magnitude of mortality is far greater than previous estimates of cat predation on wildlife and may exceed all other sources of anthropogenic mortality of US birds and mammals."[3]

Estimated annual deaths of lizards and small mammals are even higher, perhaps exceeding 22 billion. The authors broke out their estimates by "owned" cats and "unowned," or feral, cats and found that the latter have a greater impact than the former.

Many cities try to monitor and manage feral cat colonies through trap-neuter-return (TNR) programs. Loss, Will, and Marra do not believe these programs will work, and there is an active and often emotional debate about this in many parts of the country. The number of urban colonies of feral cats is often much larger than people realize; for example, Loss, Will, and Marra noted that there were currently more than three hundred such colonies in Washington, DC.

For cats that are not feral, both bird and cat advocacy groups recommend keeping them indoors, and they promote the use of "catios," or cat patios. Other options include using "rainbow collars," designed to make cats more visible to birds, and predator-proof fences and preserves such as those effectively used in New Zealand. But it remains a contentious and emotionally fraught topic, one that often seems to pit our love of birds against our love of cats, and without an easy or simple solution.

On the Catio Tour

Catios, or cat patios, are essentially enclosed spaces that permit cats to be partially outdoors while in fact restricting their contact with and, in turn, predation of birds (and keeping the cats safe from cars and other threats). Karen Kraus of the Feral Cat Coalition of Oregon (FCCO) got the idea for catios from a tour of chicken coops in Portland, Oregon. Promoting catios is now a joint undertaking of two local groups that are usually at loggerheads: the Audubon Society of Portland and the FCCO. This alliance of bird lovers and cat lovers, though unusual, is not so surprising, Kraus says. Surveys suggest that people care about both birds and cats, and increasingly there is a need to find creative solutions that merge agendas of conservation and humane treatment of animals.

One of the main ways Portland Audubon and the FCCO promote catios is through an annual Catio Tour presenting various ideas and options for what a catio could look like and how it might be designed and built. The tours have become extremely popular; in 2018 there were ten catios on the tour and attendance was capped at 1,300, with about 200 people on a waiting list. Structures such as the "Taj Meow" added an element of fun to this important issue.

I had the chance to see and experience this event myself and to visit several of the catios and speak with their owners (a short film was made about the Catio Tour).[4] At each catio, I was impressed with the large number of people huddling around the structures, examining

Figure 3-1 The Catio Tour is an annual event co-organized by Portland Audubon and the Feral Cat Coalition of Oregon. One of the main organizers, Karen Kraus, stands in front of a catio on display. Photo credit: Tim Beatley

them closely, and peppering the homeowners with questions about them. Many of the attendees were looking for inspiration and guidance for building their own catios.

The tour was extremely well organized, with sign-in and check-in tables and greeters at each stop and with the homeowners available to explain the designs and answer questions. Volunteers, decked out in distinctive blue Catio Tour T-shirts, manned tables in front of homes. Upon signing in, attendees received a blue wristband identifying them as one of the lucky catio viewers. In some cases they were able to see the proof in the pudding, so to speak, with generally bemused cats actually enjoying their catio spaces.

The structures on display varied greatly in terms of design sophistication and cost. Many were a creative extension to the house—always with some form of tube or walkway giving cats direct access to outdoor areas. Catio owners on the tour were asked to estimate the costs of building their catios, and, impressively, many had been built for just a few hundred dollars (though the cost for some was in the thousands).

The Portland effort has already inspired other cities to follow suit. There are now Catio Tours in Seattle, San Jose, Austin, and Gainesville,

Figure 3-2 A proud homeowner stands in front of her catio, one of ten on the 2018 Catio Tour. Photo credit: Tim Beatley

Figure 3-3 Many catio designs, such as this one, include a tunnel or pathway that allows the cat to move from the inside of a home to the catio outside. Photo credit: Tim Beatley

Florida, Kraus told me. As she says, "It's not really about telling people what to do so much as giving them options and hopefully inspiring people so that fewer cats are free roaming." And it is a double win: good for cats and good for wildlife, especially birds.

Cats, Coyotes, and Birds

In addition to collecting data about how wide-ranging many domestic house cats are, the New Zealand "Cat Tracker" study surveyed cat owners to get a better sense of the scale of cat predation. More than 2,600 respondents answered questions such as how many birds, mammals, and lizards their pets brought home. Owners estimated on average around five "items of prey" each month for their cats. Rodents were the most frequent types of prey caught (76 percent), but birds were a close second (72 percent).

The most telling question in the survey was "Do you believe that hunting by [your cat] is a problem?" The distribution of responses indicated that although cat owners appear to realize their cats are hunting, only 5 percent answered "Yes, hunting is a big problem."[5] One-quarter of respondents said their cat didn't hunt, and another 56 percent said either that hunting was not a problem or that it was a small problem.[6] This survey seems to suggest there is a long way to go in raising awareness and a sense of concern among cat owners that real action is needed to address a huge environmental problem.

But as more research is carried out on urban wildlife, we are putting together a clearer picture of how outdoor cats, and their predation on birds, might be influenced by the presence of other animals, especially coyotes. New research by Stan Gehrt and colleagues at Ohio State University (OSU) shows that where there are populations of urban coyotes, feral or free-roaming cats may reduce their range and, in turn, their impact on birds. Gehrt has radio collared free-roaming cats and found that where coyotes are present, the cats (understandably) keep closer to buildings and to humans.

As Gehrt stated in an OSU press release, "Free-roaming cats are basically partitioning their use of the urban landscape. They're not using the natural areas in cities very much because of the coyote presence there. . . . It reduces the cats' vulnerability to coyotes, but at the same time, it means the coyotes are essentially protecting these natural areas from cat predation."[7]

These findings lead to an interesting and intriguing conclusion that coyotes may serve an ecological function in cities as a kind of bird guardian. It does not mean, of course, that free-roaming cats are not having a major impact on birds. Even in this more guarded situation, in which cats are worried about coyotes and are avoiding natural areas, there will remain lots of opportunities for killing birds; birds will remain throughout the city, including the front yards and backyards of urban and suburban homes. But it does present a wonderful additional reason to not just accept coyotes in cities but also to celebrate them and defend their presence.

The Promise of CatBibs and Rainbow Collars

What other options exist for conscientious cat owners who still want their cat to have unrestricted outdoor time? For ages, people have put bells on collars, but small bells, medium-size ones, even quite large ones (in my experience) don't seem to work. They merely allay cat owners' worries and guilt and create the false impression that birds and other wildlife must hear these sounds (which they apparently don't, unless cats are such expert hunters that they are able to prevent the bells from sounding).

A brightly colored collar cover is a lower-infrastructure option for controlling or reducing the severe impact of cat predation, at least for those free-roaming cats that are not feral but are allowed by their owners to spend some part of the day outside. A Vermont-based company, Birdsbesafe, has invented and sells colorful collars that slip over a standard cat collar. They seem to be effective at alerting birds, as well as lizards, to the presence of a cat. A 2015 study of the collars, undertaken by researchers in Perth, Western Australia, found that cats wearing them brought home nearly half (47 percent) as many birds and lizards as did cats without the collars.[8] This kind of research is, of course, imperfect; the researchers estimated that perhaps only 23 percent of predated animals are seen or found by cat owners. Another part of this

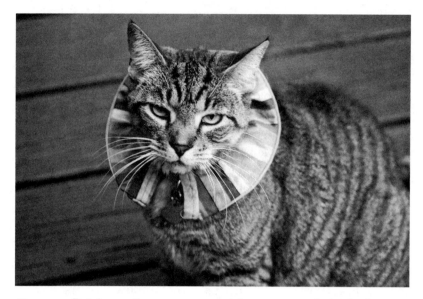

Figure 3-4 Rainbow collars are one potential answer to predation by domestic cats. Photo credit: Tim Beatley

research sought to gauge the feelings of cat owners about the collars. The authors concluded that some 77 percent of owners intended to continue using the collars.

There are other options, though not many. The CatBib has been around longer, and research suggests it is quite effective at foiling cat attacks. Invented in Oregon and now sold by a Portland-based company, Cat Goods, it is a brightly colored bib that hangs loosely from the cat's collar. As the Cat Goods website explains, the bib

> works by gently interfering with the precise timing and coordination a cat needs for successful bird catching. It works by using the simple principle of coming between the cat and the bird just at the last moment. It defeats all the cat's stealth and cunning at exactly the moment it's needed. It doesn't interfere with any of your cat's other activities. The CatBib ONLY affects your cat's ability to catch birds. A cat wearing a CatBib can run, jump, climb trees, eat, sleep, scratch and groom.[9]

Research suggests that bibs are more effective than rainbow collars. In a Murdoch University study, researchers concluded that the bibs prevented predation of birds 81 percent of the time.[10] And the Cat Goods website makes the claim that the bibs have prevented 1.8 million bird deaths since they became available on the market. They have not been universally embraced by the cat-owning community, in part because of the size of the bibs and the sense when first seeing the bibs that they must be uncomfortable for cats and interrupt natural movement (to some degree this is the point, of course). CatBib research suggests that cats become accustomed to wearing the bibs quite quickly.

These products show that there is a market and an opportunity for figuring out how cats hunt and then gently interfering with it. We need greater awareness of these resources and understanding of how effective they are. Perhaps someday such approaches could also be used with feral cats.

The Pitfalls and Controversies of TNR

What to do with abandoned or feral cats is yet another difficult problem, different from ensuring that pet cats that spend some of their time outside wear a CatBib or a rainbow collar. Most American cities harbor hundreds of feral cat colonies, many of them fed and cared for by nearby residents. What to do about feral colonies is a highly emotional topic, but in many cities the technique of trap-neuter-return has emerged as the preferred approach. Here, instead of capturing and perhaps eventually euthanizing cats that fail to be adopted, the TNR approach seeks to reduce the size and number of feral cat colonies through attrition, once the cats have been spayed or neutered and then returned to the colony site. Bird enthusiasts rightly argue that this simply returns the hunting cats back to the field to do further damage. Cat enthusiasts believe this represents the most humane path to reducing colony size and thus reducing the magnitude of the bird and animal predation problem.

There is little doubt that the number of feral cats and cat colonies in cities is high, although estimates are imprecise and vary widely. In Philadelphia, the number of feral cats has been estimated at sixty thousand, but it is very likely much higher. (Chicago estimates around two hundred thousand feral cats.) ACCT Philly (the acronym stands for Animal Care and Control Team) runs a free TNR program allowing residents to trap feral cats, drop them off, and pick them up after they have been spayed or neutered, and it even loans out humane traps.[11] This is typical of TNR approaches.

How effective TNR programs are at reducing cat populations is hotly debated. There is some evidence that such programs can significantly shrink feral cat colonies[12] and, in some cases, eliminate them through attrition, although it might take decades for this to happen. A recent study of two neighborhoods in New York City, for instance, found that after a year, sterilization rates in free-roaming cats had reached an impressive 50 percent, but the authors still concluded this was "considered insufficient to observe any changes in population size."[13] TNR will need to be of much longer duration to make any difference.

In some parts of the world, more draconian actions are being taken. One possible approach being discussed in Australia would be to outright ban outdoor cats. A few localities (and a few developments)[14] have already done this, though it would be politically difficult at a larger scale. It would certainly respond to one critique of TNR—that the life of a feral cat is a difficult and painful one, not one to be accepted or facilitated through programs such as TNR. But enforcing such a law on a broad scale would either overwhelm no-kill animal shelters or require a return to euthanizing large numbers of cats, an increasingly unacceptable option. In Australia, a national plan to control feral cat predation on native fauna has resulted in widespread aerial application of poisons (poison-laced sausages dropped from airplanes) as well as aggressive hunting programs, programs that are also not likely to be acceptable in the United States.

New Zealand has also embarked on a very ambitious bird conservation program aimed at controlling the devastating impact of non-native species, what wildlife biologist Charles Daugherty calls "camp followers": "three species of rats; three species of stoats and weasels; possums, cats, dogs, goats, pigs; I could keep going."[15] They have collectively taken a toll.

Two hundred fifty years after Captain James Cook arrived in New Zealand, most of its native birds (many flightless and thus especially vulnerable to predation) have been decimated. Zealandia, in the capital city of Wellington, has been the face of these efforts to repopulate native bird species. It is a 250-hectare (almost 620-acre) preserve on the edge of the city's downtown and, most importantly, encircled by a predator-proof fence. The fence covers a distance of about nine kilometers (more than five and one-half miles) and is an effective barrier to predators such as weasels but also domestic and feral cats. As a result, native birds have flourished, and the preserve serves as a key point of biological propagation and replenishment for the city as a whole. Zealandia receives some ninety thousand visitors per year and so also serves an important educational function. In the beginning years of this project, there was a clear "halo effect" in the sense that homes and neighborhoods close to the preserve were beginning to see the return of native birds such as the Kaka, a native parrot, to their yards and gardens. Today the program has been so successful, says Tim Park, the city's environmental partnership leader, that the halo really extends to the entire city.[16]

One of the birds that has made a recovery is the Saddleback. As Park tells it, just a couple of years ago the Saddleback was found to have nested in the city for the first time in a hundred years. And as Charles Daugherty says, the rebounding of the Kaka population has been especially impressive. Daugherty notes that today these charming and loud birds can be seen around town, a part of the life of the city once again. "I can promise you people absolutely love that; it's inspirational when you discover that first Kaka in your garden."[17]

Domestic cats and dogs continue to be a major concern (as the opening story in this chapter suggests) and also a major emphasis for the city. When it comes to dogs, the concerns have to do with off-leash dogs, which can kill birds such as young Kiwis. The city's emphasis has been on positive messaging to help pet owners reduce their effects on birds, recognizing, especially in the case of cats, that pets are "loved ones for families," and that has to be taken into account. One new requirement is that all cats must have a microchip. The approach taken by Zealandia, creating predator-free (including cat-free) areas, is a viable tool and has been used in other parts of New Zealand.

Wellington is not resting on its laurels but has been working on a larger scheme to make the city predator-free, part of a countrywide initiative and aspiration, and has developed a strategy to bring this about. A related effort has been Capital Kiwi, with the idea of bringing back the native Kiwi bird to Wellington. Kiwis are, of course, an iconic species, synonymous with New Zealand. There are places in the country where there are healthy populations, but the Kiwi has become locally extinct in the Wellington region. A key part of both efforts has been to ramp up trapping of non-native mammals in public parks and also in private backyards and the spaces around homes. Tim Park has been working to facilitate a community-based network (home-owners putting out traps and monitoring them), which has seen more than 6,500 traps set. Capital Kiwi will extend the trapping to a larger regional scale. Controversy around what to do about cats remains in Wellington, but these efforts are seen as an effective way to control at least the impact of introduced (non-pet) species on native birds.

Given these dilemmas and difficult choices, the story of Portland's catios is a refreshing one. Here, compassion for both birds and cats carries the day and brings together individuals, families, and public officials interested in the lives and welfare of both.

Care and Recovery: Wild Bird Fund and Other Urban Rehabilitators

Predation by cats—indeed, all of the urban and suburban threats discussed in this book—creates an immense need to recover and treat injured birds, something few cities and few organizations in cities are prepared to do. But some wonderful, inspiring examples exist.

Founded by Rita McMahon in 2012, the Wild Bird Fund is the only bird rehabilitation and rescue center in New York City. It has a storefront location on Columbus Avenue on the Upper West Side of Manhattan. Its stated mission is to provide "the necessary medical and rehabilitation services for injured, sick, and orphaned wildlife found in New York City."[18] The organization also has an educational mission that it pursues in several ways, including by organizing a series of bird walks in the city (called Walk on the Wild Side) and by working with New York City public schools. Visits to the clinic are possible, and staff will come to schools to present about birds. Several programs involve longer engagements of schools, including Bird Academy: Jr. Ornithologists, an eight-month program aimed at second to fifth graders.[19]

With a full-time staff of about twenty and some two hundred volunteers, the Wild Bird Fund treats more than four thousand birds each year, with many released back into the wild. At any one time, the facility is likely to be caring for several hundred birds. Organizations similar to the Wild Bird Fund can be found in other cities, such as the Toronto Wildlife Centre and City Wildlife in Washington, DC.

It is an open question whether rehabilitation and rescue centers make a meaningful difference in the large-scale conservation of birds. But it is undeniable that they have important educational value. McMahon is quoted as saying, "What we do for a single bird matters most to the person who brought it in. What we do to change people's attitudes is longer lasting."[20] This is undoubtedly true, but it might also be said that steps to save or treat a bird certainly matter to that bird, and having rescue centers like this one available and investing in them is an important part of what we owe birds and other species that are harmed and killed through no fault of their own. It might also be conjectured that if there were more bird rescue facilities, and this service could be scaled up, the conservation impacts would not be insignificant.

Chapter 4

Returning Home
Inspiring Work from London to Pittsburgh to Make Space for Migrating Swifts

These are the air pilgrims, pilots of air rivers . . .
Sleepers over oceans in the mill of the world's breathing.
—Anne Stevenson[1]

I want to know how to be as undaunted as a migrating bird,
how to sustain the perennial fortitude.
—Kyo Maclear[2]

Birds do truly remarkable things. Like migrating thousands of miles. As wildlife ecologist Caroline Van Hemert recently wrote, the urge for birds to migrate is intensely strong—there is even a word for it, *Zugunruhe*.

For birds, the urge to move cannot be contained. Its pull is so intense that a sandpiper's organs atrophy to accommodate the demands of migration. A caged robin will launch itself northward again and again, hammering against glass walls even if it has no view of the outdoors. There's a scientific term for this: *Zugunruhe*, a German word that means migratory restlessness. There's no mistaking the signs. Wings fluttering, sleeplessness, disruption of normal activities.[3]

We wait expectantly each spring for the return of our Ruby-throated Hummingbirds, and they magically find their way back to our neighborhood. I wait as well to hear the magical flute songs of the Wood Thrush, which this spring (2020) arrived on April 24. These are days to celebrate and remember.

The bird world is full of similar magical feats. The Arctic Tern is the bird species that migrates the farthest, traveling "from the high Arctic to the Antarctic."[4] Several recent studies have utilized small transmitters to document this. One recent study tracked the migrations of birds nesting on the Farne Islands, off the coast of Northumberland, England. These birds travel to Antarctica during the Southern Hemisphere summer, typically stopping over on the west coast of Africa and the east coast of South America on their way, apparently guided in part by wind patterns. One Tern in this study was found to have traveled 96,000 kilometers (about 66,000 miles), a new official record.[5]

Van Hemert noted that the record for a single continuous flight was made by a Bar-tailed Godwit, flying continuously for eight days and covering an astounding 7,000 miles from Alaska to New Zealand. "Unlike the magician's tricks that lose their magic once the screen has been removed, birds continue to amaze us with their physiology, endurance and flat-out grit. Even today when satellites indisputably track birds across computer screens, long-distance migrants show us how extraordinary the ordinary can be."[6]

We are duly amazed by these remarkable feats, and our knowledge about how they do them remains surprisingly limited. We think we know that navigation over such extraordinarily long distances is possible because of the birds' ability to feel and be guided by Earth's electromagnetic field. Only recently have scientists identified a protein in the retina of birds' eyes that helps them detect this electromagnetic field.[7]

Just keeping alive in the harshness of the environments they find themselves in is an accomplishment. That tiny Golden-crowned Kinglet lives on the edge, and it must be smart to battle the elements and to survive. Minneapolis birder Val Cunningham wrote of this bird, like many, as "tiny and tough," able to maintain its internal temperature of 111 degrees Fahrenheit when the outside is 30 below, fueling up, no less, on small insects in the midst of winter![8] They share body heat by huddling together with other Kinglets, "shivering constantly, conserving the heat this generates by fluffing out their feathers."[9]

Refuge for Migrating and Nesting Birds

But a key part of migration is having habitat for shelter and food all along the way. Globally, Swifts illustrate both the challenges and opportunities for cities around the world in offering refuge for migrating birds. In the Americas, Chimney Swifts breed throughout southern Canada and into the southern United States, and they migrate into the Upper Amazon Basin (Peru, Ecuador, Chile, and Brazil) for winter. Vaux's Swifts, their smaller counterpart, breed just south of the Yukon and down into California, and they migrate into Central America for winter. In Europe, Asia, and Africa, they migrate from as far north as the Arctic Circle to lands south of the Sahara as they follow insect populations.

One of the remarkable things about all Swifts is that they have adapted to live within structures created by humans (chimneys). They depend on these artificial spaces for roosting during migration and for nesting and raising young when they arrive. But as building design has changed, they have found themselves with dwindling habitat.

The first thing Edward Mayer, the founder of Swift Conservation, showed me as we sat down at the Wellcome Collection in London to talk about his work were images of a new Swift house he and his organization had helped to design. It is a clever structure, a combination house for Swifts and bat house: an inconspicuous vertical grey pole, wider at the top. It is its inconspicuousness that recommends it—it will fit well into the city's sea of cell towers and grey CCTV platforms. And utilizing it will often be easier than getting the planning permission necessary to install Swift boxes, at least in the older parts of London, where many buildings are listed as historic.

The poles, known as habi-sabi Swift and Bat Columns, have already been installed in several locations in London, and Mayer is hopeful that interest will increase from local councils. They are not inexpensive, with a base price of 6,000 British pounds. There is a great need for more nesting spaces for Swifts, Mayer told me. I would later discover how common a problem this is in many places, including the United States.

"We get a lot of resistance to putting up Swift boxes," for various reasons, he said. One seems to be a sense of fear about sharing spaces of one's home with wildlife.

These and other new homes are needed for the Swifts because the trend has been in the direction of gradual loss of both the natural and built spaces that have served as their nesting sites. In the United Kingdom, Common Swifts (*Apus apus*) are the only native Swift species, and their numbers have been plummeting. Mayer tells me their population has declined by more than 50 percent in the past two decades.

Mayer founded Swift Conservation as a nongovernmental organization in 2002 (it began as London Swifts, but the name was quickly changed to emphasize its broader geographic reach). Mayer was no Swift expert but had taken early retirement from the Tate Gallery, where he was head of facilities and security for many years. His involvement with Swifts came about in an unexpected way, the result of his composing a letter to the editor of the local newspaper to complain about the decline of Swifts on his street and a careless local council project involving a roof replacement at the height of Swift nesting season.

Mayer is such a passionate advocate for Swifts today that it is hard to imagine these birds were not a lifelong interest or love. He and his organization have become a kind of clearinghouse for efforts to design with Swifts in mind. His organization's website serves as an ongoing catalog of projects and activities in London and beyond.

A key problem has indeed been the decline in Swift habitat and the ways, especially following World War II, that new buildings and renovated buildings have become overly sealed and air-conditioned, taking away the eaves and other spaces where Swifts could nest. As an example, Mayer offered his own childhood neighborhood of Gordon Square in London, which was largely flattened by German bombing during the war and later rebuilt in a way that excludes Swifts.

"Most people don't even seem to know they've got them in their houses," he said. And if they do, there seems little appetite for sharing space. "We lack a tolerance for harmless things." Not just harmless, though, I think; it is a missed opportunity to share in their animated lives and to wonder over and be entertained by their antics, chatter, and gravity-defying flying skills.

"Buildings matter," Mayer told me, but so also do the gardens and green spaces around them. He pointed to another insidious and largely unintended change: as a result of London councils shifting toward resident-only parking as a way to reduce the impact of cars, residents have paved their gardens to create new parking spaces that they can rent out. There has been, he believes, a pretty significant loss of greenery and the insects the Swifts need for food.

Mayer worries about the studies showing precipitous declines in flying insects and also the changing patterns of land use and other dangers Common Swifts face during their migration to Africa.

Common Swifts are almost continuously flying, almost 100 percent of the time, Mayer said, during the first three years of their lives. I wonder how they can do that, especially at night. They enter a kind of stupor that allows them to fly and sleep, on a kind of autopilot.

There are plenty of signs that attitudes are changing and that levels of awareness and concern about the plight of Common Swifts is on the rise.

I asked Mayer what actions are most important for Swift Conservation in addressing the declining status of Swifts. Raising awareness is a key, and he has personally given more than 350 public presentations. Encouraging the formation of local Swift groups is another important activity, and there are now some sixty Swift groups around the United Kingdom engaged in a variety of advocacy and conservation work.

The encouraging part of this story is that this is a species that we know how to help, and we can help, through installation of Swift nesting boxes. There is the goal of installing a minimum of 20,000 Swift nesting places each year. This, Mayer told me, is the minimum needed just to replace the nesting spaces lost each year. That might seem like an ambitious, maybe unrealistic, goal, but he says that each year in the United Kingdom, 250,000 to 300,000 new homes are constructed. What if just one in ten of these homes were to come equipped with a Swift box? That would be a significant change. And, as he says, that does not even consider the other kinds of structures that could accommodate Swifts—factories, schools, hospitals, and lots of infrastructure, such as bridges; he mentioned the example of a bridge project in Spain he consulted on that included Swift nesting spaces.

Mayer couldn't say how many Swift boxes and other Swift nests are installed each year or how close they are to meeting this annual goal. But he does believe there has been a significant uptick in installation of nesting spaces in new buildings and development projects. He pointed to examples such as the Great Northern Hotel, the London Zoo, and a church tower in Reading, Berkshire. And he noted that they have succeeded in getting more companies to manufacture and sell such products. They are also actively training architects and planners.

Mayer mentioned one company, Manthorpe Building Products, that developed a special plastic Swift brick that can be easily inserted by bricklayers. It was designed in collaboration with the Royal Society for the Protection of Birds (RSPB) and Barratt Homes.[10] Barratt installed nine hundred of them in a new housing project called Kingsbrook, in Buckinghamshire, recently described as "Britain's most wildlife-friendly housing development." There is an emphasis there on designing in more holistic habitat for birds, bats, and hedgehogs and lots of green corridors, wetlands, and hedges. Some new residents of this 2,500-home development were already attracted to it by its emphasis on wildlife. A representative of Barratt Homes commented, "One woman told us she had moved in specifically because the house was designed to attract swifts."[11]

For Mayer, this is one of the biggest challenges and one of the most important things to work on: getting folks to welcome wildlife and birds back to their homes and their neighborhoods. This is about creating quality of life and moving away from "grey, miserable concrete areas." What kind of place does he imagine? "Millions of swifts screaming around, with a few bats as well."[12]

I had the chance to visit the Kingsbrook development in June 2019 to see firsthand the progress made to include Swifts and other wildlife. I was able to walk about, get the sense of this new approach to bird- and wildlife-friendly building, and sit down and discuss its design with key staff from the RSPB.[13] The development's spatial form is very much reminiscent of a compact, walkable country village, though not a far walk from the larger historic city of Aylesbury.

The key bird-friendly design feature is the inclusion of some nine

Figure 4-1 A specially designed Swift box allows builders to quickly and easily insert Swift habitats into their buildings. Photo credit: Tim Beatley

hundred Swift boxes, installed on the sides of many, but not all, of the homes. As many as six Swift boxes can be found on some walls, and as the RSPB's Adrian Thomas explained, it is the ecology "that drives the clustering of the boxes because the Common Swift like to be in a semi-colonial setting." Flight heights and aspect were also considered in deciding which walls to install the boxes on, as well as some home construction issues; some of the homes had loft units that made installing the bricks more difficult. All told, this high number of boxes is biologically significant, said Thomas. The boxes can also accommodate other birds, especially the House Sparrow, which in the United Kingdom has experienced a precipitous decline. There are also House Martin cups installed along eves, and there is an emphasis on bird-friendly gardens. Barratt has committed to planting a fruit tree in at least one in every four gardens, which will also provide food and habitat.

Birds are not the only species taken into account. In designing the overall layout of the community, priority has been given to ensuring generous green corridors for the movement of various animals, including hedgehogs. The backyard gardens feature "hedgehog highways," essentially openings between fences that permit hedgehogs to move between and through the gardens. Full buildout of this project will likely take some fifteen years. One of the most impressive things will be the amount of green space protected: some 60 percent of the larger development site will be set aside as protected green space, and much of that will be subject to habitat construction and restoration. Natural stormwater features will provide habitat, and native hedges and wildflower meadows will be planted. The goal is to be "net positive" for biodiversity, though what this means in practice is still a little unclear. Extensive predevelopment surveys of birds, bats, and other animals should help provide baseline numbers for answering this question. Only a small amount of this can be seen in the first stage of the project, but the overall plans seem to suggest a considerable improvement in the biodiversity of the larger site.

Especially encouraging is the way this bird- and habitat-friendly approach is being received by Barratt Homes, the largest home builder in the United Kingdom, and housing purchasers. The RSPB's Adrian Thomas and Paul Stephen explained that ahead of the project, the RSPB commissioned a marketing study to get a sense of how prospective buyers would see the wildlife dimensions. They were pleasantly surprised to find that a "huge majority" of respondents were attracted to the idea. And the faster than usual production and sale of homes, three hundred per year, seems to speak to this interest. Some potential buyers, as mentioned, have specifically come to Barratt wanting these Swift boxes and other wildlife features. As Thomas told me, wildlife- and bird-friendliness goes over well with prospective homeowners because of the green spaces and green qualities of the neighborhood, a win-win in his mind. Quality of life for homeowners can be enhanced at the same that bird and wildlife habitat is enhanced.

A few days earlier, back in London, I had set off for Walthamstow Wetlands, one of the best places to watch Common Swifts and other birds. Now it's a wonderful public park and urban bird preserve, but for several hundred years it was a place of industry, most recently serving as a water supply for much of London. The site of the Thames reservoir is quite large—more than two hundred hectares, some five hundred acres—with ten reservoirs, built between 1863 and 1910. The

Figure 4-2 The wildlife-friendly development of Kingsbrook, near the historic city of Aylesbury in the United Kingdom, includes Swift boxes throughout. Photo credit: Tim Beatley

large aboveground basins (there are water reservoirs belowground also) are now managed as wetland and bird habitat, and the historic brick buildings have been converted to a visitor center.

On the day I visited, walking from a nearby London Tube station, a "sighting board" told me what birds had been seen and where: "Swifts hawking for insects over Reservoir 4 and East Warwick." Staff had prepared me with information that the Swifts would be flying and feeding pretty high above the reservoir and would thus be harder to see, but they were there indeed and could be easily watched.

The most impressive building on-site is also one that sports a new and very large Swift tower. The so-called Engine House, it originally housed the steam pumps that moved the water. Now it is a café and visitor center. The original chimney of the structure was lost in the 1960s when the facility shifted from coal generation to electricity. Not until 2017 did the chimney get replaced, reconceived as a Swift tower. It is 24 meters (nearly 80 feet) tall, with small Swift openings on each flat side, fifty-four in total. The interior of the tower provides roosting habitat for bats. But the tower has apparently not yet been discovered by the Swifts, and no Swifts have yet taken up residence. So the London Wildlife Trust, which runs the wetlands park, has been broadcasting Swift sounds (heard as well by all the kids and families walking by the tower) to try to attract them.

The reservoir and wetlands are now an interesting blend of nature and industrial heritage. The renovation of the Engine House (with its distinctive "Brown Brindle engineering bricks") has been winning awards, and the new tower has been described as "signalling repair and transformation: repair of civic infrastructure [and] transformation from pollution to ecology."[14] The Engine House is also a place to pick up a map and rent a pair of binoculars. You can also buy your own Swift house in the gift shop.

This bird haven is now a Ramsar Site (a wetland of international significance)[15] and a remarkable resource for the residents of London, just a short trip north from the city center. When I visited, it was full of people jogging, strolling, lounging, and picnicking. In addition to the Swifts, I saw Cormorants, Greylag Geese, Common Terns, and Great Crested Grebes, among many others. The experience of strolling around the reservoirs is remarkably biophilic. The colorful and diverse flora that has pioneered these reservoirs' sloping edges is remarkable to see and enjoy, with a diversity of wildflowers, including foot trefoil, cinquefoil, black knapweed, bindweed, stonecrop, and impressively beautiful common mallow.

A Similar Story with America's Swifts

The challenges facing the Common Swifts of the United Kingdom are challenges equally daunting for migratory Swifts of North America. As people tear down or cap old chimneys, or build new homes without chimneys, the Swifts' habitat is shrinking. But the Vaux's Swifts (*Chaetura vauxi*) that pass through Portland, Oregon, have benefited from some visionary work to protect their mass roosting location at Chapman Elementary School.

As the sun began to set, I headed to the school to watch a bird spectacle that has become a Portland tradition, along with my filmmaker

Figure 4-3 At the Walthamstow Wetlands in London, a seventy-nine-foot Swift tower provides fifty-four nesting sites. This structure replaced the original chimney, which was demolished in the 1960s. Photo credit: Tim Beatley

colleague Antony Cooper. This was an event we wanted to try to capture on film.[16] Every evening in September, migrating Vaux's Swifts take up temporary residence, converging and swirling in unbelievable frenzy and energy and eventually descending down the school chimney. As many as eight thousand roost there each week at its peak.[17] Hundreds of residents arrive to lay out a blanket and enjoy a picnic while waiting for this natural spectacle to begin. Many kids bring cardboard boxes (another tradition) and slide down the steep hill facing the school chimney. It was heartening to see so many people mesmerized by a bird that weighs less than an ounce. We spoke with a number of those sitting and watching—for one couple, it was their eighth season coming to watch the Swifts. Seeing and hearing the Swifts was clearly a significant and meaningful thing for many of the attendees, something beyond just entertaining.

Bob Sallinger, director of conservation for Portland Audubon, met us that evening at Chapman School and explained more of the background. The story is an uplifting one—kids attending the school loved the birds and wanted them kept safe. "For many years the kids would go to school with jackets and sweaters and they would keep the heat off the entire month while this was occurring." With the help of Portland Audubon, funds were found to replace the furnace and also to secure and save the chimney for the Swifts, allowing it to become a permanent roost.

The Swift watching audiences can be quite vocal, and they were that day, as drama often unfolds. On the night of our visit, we filmed a Cooper's Hawk that perched ominously at the opening of the chimney. The crowd immediately booed and later clapped as the Hawk flew away (the Swifts did not seem to notice or be troubled at all by the Hawk's appearance). The evening had a rock concert feeling to it—an impressive reverence for a species other than *Homo sapiens*.

We need to do more cheering for birds (both the Swifts and the Hawk!).

For Bob Sallinger, this is a remarkable story about celebrating the nature in our midst in the cities and suburbs where we live: "It's an incredibly positive thing to see a community come together like this, in the middle of the city, around nature." It is also an important moment of awareness raising and education. More than two hundred species of birds migrate through Portland, Sallinger notes, and the spectacle of Swifts will certainly help in showing what an important role cities can play when it comes to urban wildlife.

Farther east, where I live, Chimney Swifts (*Chaetura pelagica*) are facing similar losses in their habitats. The story of the Swifts at Shepherd University, a small college in Shepherdstown, West Virginia, offers a glimpse into the gradual loss in nesting and roosting habitats for Chimney Swifts and the difficulties in replacing that habitat with artificial structures.

The immediate call to action came as a result of the impending loss of a major Swift roosting chimney on the campus. Sara Cree Hall, which dated to the early 1950s, had a large chimney that served as a major migratory roosting tower for Chimney Swifts. The building was demolished (presumably to make room for a more updated building) and the Swifts lost important habitat. However, the university has been sympathetic to the plight of the Swifts and has been working with the Potomac Valley Audubon Society (PVAS) to fund and build a Swift roosting tower on another part of campus. In the interim, the university has uncapped a smaller chimney on another building it had previously capped as a temporary mitigation measure.

Spearheaded by the PVAS, a design for the tower has been commissioned, and fundraising is underway. But there are obstacles; putting the project out to bid has resulted in some pricey bids, much higher than anticipated, so the project is temporarily on hold (and it seems more fundraising will be necessary).

If the gradual capping of the chimney has been a big part of the problem, is there a chance to engage in a program to uncap chimneys? Does that ever happen, I wondered, and are there examples of local campaigns or city initiatives aimed at this, perhaps even places providing financial or other incentives?

When I spoke with John Rowden of the National Audubon Society, he did not know offhand of such an initiative and wondered aloud how chapters would actually go about advocating for this. The trend to cap, he explained, was often motivated out of a desire to exclude animals such as raccoons, but it would seem very possible to partially uncap chimneys so that they still permit Swifts to come and go but might keep out larger critters.

A

Figure 4-4A, B, C

Residents of Portland, Oregon, come together to watch migrating Vaux's Swifts converge and roost in dramatic fashion at the chimney of Chapman Elementary School. Photo credits: Tim Beatley

B

C

The National Audubon Society has been dedicated to addressing the loss of Swift habitat and has partly funded Swift towers in several American cities. I went to Piedmont Park in Atlanta, Georgia, to see one of the newest of these. Nikki Belmonte, executive director of the Atlanta Audubon Society, explained that the design will serve as both roosting and nesting habitat for Chimney Swifts. The project was a partnership with the Piedmont Park Conservancy. It is a prominent structure, twenty-four feet tall. The city had not approved such a structure before and was concerned that there should be no risk of it falling over. Belmonte explained to me that they had partnered with a local artist to design and place artwork on the exterior. In addition to the tower itself, a native plant garden has been planted around it. They refer to the site as an "exhibitat."

Belmonte sees these towers as low-hanging fruit, important opportunities to engage the public. Atlanta Audubon is a regional organization covering some twenty counties, and she hopes eventually to see a network of Swift towers there. I asked her how many towers were needed. She said she didn't know (no one knows), and the science concerning this is limited. But more towers, many more towers, to compensate for the increasing loss of habitat for Chimney Swifts, seems the correct answer. "As we continue to develop housing, office parks, we're taking down more trees, we're capping chimneys," she said. "In fact, some houses don't have chimneys anymore. Habitat is shrinking."[18]

The Swift tower at Piedmont Park has become a popular stop and staging ground for bird walks. It is a visually distinctive structure, one that calls out for a conversation. And for now, it is the only one of its kind in Atlanta.

Swift Towers to Scale

An even more ambitious effort can be seen in the Pittsburgh area of Pennsylvania, where the Audubon chapter there has spearheaded the construction of not one but a network of some 150 Swift towers, like the Atlanta tower, mostly located on parks.

Jim Bonner, executive director of the Audubon Society of Western Pennsylvania, which has spearheaded this effort, explained how they got into it.[19] His own involvement grew from a personal interest and special connection: he and his wife live in an older Victorian home in a smaller town north of Pittsburgh, and each year Swifts nest in their chimney. They look forward to seeing these Swifts and the others in the neighborhood, as well as the hundreds that roost in the school chimney across the street. The Swift is a "cool bird," he told me. "People in general are fascinated with swifts."

They began working on Swift towers slowly. A fundraising campaign led to a goal of 100 Swift towers, and then a grant from the Pittsburgh Foundation made this a reality. In the end, they erected 7 to 15

Swift towers (used both for nesting and for a small number of roosting Swifts) in each of Allegheny County's nine regional parks, for a total of around 150. Bonner believes this represents the largest concentration of purpose-built Swift towers anywhere.

I asked Bonner if he believed that building this many Swift towers would make a difference; would it bring the effort to a kind of biological scale? He responded that he didn't know and that much more research is needed. They are hoping to have a better sense after they monitor their existing towers to better understand whether and how they are being used. Decline in insects may have an even greater impact on Swift populations, and they were hoping to get a better sense of the Swifts' diets and how they might be changing. Bonner was happy to see that county parks are taking a more natural approach to management, putting in meadows, letting the grass grow taller. These approaches may be important (though again, more research is needed) in enhancing the availability of insect food for the Swifts.

But I find the construction of 150 Swift towers impressive and encouraging. Bonner and his staff have clearly had a major impact in raising awareness and shifting public attitudes locally. He told me about a county commissioner who couldn't stop talking about Swifts, which he saw as a good sign. The towers are also being viewed as an opportunity to engage the public, with educational kiosks and scannable bar codes that encourage residents to go online and report on the Swifts they are seeing and hearing.

And they are doing many other things, including working with schools; at least one school has a Swift tower on-site and engages in an effort to involve students in its monitoring. A high school recently hosted a Swift watching event called Swifts Night Out.

Maintaining the open chimneys has become another priority, and they have mapped about two dozen large roosting chimneys in the area. They have been working with businesses to convince them to protect and celebrate these Swift habitats. Bonner told me of one success story. The Church Brew Works is a brewery (with the distinctive motto "And on the 8th day God created beer") operating in a former Catholic church. The brewery had Swifts in its chimney, and Bonner was able to convince the owners to save them. They have organized

Swift Night Out events, bringing residents out to watch the roosting Swifts and to drink beer. Bonner said, "They're looking at that now [the arrival of Swifts every fall] as an asset rather than a liability."

They have also reached out to chimney sweeps, who are often responsible for convincing homeowners they need to install spark arresters or chimney caps, which have the effect of excluding Swifts. Might they suggest removable spark arresters, which could be installed before winter and taken out each spring, creating an additional economic opportunity for the sweeps?

Still, there are obstacles. Bonner would like to see more Swift towers in the city, but the regulatory process is cumbersome and lengthy. Fragmentation of local governments in the Pittsburgh area—133 in all—is another impediment. Nevertheless, Pittsburgh is emerging as one of the leading Swift-centric cities (and regions) anywhere and an inspiration to other communities.

It would be hard to find a species of migratory bird more wondrous and intriguing than Swifts, of course. Their behavior is astounding. How is the Common Swift able to spend so many months continuously on the wing? How does the Chimney Swift find and return to the same roosting chimneys each year; how can they be found like needles in an urban and suburban haystack?

Swifts are not doing well, as we have seen, but the work in many places, from Atlanta to Pittsburgh to London, shows how much people in these cities care. And there are clear and tangible beneficial steps that individuals, organizations, and local governments can take: installing Swift boxes, building Swift towers. And, of course, one of the most hopeful things we can do is to congregate in public places, where we can, to marvel and gasp at their miraculous lives and to cheer them on.

Chapter 5

Replacing Habitats Lost

The Story of the Burrowing Owls of Phoenix and Efforts at Urban Relocation

If you ever find yourself on the open rangelands of
the West, be sure to tip your hat to the Burrowing Owl.
You may get a bobbing "howdy" in reply.
—BirdNote[1]

R apid urbanization around the world is another contributor
to habitat loss. In a remarkably short period of time, we have
shifted from a largely rural and agrarian planet to an urban
planet, with more than half of the world's population now living in
cities. Much of this urbanization is happening in the form of urban
sprawl—low-density growth, with an emphasis on automobile mobil-
ity, and a rapid expansion of roads, pavement, and impervious surfaces.

For the Wood Thrush, which depends on mature deciduous forests,
the loss of these habitats has been devastating. I spoke with Clark
Rushing, now a professor at the University of Utah, who has been
modeling the complete full-year life cycle of Wood Thrushes.[2] The
numbers and trajectory for this magnificent bird are not looking good.
There are many reasons for their decline, and habitat loss is a big one,
Rushing told me, but his modeling work indicates that it is a function

of reduced habitat in both breeding grounds and wintering grounds. Both places have seen a sharp decline. Rushing pointed out that near my home in the eastern United States, despite the regreening after colonial settlement, the past several decades have seen a significant decline in mature or older-growth forest, the habitat the bird needs. "A lot of that habitat has been lost over the last couple of decades," he told me.

He pointed to recent forest harvesting and clear-cutting in North Carolina to supply European markets with wood pellets (ironically, to support a form of renewable energy).[3] Already, some fifty thousand acres per year are being cut in North Carolina to satisfy pellet plants, and production (and thus harvesting) is increasing.[4]

And much forest loss has resulted from urbanization. We talked about how much forest had been lost along the Atlanta to Raleigh corridor, especially Interstate 85. "All these cities are growing pretty rapidly," he noted.

Rushing believes it is important to protect and set aside even small forested areas in and near cities, though the smaller these forest patches are, the more vulnerable nesting species such as Wood Thrushes are to parasitism by Brown-headed Cowbirds and predation by cats and other animals. He mentioned the explosion of white-tailed deer populations and the loss of understory in forests (from overbrowsing) in urban locations such as Rock Creek Park in Washington, DC.

Rushing's models indicate that habitat loss on both ends of the Wood Thrushes' migratory cycle is important, but more important, the research finds, are the losses to breeding grounds. It makes for a decidedly complex conservation message: we need to protect local habitat but faraway habitat as well. And the local habitat, especially in and near cities, will require active management.

Understanding of what is going on with the Wood Thrush remains complicated. One challenge, Rushing said, is to move toward more finer-scale analysis, recognizing the great regional variation in how the species is doing. A 2016 paper by Clark Rushing, Thomas Ryder, and Peter Marra published in the *Proceedings of the Royal Society* identified seventeen different geographic subpopulations and five primary wintering areas in Central America. In some areas, Wood Thrushes were doing well; in others, less so.[5]

A recent World Resources Institute report on global urbanization predicted an 80 percent increase in the spatial extent of cities and urbanized areas between 2018 and 2030 (a tripling of land area compared with the baseline year of 2000).[6] The expansion of roads and infrastructure, housing, and urban sprawl means the loss of important habitat for birds.

As the global population increases and consumption in the richest countries accelerates, the impacts on habitat loss and on biodiversity are growing. The United Nations Environment Programme's "Global Resources Outlook 2019" report summarizes well these global resource demands. The report estimates that 90 percent of the biodiversity loss is a result of the flows of resource extraction and processing, which include agriculture and aquaculture, harvesting of forests, mining, and oil and gas extraction: "It is a story of relentless demand, and of unsustainable patterns of industrialization and development. Over the last fifty years, material extraction has tripled, with the rate of extraction accelerating since the year 2000."[7] The authors of this report predict that if historical trends continue, global resource extraction will double by 2060.[8] We will see a likely increase in cropland alone of 21 percent, "as increases in yield would not be sufficient to compensate for the increased demand for food." Significant and continuing global habitat loss for birds and other species is the inevitable result of these high levels of resource extraction.

Resource extraction is already having a serious impact globally on birds, though we do not tend to make connections between our consumption patterns and the plight of birds. In the boreal forests of North America, about one million acres of forest are lost each year, much of it used to produce paper products for the American market. The boreal forest is also the breeding ground, a bird nursery, for billions of the songbirds that Americans love and care about, yet this connection is rarely obvious, and it is rarely a factor in our choice of, say, paper towels or toilet paper.[9]

Shorebirds have experienced a precipitous decline globally as a result of the loss of coastal wetlands and tidal flats. Scott Weidensaul writes compellingly about the land use changes occurring in key migratory zones such as along the coast of the Yellow Sea in China, where mudflats and bird habitats have been taken away through land reclamation and industry. Bird species such as Knots and Godwits, which migrate thousands of miles, depend on these declining areas to fuel and sustain their remarkable journeys, and it is no wonder that many of these shorebirds are witnessing steep declines. Weidensaul wrote, "The loss of safe, resource-rich places to rest, refuel, and winter means that increasing numbers of breeding-age adults simply don't survive the journey, or arrive on the nesting grounds late and in such poor condition that they haven't the time or energy to breed."[10] The news is not all bad, and some shorebird species have managed to adapt to changing conditions and land use patterns, but the prognosis is not good.

Loss of habitat is often accompanied by the creation of serious new dangers for birds, for instance, the dangers of waste pits and chemical ponds from oil, fracking, and mining operations. Many birds are attracted to such waste traps and end up covered in chemical sludge and oil, which kills potentially several million birds or more per year.[11] The burning of flare gas represents another danger to birds. Shifting politics and lax environmental enforcement have further placed birds at risk. The Donald Trump administration has chosen to reinterpret the provisions of the Migratory Bird Treaty to prohibit only intentional killing of birds. The failure to prosecute oil and mining companies, and to seek fines for bird deaths under the treaty, means that there is currently no incentive for companies to take steps (such as placing netting above waste pits) to minimize loss of birds.[12] A failure to prosecute these cases and to seek fines has also resulted in reduced funds for needed wetland and habitat restoration.

Birds are also frequently found to be incompatible with certain urban land uses and in turn are controlled or displaced, for instance, when they are in too close proximity to airports and military bases where there are concerns about plane strikes. Recent examples include decisions in San Antonio, Texas, to disperse a large flock of Cattle Egrets at Elmendorf Lake, viewed as a threat to planes operating out of Joint Base San Antonio.[13]

Urban sprawl and processes of urbanization also represent a serious threat to habitat. I recently visited with several staff members of the Atlanta Audubon Society to discuss birds in that city. It is a city notorious for its spreading low-density growth. Atlanta's motto is "City in a

Forest," and much of that forest canopy remains. But much of it is being lost over time, as new development seems often to proceed mainly by clearing a development site, rather than starting with the existing trees and vegetation and planning and designing to preserve as much of that canopy as possible.

I asked Nikki Belmonte, executive director of Atlanta Audubon, what she worried most about. There are multiple threats, of course, but she said she thinks the biggest challenge is "loss of habitat, and the loss of quality of habitat." Even where there are parks and green spaces, they do not necessarily contain the natural habitat needed for birds. "You see a lot of green here in Atlanta," she said, but it is increasingly not the green needed. "We have a lot of invasive plant species that are taking over our native forest canopies and our native ground covers. And that is changing the whole landscape."[14] Making room for birds in cities should not be hard. Indeed, Phoenix, Arizona, provides an inspiring story about the ways this can happen.

The Burrowing Owls of Phoenix

Sitting at the gate at Phoenix Sky Harbor International Airport, about ready to board an American Airlines flight returning home, I couldn't help but overhear an excited discussion among a group of fairly elderly tourists next to me. They were reliving the past several days of their visit, which had included a visit to the Grand Canyon (and a hair-raising jeep safari ride).

Phoenix is the starting point for many natural adventures, certainly, and there is immense natural beauty not far away in just any direction. But it was an interesting contrast to the experiences I had been having over the previous couple of days, which were decidedly more urban and suburban. I had been spending time learning about and watching Burrowing Owls, not in a faraway national park but living in the city, among the car traffic and highway noise, between the sprawl and suburban tract houses and strip malls. There might well have been an urban safari to visit these wonderful creatures (though to my knowledge there is none currently).

This is the unique story of efforts to relocate and reestablish Burrowing Owls in the Rio Salado Habitat Restoration Area near downtown

Phoenix, Arizona, and in other places around Phoenix, a growing and sprawling metropolitan area. It is a story of how a charismatic Owl might coexist with urban and suburban neighborhoods and how life in this city can be made better by having these Owls around us. I set out to capture a bit of this story on film, which led to a short documentary.[15]

It would be hard to conjure up a more endearing critter than a Burrowing Owl (*Athene cunicularia*). As Cathy Wise, education director for Audubon Arizona, commented to me, residents are surprised by these Owls and find they are quite different from what they expect—they are Owls that are active during the day, they like to live in groups, and they live underground![16]

When you first see one of these small and incredibly charismatic birds, you realize they are like no other Owl. The eyes and near 360-degree turns of the head on this small ground-oriented Owl are impressive. Often standing on a single leg, they are attentive and observant. They are not high flyers at all but swoop close to the ground, alighting on a low tree bough or the ground or on one of the cross-shaped perches placed near the burrows. True to their subterranean homes, they are ground-hugging birds.

A major part of the story in Phoenix is the design of unique artificial burrowing structures and, as more is learned about what the Owls need, how these makeshift designs will need tweaking over time. Burrowing Owls are not endangered in Arizona, but they are a species of concern and a species in decline. How they will do in more urban settings is not clear, but the presence of many artificial burrows will help. Burrowing Owls have been known to cleverly learn from the alarm calls of other species with which they have shared space, notably prairie dogs.[17] Burrowing Owls have also been known to seek human proximity as a way of shielding themselves from a predator.

Artificial burrows are needed to mitigate the loss of natural burrows. Burrowing Owls are remarkably adept at moving in and out of these underground habitats, but they are unable to dig them themselves

---

Figure 5-1A, B (opposite page)

Artificial burrows for Burrowing Owls have been installed in a number of places around Phoenix, Arizona. Highway and road construction projects especially have displaced many of the Owls. Photo credits: Tim Beatley

A

B

(Burrowing Owls in Florida are the only subpopulation able to dig their own burrows, likely a function of the sandy soils there). They have to rely on burrows excavated by other animals—especially prairie dogs in the West, but also ground squirrels and badgers. As the range of these burrowing mammals has dramatically declined over time, habitat for the Owls has declined as well.

About one hundred Burrowing Owls have been relocated to Rio Salado (Salt River). There are five relocation sites, including the 16th Street location that we visited and filmed on that day in 2019. Cathy Wise, with Audubon Arizona, met us on-site, introduced us to some of the volunteers, and explained the tasks for the day. When we arrived at the site, volunteers were already working vigorously. Their job that day was essentially to help update and enhance a series of artificial Burrowing Owl burrows. This event was part of a larger Arizona State University week of service, and the volunteers were staff and students from the university's College of Health Solutions.

At a certain point, the pounding of stakes and other noises of construction were too much and a male Burrowing Owl came out to complain, as he would do several times during the several hours of construction. He would make a circle flight pattern around the group and perch on a stake. His vocalizations were charming, accompanied by an animated up and down move as if to add extra emphasis to what he was saying.

This habitat enhancement work is a collaboration between Audubon Arizona (which runs a visitor center at Rio Salado) and a local nonprofit called Wild At Heart. Wild At Heart has become the organization with the most expertise in relocating Burrowing Owls. It has developed a process that seems to work well. With projects such as the recent expansion of Highway 202, Wild At Heart is commissioned to close natural burrows that are in harm's way and to trap Owls and relocate them to new sites with artificial burrows. The process also involves a thirty-day stay at the nonprofit's aviary intended to break the Owls' "site fidelity"; if released earlier, they would tend to return to their original nesting sites.

Once they are ready for relocation, they are taken to one of the sites, such as the 16th Street location. They are kept for another thirty days in a tent that encompasses a grouping of artificial burrows, allowing

Figure 5-2 A sign announces the location of a volunteer day for Burrowing Owls at the Rio Salado Habitat Restoration Area in Phoenix. Photo credit: Tim Beatley

the animals to acclimate to the site. After the acclimation period, the tent is taken away. "In most cases the birds will stay," said Wise.

I asked her how well the Owls at Rio Salado were faring. "In general the Owls are doing well," she said, but it was hard to know for sure. "One thing to remember is that the owls that have been relocated are birds that would have been displaced, with nowhere to go otherwise."

So, in a way, the Owls have no choice and no other option when a highway or other project comes along.

Greg Clark is Wild At Heart's Burrowing Owl habitat coordinator, the main expert on Burrowing Owl translocation and the main designer of the artificial burrows.[18] Now in his seventies, he is a retired engineer and previous owner of several companies. His engineering know-how has undoubtedly come in handy. On the day we met, he was directing the volunteer crew in assembling burrow extensions that he believes (and science is suggesting) will do a better job of protecting the Owls.

This is not something new for Greg. He has been a volunteer with Wild At Heart for more than twenty years. He told me that during that time, the group has relocated between 2,000 and 2,500 Burrowing Owls and installed around six thousand artificial burrows (not all in the Phoenix area). He explained how they discovered the basic design of the burrows, which he has been modifying and tweaking over the years. It started with efforts to relocate prairie dog colonies. The artificial burrows did not work very well for the prairie dogs, but as it turned out, the Burrowing Owls moved in.

Clark initially encountered a lot of skepticism about building the burrows in larger numbers. "It was not considered practical to put in large numbers of burrows," he told me. "As a mechanical guy, I could see that this project could scale up."

And scale up he has. Clark has supervised volunteers who have done the work to install the six thousand artificial burrows, and this emphasis on volunteer work is something he cites as a key element of the effort. "The people who lived near burrowing owls could have a direct conservation impact," he said. "It was right next to where they lived . . . and they could directly help that owl."

On this day, the crew was attaching new aboveground tubing, later to be covered with dirt and stones. Stacks were placed in the ground, and wire was used to attach and secure the tubing to the ground and the opening of the tube to a hard tile sitting directly below it. Most important, these tube extensions come with a new, much wider opening, which Greg explained will allow adult Owls and their chicks to more quickly and easily retreat to the safety of the burrow in the event of a predator. And it was also a partial answer to the problem of

Figure 5-3 Volunteers at Rio Salado help install enhancements or extensions to artificial Burrowing Owl dens. Photo credit: Tim Beatley

mischievous kids who have apparently been throwing rocks down the openings. Part of the enhancement is to lower the opening to the burrow; another is to help chicks needing a fast escape.

This site was one of five located at Rio Salado. These relocation sites are unusual because they are on publicly owned land, with the potential for residents to legally visit and see the Owls. On the other side of the road, the site is flanked by numerous light industrial companies. I wondered immediately whether anyone who worked there had noticed these Owls. About an hour into our visit, a young man came by and said that he enjoyed his daily visits to the Owls. He didn't really know much about them, he said, but enjoyed them. There are no prominent signs announcing their presence, only a very small placard with information on the relocation efforts located along the fence line.

Burrowing Owls turn out to be all around the Phoenix area and, unfortunately for them, often are in the way of projects such as the Highway 202 expansion and the general sprawling development patterns. This is a metropolitan area that has been growing and will continue to grow. Despite the work of this enthusiastic group, it is an open question whether there will remain a place for Burrowing Owls in this city.

To build the burrows, a trench must be dug with a backhoe. The tubing extends four feet down and leads to a five-gallon bucket, creating a belowground chamber, though recently they have concluded that these probably need to be larger. The main predator worry is raptors, and for much of the day a Red-tailed Hawk could be seen soaring nearby. Cooper's Hawks and coyotes are key threats in Phoenix, but so are dogs. During the nesting season, the chicks need to be able to scurry quickly back into the nearest opening. The additional length and bend in the tubing added by the volunteers will help protect the chicks. Burrowing Owls have also been reported to mimic the sound of a rattlesnake as another clever defense.[19]

The 16th Street site is adjacent to Rio Salado, which on this day was, unusually, flowing with water, the result of an unusually rainy period. The site is flat, which the Owls like, but with a bit too much vegetation around, which the Owls don't like because it tends to obscure their view of potential predators. One advantage of the Rio Salado sites is that the Owl burrows are essentially located in a public park, on publicly owned land. Most often, Owl relocation sites are on private property and thus not in places the public can see. And, as Wise noted, it means also that volunteers can come back and see the Owls and visit the site they helped to create.

The Rio Salado sites might have reached their capacity for more burrows and more Owls, Wise told me. The limiting factor, especially at the 16th Street site, was availability of food. Normally, this site would likely see three nesting pairs. A few years ago, a study of on-site food sources concluded that the Owls did indeed have enough food, but this is a perennial concern in more urban locations.

At the end of the workday, the volunteers took a group selfie. They seemed quite happy about what they had done, and they clearly had some clear and tangible results from their labors. The volunteers were an impressive and dedicated group. A somewhat smaller group than expected, they worked hard to finish the burrow enhancements. Cathy Wise spoke to us of the value of this kind of community engagement. The Owls are wonderful ambassadors, as she called them, noting how engaging and inquisitive the birds are and how they really seem to

Figure 5-4A, B

Volunteers work to enhance Owls' burrows by extending the burrows' tubing, providing Owl chicks with more protection and easier escape from predators. Photo credits: Tim Beatley

Figure 5-4B

make an impact on people. "I'm seeing now more than ever," she said, "there's a real desire in people who live in the city to do something good for the environment, to give back and to be a part of conservation, not just watch it on TV or hear it on NPR; they want to actually get their hands dirty."

Later in the day, equipped with specific instructions on where to find a larger colony of Owls, we went in search of the Laveen neighborhood. Although still within the boundaries of the city of Phoenix, this site felt much more remote. We drove down several dirt roads until we finally found a gravel road on the edge of a floodplain canal with the backyards of a subdivision backed up to it. There, we found an inconspicuous row of artificial burrows poking out of the ground, aimed at an angle in the direction of the homes across the way. They seemed almost like cannons ready to fire upon the houses.

As we walked quietly around the site, we saw four or five Owls. They generally seemed more shy than the male we had gotten to know earlier in the day at 16th Street. No wonder, given the setting. Even though there was a family some distance away flying a kite, there were few other people around, and it was clear that few cars went down the road we had traveled. It seemed like a good place for these Owls.

As I quietly walked by, I would see a head pop out and then disappear back into the burrow. In the case of two Owls, one perched on top of the burrow, they flew away and, interestingly, crossed the flood channel ending up on the outer fence of the houses, in one case flying directly into the backyard of a home. I wondered whether that family had a personal relationship with that Owl. It seemed plausible that the residents of the house would at least be aware that Burrowing Owls lived nearby.

On Saturday morning, following the Friday workday at Rio Salado, I traveled by myself to Estrella Mountain Community College in Avondale, a city of about eighty thousand to the west of Phoenix, and spent the morning watching (and trying to get a bit closer to) Burrowing Owls. It is an interesting site that shows how the Owls can find space in the messy matrix of suburban land use. Here, as many as forty artificial burrows are clustered along the edge of the parking lot for the college's performing arts center. On the other side is an open field, with

Figure 5-5 In many parts of Phoenix, Burrowing Owls coexist with human development nearby. Photo credit: Tim Beatley

single-family homes beyond. The line of burrows continues around the perimeter of a solar farm.

Many Owls were out and about that morning, even as midday approached. It was still relatively cool for Phoenix, with temperatures in the upper sixties. I found one Owl poking his head out of a natural burrow underneath a utility shed, happily hanging out in the shade created by this structure.

It was the first real chance I had to see how the Owls moved into and out of the openings of these burrows. Here, the burrow openings were of the narrow kind, but they did not seem to slow the birds down. The Owls seemed to compress their bodies and effortlessly slip in and out of the burrow openings, much as prairie dogs do.

Because it was a weekend day, the parking lot was mostly empty. I found myself wondering whether the faculty, staff, and students of this community college noticed the Owls, whether they knew they were there and perhaps had some pride about their living there.

The Promise and Limitations of Relocation

As this story suggests, it is indeed possible to find ways to restore and relocate a species such as the Burrowing Owl within a city such as Phoenix. And the proximity to urban and suburban homes and residents, while a mixed blessing, offers the prospect of watching and enjoying these wonderful birds.

The Phoenix story does raise serious policy and planning questions about whether in this city there is enough of an effort to protect the birds and avoid their displacement in the first place. As Cathy Wise noted, perhaps we should rethink projects like the Highway 202 expansion. "If we were thinking differently about transportation," she said, "those owls would not have needed to be moved." It points to the need to give Burrowing Owls and other birds and animals more status in the planning and development process. This is not likely to happen in Phoenix; though, to its credit, the city is expanding its light-rail system and is trying to promote denser, more compact growth, at least in the city limits.

The State of Florida takes a different approach, one that imposes a more rigorous set of conservation requirements on those agencies or developers whose projects might affect Owls. Although the Burrowing Owl is not federally listed (under the federal Endangered Species Act), in Florida, at least, it has been designated as threatened under state law. The Florida Fish and Wildlife Conservation Commission has prepared a Species Action Plan,[20] and it also imposes an impressive set of Burrowing Owl protection guidelines. Any development that might impact Owls or their burrows must obtain a so-called incidental take permit requiring avoidance and minimization, where possible, and mitigation and compensation where this is not entirely possible. Issuance of a take permit is allowed only "when there is a scientific conservation benefit to the species and only upon showing by the applicant that the permitted activity will not have a negative impact on the survival potential of the species."[21] Interestingly, the guidelines discourage translocation, suggesting that it is still too experimental. It is not clear how stringently implemented these standards are as a matter of practice, or how difficult it is to obtain an incidental take permit, but the Florida approach seems a step in the right direction in giving greater protection to Burrowing Owls than seems the case in Arizona.

In the meantime, relocation efforts like those we filmed at 16th Street will continue and will be a necessary and helpful step. I find myself mentally returning to the scene of those departing tourists who had such a great visit to the Grand Canyon. Might there not be a similarly enjoyable, but of course quite different, kind of urban tour that includes the Burrowing Owls? Could it be a Burrowing Owl safari? Plenty of people still don't know there are Burrowing Owls in and around the city, so it would have to appeal to local residents as well as tourists. It could generate some jobs and income, some of which might be steered toward further Owl restoration and relocation, but in any event it would help to raise awareness about this remarkable little Owl living among them.

The Value of a City with Burrowing Owls

My experience with Burrowing Owls brought to mind Carl Hiaasen's young adult book *Hoot*. I found it and read it again, realizing just how on-target the story is in capturing the essence of the state of Burrowing Owls today. The story involves a group of middle schoolers in

South Florida who discover and eventually work to stop a new development from taking place on land that's home to several pairs of Burrowing Owls. The story has all the key elements of the ethical dilemmas and quandaries we face with Owls and birds more generally: Is it right or acceptable to kill and displace the Owls to accommodate new development?

The father is the voice of adulthood and rationality, explaining that the developer owns the property. "Just because something was legal didn't automatically make it right," thinks Roy, the main narrator in the book. The story ends well, with kids from the middle school organizing a surprise protest and the company agreeing to set the land aside as a permanent sanctuary for the Owls.

Hiaasen's story and the real-world dynamics in Phoenix suggest that although not always easy, there will almost always be ways and places to accommodate Burrowing Owls in cities. It is the right thing to do to make room, but it is also the smart and wise thing to find ways to ensure that kids and adults live in cities with such abundant wonder and wildness.

Chapter 6

Vertical Bird City
Singapore, Hornbills, and Beyond

No child should grow up unaware of the dawn chorus
of birds in spring.
—Rachel Carson[1]

The headline in Singapore's *Straits Times* read, "Visiting Pair of Hornbills Thrill Condo Residents." A pair of Oriental Pied Hornbills had been perching on balconies in the Country Park Condominium development in the Bedok section of the city.[2] Although Hornbills were thought to be extinct in Singapore for over a hundred years, Dr. Lena Chan of the National Parks Board (NParks), an internationally known expert on urban biodiversity, said sightings are not uncommon these days. "It is not unusual to see them in built-up areas," she said. "The hornbill has been able to adapt to a more urban environment."

What is most distinctive about this bird—of course, as its name suggests—is its hornbill, or, more accurately, its casque. More than the beak or bill, it is the larger odd structure above and attached to the bill. *Webster's* defines a casque as "a piece of armor for the head," or, in other words, a helmet! And what a helmet this is. There is a remarkable diversity among Hornbills in the shape of their casques, as well as in the overall color and shape of their heads and bodies. They are distinctive, unusual-looking birds that get your attention.

The native habitats for these species are dense forests, and with the land clearance that occurred in Singapore as it developed, few of these species were left to be seen by the mid-twentieth century. The last formal record of the Oriental Pied Hornbill (*Anthracoceros albirostris*) was in 1855, and there was a remarkable gap in time before this distinctive bird species was seen again in Singapore, in the mid-1990s. The return of the Hornbills is a testament to a concerted effort in Singapore to make this urban high-rise city a more welcoming habitat. The Hornbills, specifically the Oriental Pied Hornbill (the main focus of this chapter), have benefited from use of cutting-edge technology to gain a better understanding of their nesting habits, and the city-state has also expanded general efforts to become, literally, more green—with elements of the lowland tropical forests the Hornbills traditionally called home. More high-rise and densely built up than Phoenix, Arizona, and the Burrowing Owl habitat, Singapore has taken a different approach that reflects a more jungle-like ecosystem, focusing on the facades of buildings and connected green spaces.

Singapore has now developed, and rightly deserves, an international reputation as a green and biophilic city. It has done this through a series of related policies, including a requirement that new high-rise buildings (mostly what is built in this space-limited island metropolis) replace the nature lost by designing in new "vertical greening," or vertical forms of nature. Singapore has also invested in tree planting and in multiple interlocking layers of tree canopy that are good for birds. And there are efforts to replace flood control channels with more natural streams and waterways, as in the dramatic case of the Kallang River, which now meanders naturally through Bishan Park, the country's most popular park. (Most agree this was what led to the arrival of arguably the city's most famous animals, the family of smooth-coated otters known as the Bishan otters.)

Bringing Back the Hornbill

Some fifty-four Hornbill species are found around the world, mostly in Asia and Africa. Eight species are native to the larger region around

Figure 6-1 Oriental Pied Hornbills are now seen in Singapore, having benefited from an extensive nest box program there. Photo credit: Kawai Choy for Singapore NParks

Singapore. A Hornbill conservation effort called the Singapore Hornbill Project (SHP) began in earnest in 2009. With a primary focus on the Oriental Pied Hornbill, the SHP was a collaborative effort involving NParks, Wildlife Reserves Singapore, and several Singapore universities. The project was initiated by Marc Cremades, a bird expert and researcher formerly with Jurong Bird Park, and Ng Soon Chye, a well-known birder and a physician and professor of gynecology. The core of the effort involved designing and installing artificial nest boxes to accommodate new nesting birds. These are birds that don't build nests but rather search out and occupy tree cavities, which become their nests. So, as natural nests have been in decline, creating artificial nests to replace them has been key. More than twenty of these nest boxes have been designed and installed, each seemingly more sophisticated than the last one.

Made largely from plywood, the boxes are designed with a distinctive diamond-shaped opening. These "intelligent" nest boxes are designed to monitor the birds and to collect scientific data about them. Cleverly, the design includes an exterior perch that is also a scale for weighing.

The boxes come equipped with sensors that measure temperature and humidity. There is another scale below the main nesting basket. And there are multiple cameras filming and monitoring the birds, including infrared cameras both inside and outside of the nesting box, as well as a dome camera installed on the inside. Many things have been learned by this close monitoring. One of the more interesting is how the mom Hornbill teaches the chicks to poop outside the nest, which happens only after the chicks open their eyes.

Success of this effort can best be measured by the numbers of birds now seen in or around the city, as the opening news headline suggests. The number was estimated in 2012 at between seventy-five and one hundred individuals. There are photos of these birds appearing on balconies and perched in other places in the dense vertical city where residents can see and enjoy them. As Cremades and Chye noted, "It is a powerful message to children and adults to see a bird of this size making a comeback in the city."[3] Their size and color make them something striking to witness and likely unexpected in an urban setting.

As researchers continue to monitor the Hornbills, they will be able to expand their efforts to create habitat for Hornbills and other bird and animal species. "Throughout this project, the hornbills have shown us their great adaptability by discovering new habitats in the core of the city," said Cremades and Chye. "We must enhance these zones that are often havens for wildlife. Replanting local plants for feeding large populations of animals is the next necessary step for the long-term comeback of the hornbill in our city."[4]

Although current Hornbill population numbers are not available, Lena Chan, of Singapore NParks, told me their numbers are healthy and likely growing. There are frequent sightings, some (again) from balconies, often to great delight. A profile of cofounder Ng Soon Chye summaries what the SHP has accomplished in a short time: "From being seen primarily on Palau Ubin [a separate and less developed island located in the northeast], the bird became sighted quite frequently all over mainland Singapore within a decade."[5]

Biophilic City in a Garden

Singapore represents an unusual model for future cities and is a place that demonstrates the potential for biodiversity and urban density to coexist. Several years ago, Singapore changed its official motto from "Singapore, a Garden City" to "Singapore, City in a Garden," a small but profoundly significant change. It is a place that aspires to immerse its citizens in nature but also houses the vast majority of them in high-rise structures (and 80 percent of the country's population lives in social housing, itself an impressive story). Lately, NParks has been speaking in terms of "Biophilic City in a Garden," giving even further emphasis to the natural setting and context.

Some of the most dramatic examples of vertical nature have happened in the past five years or so, and the city and its designers and developers, with the financial assistance of government, do appear to be breaking ground in forging new vertical models of nature. The work of local design firm WOHA has been getting special international attention. Included among WOHA's portfolio of work are the Parkroyal on Pickering hotel, the Oasia Hotel Downtown, and, most recently, a mixed-use social housing development called the Kampung Admiralty. I have had the pleasure of staying in the first two of these and touring the third. They break ground in some important ways and suggest the potential value this development model might have for birds.

Parkroyal on Pickering is perhaps the most internationally recognized building in Singapore, at least among those in the green building world. Its skyparks—a series of planted ledges—are its most notable green feature, but the draping plants encountered when walking up to the building from the street are also visually striking. This building provides more park space and greenery than the historic park across the street.

The Oasia Hotel Downtown is striking in a different way. It is a taller structure, more in the traditional form of a high-rise building, most of it a hotel. From street level, its most prominent feature is the system of facade trellising that covers its exterior. It has been planted with twenty-one varieties of flowering vines; indeed, the idea is that no matter what time of year it is, something will be in bloom.

I like very much the idea of a "blooming building" and the notion that we might judge a building (and a city) by whether and how often it blooms. In an interview at the WOHA office, Wong Mun Summ told me that he designed the building explicitly with animals and wildlife in mind.

Figure 6-2 The exterior of the Oasia Hotel Downtown in Singapore was de-signed with birds and wildlife in mind. It includes an aluminum exterior trellis planted with twenty-one species of flowering vines. Photo credit: Tim Beatley

There are a number of co-benefits of this exterior as well. It helps shade and cool the structure and reduces its energy consumption and its carbon emissions.

Much of the greenery and nature of Oasia cannot be seen from the ground, however. There are four levels of sky gardens, including Level 6, where guests check in. These levels are in the form of open-air parks, with trees and greenery and places to sit outside. In contrast to many other conventional hotel buildings, these spaces are not sealed and air-conditioned. Wong told me that there are pleasant breezes to enjoy on these skypark levels and that it is cooler there than on the street level below. That certainly squared with my own experiences of these spaces.

But how good is a building like this for birds? In 2018, WOHA commissioned a biodiversity and social audit of Oasia and found some interesting results.[6] Biodiversity surveys of the building were done over a roughly seven-month period, and two nearby public parks and a nearby green patch for were surveyed for comparison. Although Oasia's interior and facade were found to have fewer birds, some six species were recorded there, including Yellow-vented Bulbuls, Black-naped Orioles, and Olive-backed Sunbirds. And the insect diversity was considerable.

The study notes the issue of the small area of nature in Oasia compared with that of surrounding parks and that such structures are better thought of as corridors and stepping-stones. It may also suggest that with vertical structures such as Oasia, where birds must find upper-level skyparks, more active attempts to attract birds and to accommodate a diversity of bird species may be necessary. And it is also important to note that the surveys were conducted only a short number of months after the building was completed.

A more recent WOHA development, the Kampung Admiralty, is likely to offer more attractive bird habitat. It is designed as a series of tiered levels with the top level covered with native forest. The structure provides social housing for seniors, a day care center for children, and a medical center. On the ground level is a "people's plaza," a beautiful shaded public open space. On one of the top floors there is a food-producing garden.

Clearly, an important part of the answer is to do what is possible to ensure, for birds and other species, that each new structure helps contribute to an integrated bird- and biodiversity-friendly urban environment. One building alone cannot do that, but it can help to stitch or weave together the many different habitats and habitat patches that will exist in a dense, highly developed city such as Singapore.

Because of the policies now in place, much of Singapore's future growth will happen through the construction of green towers such as those designed by WOHA. For birds, this may be a mixed picture, at least in the short term. The global trend is in the direction of vertical structures that blur the lines between building and park. Architects such as Stefano Boeri and Vo Trong Nghia have been similarly innovating new vertical green models.

Few green buildings have gotten the amount of attention of Boeri's Bosco Verticale, or Vertical Forest, in Milan, Italy. The project consists of two residential towers encircled by large mature trees in planter boxes. This is how Boeri described the project's greenery, with the intention of creating new spaces in the city for birds, insects, and other animals:

> Vertical Forest increases biodiversity. It helps to set up an urban ecosystem where a different kind of vegetation creates a vertical environment which can also be colonized by birds and insects, and therefore becomes both a magnet for and a symbol of the spontaneous re-colonization of the city by vegetation and by animal life. The creation of a number of Vertical Forests in the city can set up a network of environmental corridors, which will give life to the main parks in the city, bringing together the green space of avenues and gardens and interweaving various spaces of spontaneous vegetation growth.[7]

The towers include balconies with mature trees, some eight hundred in all, and 4,500 shrubs and 15,000 plants. Boeri is said to have selected the tree varieties, many of them fruiting, with birds in mind.

Richard N. Belcher and colleagues conducted one of the first surveys of the birdlife found on these structures, what they call Dense and Green buildings, comparing them with Normal Dense buildings.[8] The study concluded that the Dense and Green buildings, one of the three being Bosco Verticale, do indeed support greater bird diversity, consistent with an earlier study finding greater bird use of green walls as compared with barren building facades. Nevertheless, the number of species found on a green vertical structure like Bosco Verticale was still only a small number of the bird species that might be encountered in Milan.

How to think of the habitat value provided to urban birds in vertical growth such as Oasia and Bosco Verticale remains an open question. Belcher and colleagues are probably correct that the extent of diversity and abundance of birds found on such buildings will depend greatly on the extent of that in other nearby parks, greenery, and trees and the "available pool of nearby bird species." Structures such as these can best be thought of as stepping-stones, though they can clearly be designed to enhance nesting, perching, and foraging value, as with the fruiting trees in Bosco Verticale.

The dense vertical city model of Singapore will ultimately depend a lot on the network of green spaces and nature that exist and how they are connected (or not) to one another. Vertical buildings will undoubtedly be increasingly expected to provide bird habitat, and we must do an even better job, whether the structure is thirty stories or three, in designing it with birds in mind from the beginning.

We will likely see forested biophilic towers popping up in many cities around the world in the future, designed by different firms and in different creative ways that will, it is hoped, contribute to bird-friendly cities. In Toronto, Ontario, an interesting new design for a residential tower, called Designers Walk, has been approved and will break ground in coming months. Designed by architect Brian Brisbin (Brisbin Brook Beynon Architects), it will include some four hundred trees, with a unique design that allows the trees to grow up from the building's floor plates. The result will be wonderful green terraces that bring nature inside, while enhancing nature and greenery for the surrounding neighborhood. As Brisbin explained in an interview, he very much sees the tower as an ecological waypoint in this city. The city has set some ambitious tree-planting goals that will be difficult to reach without towers like this, but, more profoundly, Brisbin hopes these forested towers will connect to one another, to parks, and to other green elements in the city, helping to grow a rich ecological matrix that will be good for birds as well as humans.[9]

Designers Walk is also a case study in understanding how cities can come to love and desire the density they need to be sustainable in the future. There is usually resistance to new projects like this one from surrounding residential neighborhoods (the NIMBY syndrome—"not in my backyard"). Brisbin told me this did not occur in this case— rather (and surprisingly), the neighborhood residents became active advocates for the project, viewing it as a "terraced hillside community of trees."[10]

Designing for birds makes sense on its own, of course, as I argue throughout this book. But it will also help to make denser urban projects and buildings more palatable and attractive to people and existing neighborhoods (combating urban sprawl and habitat consumption at the city's edge as well). Brisbin tells the story of designing the eight-story building in which he currently lives: one key benefit and pastime for him is enjoying the songbirds that visit his terrace!

Chapter 7

Bird Appreciation
Changing Perceptions of Urban Birds

Watching a soaring turkey vulture is like meditating. Gently
rocking with the breeze, wings fixed in a shallow dihedral, a
vulture's flight looks peaceful and elegant, almost contemplative.
Although their movements are purposeful, the birds appear
relaxed and unhurried, like long, slow breaths. In times of stress
or struggle, gazing at a vulture overhead is a reminder to glide,
to sail, use the prevailing winds.
—Katie Fallon[1]

Few experiences of nature are more ubiquitous, more readily
available, than watching and enjoying birds. It can be done by
everybody, at every stage of one's life, from very young to very
old, and it is often simply a matter of directing one's gaze skyward
on the way to the car or the bus or on the walk to work, or, quite
commonly, watching birds from the windows of our homes and flats.
Increasingly, we can also watch birds via webcams, imbibing a dose of
nature therapy while at our desks. This chapter looks at the emotional
benefits of bird-watching and highlights a few birds that are underappreciated but present in urban areas.

Watching birds, following their flight through the air, can serve as a remarkable reducer of tension and stress; watching birds relaxes us, puts us in a calmer frame of mind. Some describe cities as complex stress-inducing machines, exacting an emotional penalty on all of us living in them.

One study in the United Kingdom of those who put up bird feeders and watch birds in that way demonstrates the motivations and benefits gained and the self-reported benefits of relaxation. Surveying 331 residents of three small cities north of London, the authors found that "most people felt relaxed and connected to nature when they watched birds in their garden" and that the "feeling of being relaxed and connected to nature increased with the level of bird feeding activities and in people who noticed birds for a greater proportion of the day. The feeling of relaxation also increased in respondents over 40 years old."[2]

"Garden bird feeding," the authors suggested, may be an underappreciated source of people's daily dose of nature. For many people, watching and listening to the birds around them and maintaining one or more bird feeders is an excellent way of obtaining their minimum daily requirement of nature.

There is something to be said for the impressive ability to take direct personal action to enhance the quality of the natureful environment you live in—set out the feeder, maintain and clean it, and the birds will repay you manyfold.

"Here we show that the act of maintaining and watching a bird feeder increased self-reported feeling of relaxation, so contributing towards reduced levels of stress," the authors wrote. "Although we do not show causation, we do not believe that it is too great a leap to conclude that people who feed birds more regularly and feel connected to nature from doing so, feel a deeper connection to nature. Watching birds at feeders and listening to their song provide opportunities to reinforce this connection within one's own garden."

Although the authors concluded that the psychological benefits gained by watching birds is the most important motivation, it is also clear that residents who maintain feeders are exhibiting concern about the welfare of the birds themselves. "Indeed, many people feel passionately about the welfare of their garden birds, shown here by their willingness also to invest time in offsetting associated risks, such as by following best practise guides to reduce the risk of the spread of disease."

It is important to recognize the robust and growing literature that establishes the health benefits of contact with nature. A recent study of a large data set (some ninety-five thousand records) in the United Kingdom examined the relationship between neighborhood greenness and depression and found a strong relationship: the greener the place you live in, the less likely you are to report depression. There are thus clear "protective benefits" from living near trees, greenery, and birds. These "psychological ecosystem services," as the authors called them, are significant indeed: "With rapid urbanisation and progressive urban densification, optimisation of individual-level exposures to green can be one of the most enduring public health interventions achieved by urban design and planning."[3]

In 2017, I wrote a guest column for the Island Press blog titled "Bird Therapy." I did not know at the time that these words, and the idea of birds and bird-watching as an effective form of therapy, had special meaning for British teacher Joe Harkness. Harkness is the author of the recently released book *Bird Therapy*,[4] which recounts the story of his own nervous breakdown, his diagnoses of obsessive-compulsive disorder and generalized anxiety disorder, and his gradual recovery through birds and bird-watching. *Bird Therapy* is part guidebook to birding, part tribute to the birds Harkness loves the most, but mostly a first-hand account of and argument for the deep and practical therapy birds are able to provide and their power (and the power of bird-watching) to enhance and improve mental health. At numerous points in the narrative Harkness describes moments when birds helped to calm him, to soothe his anxiety, to invoke a mindfulness about what is around him.

"Birds and nature are my anchor to the present," Harkness reflects in the book's final chapter. "They're constant and reliable, in a way that people rarely are, perhaps a reason why I and many others turn to them at times when nothing else seems to help. Even when the world around us is a dark place, the birds still sing, they still migrate—they're just there, being, in a way that perhaps we all aspire to ourselves."[5]

In telling stories of birding in the United Kingdom, Harkness makes a strong argument that birds help us break out of our highly individualistic shells, providing opportunities for friendships and interactions with others, getting physical exercise, engaging in altruistic actions and behaviors, cultivating curiosity and lifelong learning, and deeply getting to know the places and nature around us.

Increasingly we recognize that the mere acts of watching and listening to birds will make us healthier and happier, will help to reduce stress in our lives, will help to heal what ails us, mentally and physically.

The past decade especially has seen the emergence of an impressive body of research showing the power of nature—it calms, refreshes, positively changes our mood, enhances cognitive performance. Nature is good for us. We've probably always known this, but the growing empirical research is adding evidence, and though these studies still fall short of causality, there is strong correlation that is more than suggestive.

Increasingly we are overcoming the traditional bifurcation in our view of nature. We have often thought of nature as something different and distinct, a place to visit occasionally on a summer break or holiday. It is often seen as something remote, a place we must travel to, perhaps a national park or a national wildlife refuge. But what we need today especially is what many of us have been calling "everyday nature," the nature that is all around us where we live and work and where we spend most of our time.

Here is where birds play an especially important role. They are not only far away but also close by. Indeed, they are the ultimate form of everyday nature—fascinating, delightful, beautiful—and they are outside our window, in our backyard, perched on a tree we walk by every day. The chance to hear or catch a glimpse of a bird during the course of an otherwise bland or uneventful day can make all the difference. Birds represent a remarkable reservoir of readily administered doses of urban nature.

The *Guardian* recently reported that doctors in Shetland, in Scotland, are now authorized to prescribe "rambling and birdwatching." Nature prescriptions are on the rise, and the Royal Society for the Protection of Birds (RSPB), one of the largest environmental nongovernmental organizations (NGOs) in the United Kingdom, has prepared calendars and a list of walks to help. "Patients will be nudged to go hill walking on Shetland's upland moors, and directed towards coastal paths to watch fulmars, to beachcomb for shells, draw snowdrops in February, and spot long-tailed ducks, oystercatchers and lapwings."[6]

A 2017 study by researchers at the University of Exeter sought to explore the relationship between how green a neighborhood was and the extent of birdlife present and residents' mental health. They found, not surprisingly, that "people living in neighborhoods with higher levels of vegetation cover and afternoon bird abundances had reduced severity of depression, anxiety, and stress."[7] We enjoy having birds around us; our lives are improved immeasurably by their presence; we feel better and less stressed when they are nearby.

Activating Bird-Friendly Backyard Habitats

Enhancing bird habitat through efforts in our own backyards can be very beneficial for birds and humans. Portland, Oregon, has an impressive and instructive Backyard Habitat Certification Program. It is a serious program requiring real commitments, with site inspections and verifiable habitat thresholds; to achieve the highest level of certification, platinum, a minimum of 50 percent of the backyard must be planted with bird-friendly native plants.

Nikkie West, co-director of the program for the Audubon Society of Portland, spent some time explaining to me the benefits of the program and the mechanics of how it works.[8] It is jointly run with the Columbia Land Trust, a land trust whose main landholdings are outside Portland. The program launched in 2009 within the borders of the city of Portland, and since that time some 5,200 properties have been enrolled. The program has gradually been expanding its geographic range with the goal of seeking participants in all four counties of the Metro Portland area within the next two years.

There are other backyard habitat programs, including one run by the National Wildlife Federation (which West went out of her way to compliment). Yet the Portland program is different, partly because it is a program in which homeowners actually have to do things to gain certification. This, West told me, is sometimes a shock to homeowners: "You mean my bird feeder isn't enough?" There are three levels of certification and specific, verifiable requirements for each level. The process begins when a representative from the program comes to inspect the yard and undertakes an initial assessment. The technician meets with the homeowner to discuss the results and to understand the participants' goals. That first meeting usually lasts around an hour and a half. An initial plan to meet baseline certification is prepared, and resources are provided, such as information about where to purchase native plants and coupons that provide discounts at one of the five native plant nurseries Audubon has developed relationships with.

The participants, even before doing anything, receive a sign to put up indicating their intent to create a certified yard. I asked West whether this tended to create a sense of psychological commitment to following through. She agreed that indeed it did.

The personal connection is a key difference in this program. The fact that an actual human being comes to the home and the homeowner has a face-to-face discussion with someone who knows what can and should be done to make the yard bird-friendly is highly valued by participants.

What motivates people to participate in what is clearly becoming a very popular program? West told me she thinks it is several things, including, certainly, concern for birds. But it is as much a sense of connection to community, and of wanting to do something that helps address larger environmental problems, that seems to motivate many. "I think people feel a strong sense of community around this," she told me, and believe that "our combined actions do matter." She noted that Portland is a community growing and changing, and for many participants new to the community this is an important way to connect with, and commit to, this new home.

West told me that the impacts of participating can be transformative. She related the story of a woman who had planted elderberry shrubs and each morning would lament the need to trim the unruly bushes. One morning, a flock of Bushtits visited during her breakfast, feasting on the berries—everything changed for her in that wondrous moment, and no longer would she worry about the out-of-control shrub!

Yards do not gain certification until later, after actions specified in the prepared plan, such as removing invasives or putting in new native plants, have taken place. Program volunteers (there is a more specialized group of about thirty who do this) return to the home to see that these actions have occurred. Once certified, the participant gets a new sign to replace the one that says the yard is "in certification." West told me that seeing the signs is the number one way that new participants find their way to the program. Hearing about the program by word of mouth, from friends and family already participating, is the second most common way of learning about the program.

Another unique aspect of this program is its ongoing nature. As West said, the program "sticks with" participants over time. Once participants become certified at one level, there is always the hope that they will work toward a higher level. The program stays in contact through follow-up emails and a quarterly newsletter, sometimes announcing plant sales and discounts at local nurseries.

We discussed how the program is funded. It started as more of a grants-based program but now operates more as a fee-for-service program, with much of the funding coming through contracts with local government partners. These local governments, including the City of Portland, have come to see the value of this effort for advancing on the ground a number of local environmental goals, from stormwater management to biodiversity conservation.

I asked West what the larger cumulative impact of these more than five thousand certified backyards is likely to be and whether they will make a difference. "It is tricky," she said, to understand the impacts on a larger landscape level, or what they will mean for birds, but she is convinced that the program matters, and there is no question that the size and scale of the efforts are unusually impressive.

What to do, and how to make a difference, are things that for many people can be overwhelming. This program provides clear guidance, actual face-to-face help from staff and volunteers with horticultural and landscape design experience. And there is constant encouragement, and resources made available over time, to ensure success.

As with the work on catios described earlier, other communities around the country have been inspired by this approach to certified backyards and have sought to emulate it. West consulted her computer and indicated a list of at least thirty-five places that had contacted her about the program. From Fresno to Chicago to Tucson, she has shared Portland's model with others.

Cities such as Atlanta, Georgia, have started their own versions but are mostly far behind Portland. Nikki Belmonte explained that the Atlanta Audubon Society's Wildlife Sanctuary Program has 550 properties certified. But this is a serious number and a good start. Belmonte said that Atlanta's effort has sought to focus more on larger public parks and landscapes. Her program essentially has no paid employees and is entirely run by volunteers.

One question Nikkie West gets often (and one I asked her) is whether participants must, or should, use only native plant species. The evidence does seem to back up this position. Recently a citizen science project called Neighborhood Nestwatch researched the reproduction of Carolina Chickadees in Washington, DC. It was found that backyards planted with non-native vegetation supported much lower levels of arthropods,

> forcing [the birds] to switch diets to less preferred prey and produce fewer young, or forgo reproduction in nonnative sites altogether. ... Our results reveal that properties landscaped with nonnative plants function as population sinks for insectivorous birds. To promote sustainable food webs, urban planners and private landowners should prioritize native plant species.[9]

A major rethink and cultural reboot of the American lawn is long overdue. It is important to recognize that many forces led to its emergence as a symbol of status, including a multibillion-dollar lawn care industry and advertising campaigns that associate having a tidy turf-grass lawn with being a good citizen.[10] Being a good citizen, though, means thinking about the entire (biological) community, including birds, and I look forward to the day when we celebrate the biodiversity present in the gardens and spaces around our homes.

Falcon, Osprey, Eagle, and Other Bird Cams

There has been an explosion in the number of bird cams (and wildlife cams more generally). They have helped to stimulate interest in birds and connect us to birds, and they allow us to see the intimate lives of birds in ways that would otherwise be difficult. Seeing eggs in a nest, watching chicks hatch and eventually fledge, watching a parent deliver a freshly killed meal—all are important dimensions of birds' lives that would otherwise be difficult or impossible to witness.

Sometimes the cams show the harshness of life in the bird world. In Vancouver, British Columbia, one of the most impressive bird cams is aimed at North America's largest Great Blue Heron colony, with eighty-five nesting sites. These birds do not migrate. They live and interact with Bald Eagles, which sometimes kill and eat the Heron chicks, something witnessed by both cam viewers and on-site visitors.

The opportunity to see the biology of large birds like this, up close, is a key advantage of a bird cam. As the board chair of the Vancouver heronry, Stuart Mackinnon, said in a recent press release, "It's amazing to be able to get a birds eye view of the nesting, courtship, mating, nest-building, and egg-laying of these magnificent birds."[11] Since the cam was installed, in 2015, some 180,000 viewers have watched. It is aimed in a way that allows watchers to see as many as forty nests, to zoom in and out, and to control to some extent what is seen.

Another successful example is the Eagle cam monitoring the nesting progress of a pair of Bald Eagles at Hays Woods, a new six-hundred-acre park within the city of Pittsburgh. This cam has seen more than seven million web hits, according to Jim Bonner, executive director of the Audubon Society of Western Pennsylvania. It has been an important tool for engaging the public, he told me. An important part of the story of why there are now Eagles in the city is the improving quality of the river system there. The Eagles become a way to talk with the public about the need to further address pollution that affects them, for instance, the problem of combined sewer overloads. "Sewage is a hard thing to talk about," Bonner acknowledged. "But if you can say this is going to hurt the eagles you have, they care, [and] they talk to their elected officials."[12]

A number of cities now have one or more Peregrine Falcon cams. And Falcons have shown up in several large universities, often occupying a bell tower or another high structure. At the University of Pittsburgh a pair of Falcons nests in the Cathedral of Learning, while at the University of Texas a female Peregrine Falcon occupies the UT Tower. The Texas Falcon is known locally as Tower Girl, and whether and when she will find a mate is a major subject on campus. At the

University of California, Berkeley, a pair of Peregrine Falcons nests in the Campanile bell tower, 307 feet high, with a camera live-streaming the action to a large street-level screen temporarily given over to this purpose by the UC Berkeley Art Museum and Pacific Film Archive.

Watching and Loving Vultures

As much as raptors capture our imaginations and we welcome song-birds into our backyards, there are a few birds that most people don't care to see. Americans seem to have a deep aversion to Vultures. Perhaps it is the dark form they take and the odd-shaped head, or that they are associated with death, since Americans especially do not like to think about death and don't want to be around anything that reminds us of the end of life.

This fear has carried over into very real conflicts about how to manage populations of Vultures that converge upon and congregate at roosting sites, usually in the winter months. In many of the communities with active efforts to disperse Vultures, it seems they are triggered by one or more complaints by the public. A homeowner is uncomfortable with seeing a number of Vultures in a nearby tree and calls the town manager to complain. There is a sort of knee-jerk response of wanting to do something to address the complaint, and this often takes the form of calling in someone who works to disperse the Vultures through the use of sound cannons or flares or, in some cases, by hanging Vulture carcasses upside down, which does understandably seem to disturb Vultures.

But few towns are prepared to challenge complaints with the facts about Vultures or to see the point of complaint as a chance to educate. This seems rarely to happen; the citizens or constituents seem always to be treated as though their concerns are valid. Peaceful and informed coexistence would seem a better approach, and often just a waiting period will demonstrate that the Vultures have moved on.

Unlike many people, I grew up watching Turkey Vultures. For me, they epitomized grace and beauty in flight and tended to induce the desire to slow down and watch and daydream. Often these days, my watching is more accurately described as glimpsing. It often happens through the windshield of a car, and sometimes the lingering sight leads me to stop too suddenly and closely behind other cars at a stop sign. Like so many of the birds commonly around us, they are not likely to be paid much attention.

There was a time when this was different. Two brothers from Ohio famously rode their bikes to the Pinnacles, a natural gorge south of Dayton, to picnic and watch. Orville and Wilbur Wright were famous for the methodical and scientific ways in which they built models and tested their ideas about flight. But they also spent much of their time watching and being inspired.

A historical sign exists today close to that spot, noting how the brothers observed the Vultures "soaring gracefully above the river valley. In the summer of 1899, while watching the birds at Pinnacle Hill twist the tips of their wings as they soared into the wind, the Wright brothers developed their wing warping theory."[13]

It was the solution to an important problem: how to turn or roll the airplane. From this insight they built a kite that allowed them to test this twisting guidance—that allowed them to twist one wing downward, decreasing lift and increasing drag, while twisting the other upward with the opposite result. It makes complete sense that a Turkey Vulture would provide the answer, as the subtle movement of their wingtips allows them to do this, foreshadowing the invention of the aileron on the modern aircraft wing.

Watching Turkey Vultures is a good way to learn how to build a flying machine, but I think it is likely to induce creative thinking about just about any subject.

One person who shares my love of Turkey Vultures is Katie Fallon, author of the 2016 book *Vulture*.[14] It is really an extended essay on why Turkey Vultures are so special and why we should care about them.

For Fallon, it is an appreciation formed from firsthand contact with Vultures. She and her husband run the Avian Conservation Center of Appalachia, located in Morgantown, West Virginia. Part bird rehabilitation center, part animal hospital, part environmental education center, it received and treated some 430 injured and sick birds in 2019.

The center is home to three permanent resident Vultures: two Turkey Vultures (Lew and Boris) and one Black Vulture (Maverick). Fallon described each to me, the elements of their distinct personalities, in a way that made me feel I actually knew them.

Figure 7-1 Katie Fallon, who runs the Avian Conservation Center of Appalachia in Morgantown, West Virginia, has become a passionate champion for Turkey Vultures. Photo credit: Compliments Katie Fallon

Fallon finds herself nearly constantly needing to correct popular beliefs about the Vultures, especially about what they eat and whether they are a potential menace to livestock or pets. They are not, and she spends much time debunking these popular impressions. Turkey Vultures are not anatomically equipped to pick up and fly away with a chicken or a small dog, even if they wanted to. It is important to know that what they eat is almost always already dead.

They are known to be "obligate scavengers," meaning they feed entirely on dead animals. And thank goodness, because they perform a remarkable sanitation and cleanup service for us all.

They are also wonderful flyers, of course, graceful and peaceful. In Central Virginia, where I live, they are a frequent sight soaring above and near to cities and towns. Look skyward on any given day and you are likely to see one or more.

One chapter of Fallon's book, titled "Virginia Is for Vultures," documents some roosting sites in my home state and conflicts that have arisen. Roosting Vultures can sometimes cause damage (tearing roof materials and depositing feces), but mostly they do not.

Fallon's hope is that we will begin to actively enjoy Vultures, that we will look at them differently, that we will not only accept their winter roosts but seek them out. Go looking for them.

More than just tolerating Turkey Vultures, we might want to learn more about them, to understand and celebrate their unique role in the natural world. To that end, a number of places organize some form of celebration around Vultures. For instance, Hinckley Township, near Cleveland, celebrates its annual Hinckley Buzzard Sunday each March. OhioTraveler.com describes the event in this way:

> See buzzards (turkey vultures) come home to roost in the rock cliffs and ledges in Hinckley. This annual celebration dates back to 1957 when 9,000 visitors flocked the township to see the return of the buzzards from their winter hiatus. The event includes an early bird hike; skits, songs and stories performed in tents or in fields, displays, crafts, photos, contests and additional hikes. Don't miss this rite of Spring. Learn about the legend that surrounds Buzzard Day and why so many buzzards and people come out in March.[15]

This is how Hinckley describes itself: "With the combination of beautiful rolling hills, acres of parklands, rural home sites, and supportive community groups, those who come to live in Hinckley Township live by its motto: Small Town, Big Hearts."[16] Big hearts indeed: it is a compassionate and caring community that sees the inherent worth of Vultures.

Turkey Vultures and Black Vultures of the New World are doing fine, and their numbers may actually be slightly on the increase. Fallon has concerns about their ingestion of lead shot and, of course, about potential conflicts about winter roosting sites. But for the most part, the issues for these species are the need for more public education about them and the mostly missed opportunity to enjoy and celebrate these magnificent flyers. Their ubiquity and their especially beautiful flying abilities suggest that we should do more to actively appreciate them.

Box 7-1
What Can We Do?

- Switch to non-lead ammunition.
- Do not purchase products made of ivory.
- Support sensible regulation of the veterinary use of diclofenac.
- Support nonlethal alternatives to dispersing vulture roosts.
- Travel to see winter vulture roosts, and tell people you've come to see their vultures.
- Attend a vulture festival.
- Challenge negative public opinion and misconceptions about vultures.

Source: Katie Fallon, *Vulture: The Private Life of an Unloved Bird* (Lebanon, NH: ForeEdge, an imprint of University Press of New England, 2017), 205–10.

Befriending the Vultures of Lima

In early 2016, I had the pleasure of attending the USAID Environmental Officers Workshop in Washington, DC. It was a meeting that brought together environmental staff from posts all over the world. On one day the organizers showed a short video in Spanish, a public service announcement that described an innovative effort to use GPS-tagged Vultures to find illegal trash dumps in the area of Lima, Peru. It was a fascinating story and sent me on a search to find out how this initiative came about and what its impact has been.

Many of the details of the story of the Lima Vultures (American Black Vultures, *Coragyps atratus*) I learned from Lawrence Rubey, the USAID official in Lima who helped initiate this unique program.[17] The idea, developed in partnership with ornithologists at the National University of San Marcos and Lima's Museum of Natural History, was to use GPS-tagged Vultures to raise awareness about environmental issues, especially the problem of clandestine garbage dumps, a major problem in Lima.

Ten Vultures were eventually tagged, and they can be tracked in real time online. Residents could visit the website and watch the blinking

Figure 7-2 An innovative program in Lima, Peru, works to change the popular perception of Vultures. Photo credit: Compliments USAID

icons of Vultures to locate their current positions and where they have traveled and visited. Two of the Vultures were, for a time, outfitted with GoPro cameras, which generated some impressive footage of what it might be like to be a soaring Vulture. Each Vulture was given a distinctive name, such as Grifo, Elpis, and Captain Higgin (the Vultures were grouped into three teams, each with a captain!). The Vultures have indeed been used to identify garbage dumps, leading to the next step, the organizing of community-based cleanups.

The initiative was seen as a way to educate the public about the broader issues of climate change and environment. Learning about garbage through the creative lens of Vultures was viewed by USAID and Peru's Ministry of Environment as a broader gateway to environmental awareness and local action.

Remarkably, the Vultures seem to have captured the imagination of many in Lima, and the story has become as much about how the initiative has changed the ways the public sees this oft-maligned species. Rubey told me there had been some four million social media interactions—Facebook and Twitter posts, video views. And most telling has been the ways in which hearts seem to have softened for these Vultures. The whole idea, he told me in a recent phone conversation, was "to draw people into the website through social media and then leverage that into community action." This has certainly happened, leading to a number of neighborhood-based garbage cleanup events.

Rubey told me the campaign did seem to change the local view of Vultures from what had been a fairly negative one. "But you read through on Facebook and Twitter and you look at the comments and people are saying 'how cute, how sweet,' because each of the vultures has a persona and a name and would make posts. The response that came back was very, very positive about them as individuals, and people have favorites."

The initiative has personalized the Vultures in a way that makes it hard to demonize or dislike them. Getting up close and personal with Vultures, and creatively using the new technologies we have available to us to connect emotionally with them, is a promising approach. These new technologies, especially our smartphones, may allow us to easily see, experience, and, it is hoped, empathize with species such as Vultures.

Vultures in the Green Balkans

Vultures in the Old World are not doing well at all in comparison with the Turkey Vultures and Black Vultures of the Americas.

One dramatic recent example of the impacts of pharmaceuticals on birds can be seen in the sharp decline in the population of Asian Vultures, an unintended side effect of the widespread use by veterinarians of an NSAID (nonsteroidal anti-inflammatory drug) called diclofenac.[18] Renal failure and death result from Vultures feasting on diclofenac-infused livestock carcasses. Decline in Vulture populations in India has resulted in a public health crisis, likely resulting in an increase in the country's feral dog population and, some believe, accounting for that nation's spread of rabies and high loss of human life from the disease. Veterinary use of diclofenac was banned in India in 2006, and there has been a hopeful partial rebounding of Vulture populations. Other efforts have included the establishment of a network of captive breeding stations as well as designated safe zones. But despite steps taken to curtail use of diclofenac, there are few restrictions on other drugs equally fatal to Vultures.

The Vultures traveling through the Balkans, including the European Black Vulture and the Griffon Vulture, face a different kind of poisoning threat. Farmers frequently bait carcasses as a method for control of wolves, foxes, and other predators. The organization Green Balkans, based in Plovdiv, Bulgaria, has been working to address this program in creative ways, including by breeding sheepdogs and promoting their use as an alternative way of protecting livestock.[19] These are not the only threats to Vultures, which also include electrocution by uninsulated power lines.

Maureen Murray's work at the Cummings School of Veterinary Medicine at Tufts University has demonstrated the negative impact of anticoagulant rodenticides, including brodifacoum, popular among pest control companies. In recent years, Murray has been finding exposure to multiple rodenticides especially in Red-tailed Hawks and species of Owls.[20] These anticoagulants appear to accumulate and persist in the livers of birds.

A similar poison is implicated in the deaths and long-term neurological ailments seen in the wild Parrots populating San Francisco, including the famed and beloved wild Parrots of Telegraph Hill (made famous through Mark Bittner's book and a PBS film about them). Many of these ill Parrots have made their way to local care groups, including For The Birds and Mickaboo. In a recent study of fecal samples from these birds, all were found to have levels of bromethalin. Most troubling is that the source of the poison is unknown, and it is likely affecting other birds and wildlife.[21]

In a number of metropolitan areas around the world, proliferation in the use of anticoagulant rodenticides has become a serious problem. It has been implicated in the poisoning of mountain lions in Southern California and in the poisoning of caracals and other wildlife in Cape Town, South Africa.[22] Not surprisingly, birds suffer as these poisons enter the food chain. Lead poisoning remains a serious problem for Turkey Vultures and other birds that feed on hunted carcasses. Ingestion of lead has been a major problem for California Condors and a cause of more than two-thirds of the deaths of Condors, according to a recent study by the American Bird Conservancy.[23] A positive step has been the ban in California on use of lead ammunition in hunting, which took effect in July 2019.

Indeed, most Vulture species globally are in fairly dire condition. I got a sense of this recently during a phone interview with conservation staff at the Bulgarian NGO Green Balkans, a group spearheading efforts to conserve and reintroduce Vultures in that part of Europe. The organization has been working at this now for thirty years, with some considerable success. But the story is one of very cautious optimism.

The story behind the founding of Green Balkans is itself an impressive bird story. The NGO was formed in 1988, before the country's turn toward democracy. A uprising of student protests followed the then authoritarian government's remarkable decision to massively apply rodenticide, resulting in the deaths of an estimated million birds. The protests were held even though the risk of jail, and even death, was strong.

Three decades later, this organization is working hard to reestablish populations of Vultures. There are four species that spend time in Europe: Griffon Vultures, European Black Vultures, Egyptian Vultures, and Bearded Vultures. The status of each is threatened, the most endangered designation of the International Union for Conservation of Nature (IUCN).

My Bulgarian colleagues explained that the largest threat today is illegal poisoning.[24] This is done by farmers who bait carcasses in an effort to control predators such as wolves, which are seen as risks to their sheep. Green Balkans has developed some creative programs to address this and other threats. One of these efforts is to get farmers to consider other, less damaging methods for controlling or keeping away predators. In particular, the organization has been breeding sheepdogs and giving them to farmers as an alternative. This approach has been used successfully in Spain as a way to reduce wolf-livestock conflicts.

The changing nature of agricultural food production has meant a gradual reduction in the availability of carcasses to Vultures. Another threat to Vultures in the Balkans has been electrocution from utility lines and poles. To address this issue, the organization has been working with electricity companies to develop and install better insulation on poles and lines. The work of Green Balkans is characterized by its strong emphasis on collaboration with key stakeholders, such as farmers and utility companies.

One program Green Balkans is leading is the Egyptian Vulture NEW LIFE project, funded by the European Union (EU) and aimed at restoring populations of European Black Vultures. Called Bright Future for the Black Vulture, it is a collaboration with five other Vulture conservation groups, including the Vulture Conservation Foundation. A seven-year program, with funding of 3.5 million euros, it builds on an earlier effort, mostly successful, to undertake similar work on behalf of Griffon Vultures. Much of the effort involves propagating and releasing Black Vultures, some of which are from Spain. Green Balkans regularly collaborates with other bird conservation organizations, including the Bulgarian Society for the Protection of Birds (BSPB) and the Vulture Conservation Foundation. A similar EU-funded LIFE initiative, The Return of the Neophron, for which the BSPB is the lead, aims to address similar challenges for the Egyptian Vulture.

Much of this work on behalf of Vultures, including Black Vultures, is carried out through Green Balkans's Wildlife Rehabilitation and Breeding Centre in the city of Stara Zagora. The center receives and takes care of about three thousand birds per year. It is also an important breeding center for Vultures and includes three pairs of breeding Egyptian Vultures and a breeding pair of Bearded Vultures. The center serves an important educational function and is visited by many school groups during the year.

May 2019 brought the excited announcement that there were now two Egyptian Vultures at the rehabilitation center, each with two eggs.[25] Small progress, but cause for hope for the recovery of this majestic bird.

I asked my Bulgarian colleagues whether they were optimistic about this future for Vultures. They were trying to be, they told me, and it helped that there are many other organizations working on behalf of Vultures. They were also seeing the fruits of their efforts over thirty years to change the popular perceptions of Vultures, and they do seem to be making progress. Engaging urban populations in Bulgaria is one way to cultivate some optimism, and they have been attempting to do this. Working with urban schools is one way. Organizing Vulture awareness runs and races is another.

In discussing the chances of bringing these beautiful Vultures back from the brink, the Bulgarians mentioned the story of California Condors and how touched and impressed they were that such a thing could happen, that they (we) were able to "bring him back home." The same is possible, they believe, for their Vultures. The California Condor story is indeed an inspiring and hopeful one. From low numbers in the 1980s (as few as twenty-two Condors in the wild), an aggressive captive breeding and reintroduction program has resulted in a remarkable number (more than five hundred) now living and surviving in the wild.[26]

Around the time that I had my Skype interview with Green Balkans, extraordinary news came out of war- and disease-ravaged Yemen about a Griffon Vulture from Bulgaria, named Nelson, who had been captured by government forces there. Nelson had traveled the nearly 4,000 kilometers (2,500 miles) between the two countries, apparently not an unusual journey for a young Vulture. When he was captured, it was suspected that his GPS tag was sending military secrets to opposing rebels in this civil war. He was tied up and likely would have been killed. But there was a Bulgarian phone number on the tag. According to BBC reports, the Bulgarian group monitoring Nelson (the Fund for Wild Flora and Fauna, or FWFF, a partner organization to Green Balkans) received many emails and calls on his behalf, which set in motion diplomatic and other efforts eventually allowing the Vulture's rescue.

The BBC story noted the surprise at this sense of concern for Nelson: "The conservationists in Bulgaria marvel that so many Yemenis, trapped in a war that has become, the UN says, the world's most serious humanitarian emergency, have worried so much about a bird." The paradoxes of efforts to feed and care for a Vulture in the midst of a war, starvation, and outbreaks of cholera were also noted in the BBC coverage.

> The vulture is being fed with meat and water every hour to try to build him up. In six to eight weeks, if all goes well, he will be strong enough to be released to start the long migration back to Bulgaria.
>
> It may seem strange, perhaps even wrong, to lavish attention, and fresh meat, on a bird in a country where nearly 240,000 people are facing catastrophic levels of hunger, according to the UN.
>
> But the response of Yemenis to Nelson's misadventures, and the

threat to his life, might be better seen as an assertion of their own humanity.

Helping others, doing small favours, worrying about a lost Bulgarian vulture can brighten the most miserable times. Even in war, even in Yemen, even in the world's worst humanitarian emergency.[27]

This remarkable story demonstrates once again how migratory birds help to bind the world together. It is also a cautionary tale about war and how birds such as this Griffon Vulture are at immense risk as a result of these conflicts, often becoming casualties themselves. But as with the stories of the relief and solace afforded soldiers seeing and watching birds on the front lines, a Griffon Vulture may help us to see an end in sight, to connect to a promise of a time of peace and normalcy. Caring for and caring about another form of life, even a Vulture, seems to soften the heart and to help us exercise our innate powers of empathy.

Appreciating American Crows and Other Common Birds

Birds challenge us in our usual ways of thinking about animal intelligence.

Birds have also been caught in various acts of joyful play. Over the past decade especially, much has been learned about the social life and intelligence of corvids—Crows, Ravens, and Jays—adding immense additional curiosity and fascination to any exchange or interaction in the field.

Much of this work is due to the creative experiments of University of Washington ornithologist John Marzluff. Marzluff has been studying American Crows and other corvids for most of his career and has uncovered some surprising things about them. In a series of studies of American Crows, he has discovered a remarkable ability of these birds to remember specific human faces and to carry and even pass along the memories of dangerous interactions with specific humans.

I visited Marzluff several years ago to discuss his work, witnessing firsthand some of the tools of his trade, including various human masks used to explore whether American Crows recognize and remember actual human faces. There was the Caveman mask, worn by those capturing and banding Crows, and the Vice President Dick Cheney mask that served as a control.

Even years after the trapping occurred, these Crows recognize "dangerous" masks and people. Marzluff told me of a recent walk he took around campus wearing the Caveman mask and being almost immediately scolded by Crows, in contrast to the many other humans walking around this busy campus unnoticed by the Crows. This is remarkable, given that the trapping had taken place eight years earlier and that many of the scolding Crows had not even been hatched then (Marzluff told me he believes there is definitely social transmission, social learning, between the Crows about these dangers). That corvids are able to remember and recognize specific faces of dangerous humans, and to pass along this information to subsequent generations, shows a species at once highly intelligent and adaptable to the human world.

Marzluff has spent much of his career studying the remarkable behavior of American Crows, and the family of corvids more generally, and collecting many stories of these highly intelligent birds doing things unexpected. Marzluff and Tony Angell's delightful book *Gifts of the Crow* is the best single telling of these stories. In it, we not only hear of the creative work being done regarding masks and human recognition but also learn about the amazing feats of these birds: their ability to cleverly solve problems, utilize tools, anticipate future needs, and carry out a plan of action; their ability and tendency to give gifts to humans who have fed or otherwise befriended these birds.

The most dramatic example of Crow gifting can be seen in the story of Gabi Mann, a then eight-year-old living in Seattle who started paying attention to and feeding the Crows that appeared outside her house. In return, she would receive back from them (as gifts!) an incredible array (a collection now) of objects—buttons, small pieces of metal, a paper clip, shiny pebbles.[28] It is because the Crows love her, she told the BBC in 2015.[29] There is little doubt that she and the Crows have been able to communicate and to forge a special bond.

Corvids are known to engage in play, as the many viral videos from around the world demonstrate. In the realm of YouTube, the antics and surprising behaviors of corvids are a hit. These include the video of a Russian Crow that repeatedly slides down the snowy roof of an apartment building using a plastic lid, clearly engaged in human-like

Figure 7-3 American Crows congregate and socialize at a picnic table near Santa Fe, New Mexico. Photo credit: Tim Beatley

play. She does it time and time again, clearly enjoying herself. There are the Japanese Crows that place nuts on the street so passing cars can crack the shells, apparently in the process understanding the red and green traffic signal lights. There is the video of a Crow tumbling down a hill, rolling over and over along the way. Marzluff tells of a Magpie that rang the doorbell to remind the homeowner to put out some food.

There is even the phenomenon of Crow funerals, Crows converging upon and carefully observing when a member of their flock has died. "Crows and ravens routinely gather around the dead of their own species," Marzluff and Angell wrote.[30] Why they do so is not entirely known, but it may be that they, like humans, need to grieve. It may also be that such deaths offer a learning experience. Marzluff's recent work with doctoral student Kaeli Swift has sought to understand how Crows react to seeing dead Crows, whether and in what ways they learn from this exposure, and, again, if they are able to remember humans associated with that danger.

The ability to plan ahead is one very human-like quality that researchers are now finding in corvids. In a series of clever experiments, researchers from Lund University in Sweden were able to demonstrate that Ravens would delay short-term reward for the opportunity to use a tool or a token to barter for a more significant treat at a later time, what the authors described as "planning beyond the current moment."[31]

The more we know about the birds that co-occupy human spaces, the more interesting they become and the more likely we are to care about what happens to them. Examples include the new research that shows the fascinating bacterial contents of the stomachs of common Turkey Vultures (clostridia and fusobacteria, both toxic to humans), which permit them to digest carrion,[32] or the foraging habits of Pileated Woodpeckers that lead to creation of tree cavity habitats for other species.[33]

They fascinate and surprise; at every turn, these birds do things that at once endear and impress.

Vultures and Crows in Our Urban Lives

We are lucky that in the Americas we have a healthy population of Vultures to see and enjoy. Their threats are modest by comparison with those faced by Vulture species in Europe and Asia, most of which have experienced precipitous declines. There are many reasons for this, but notable in the Asian context was the widespread use, beginning in the 1990s, of the veterinary painkiller and anti-inflammatory drug diclofenac, which proves fatal to Vultures, as discussed earlier. Now that it has been banned, Vulture populations in India are beginning to stabilize, but most Vulture species there, such as the White-rumped Vulture and the Slender-billed Vulture, remain critically endangered. And despite the official ban, diclofenac is still in use and is still legal in Europe. Add to that intentional poisoning of carcasses, and the other hazards these majestic birds face, and the prognosis is unclear.

All of the Vultures, including Turkey Vultures and Black Vultures, that we see every day here in Virginia continue to suffer from bad public relations and a sense that they are ugly, scary, or associated with death. Their immense value and their public health benefits are not appreciated, and their beauty and flying acumen are rarely discussed or even mentioned. Flying high above us, thermaling with nary a movement of wing or feather, they are mostly unnoticed or misidentified as Hawks or other birds of prey. We would do well not only to notice them but to celebrate them and, at least occasionally, to profess our love, as Katie Fallon does, for this bit of soaring magic in our lives.

And we are lucky as well to be able to see, hear, and experience daily the antics and boldness of American Crows and other corvids. The status of these smart birds is rising, to no small degree a function of the capturing of their antics and cleverness through smartphone videos. It's about time that the reputations of these wonderful birds gets a major rehabilitation. In actively welcoming all kinds of native birds to our backyards and cities, we stand to gain a lot.

Chapter 8

Design for Safe Passage
Cities Such as San Francisco Lead the Way with Bird-Safe Buildings and Design

Once upon a time, when women were birds, there was the simple understanding that to sing at dawn and to sing at dusk was to heal the world through joy. The birds still remember what we have forgotten, that the world is meant to be celebrated.
—Terry Tempest Williams[1]

In a world in which perceived differences often divide us, birds are something we share. As balkanized and divided by national and subnational boundaries as we might seem, by virtue of their annual migrations, birds weave our world together.

There are eight major migratory bird flyways and few parts of the globe birds don't touch. Some birds, such as the Arctic Tern, which migrates from pole to pole, cover much of the world over the course of a year. According to the Bulgarian Society for the Protection of Birds, a species such as the Egyptian Vulture spends its summers in the Balkans and travels 4,000 kilometers, about 2,500 miles, to African countries that include Chad, Ethiopia, and Sudan.[2] Do humans in these disparate parts of the world see that they share this remarkable bird? Perhaps not, although there are joint conservation efforts underway. I see great potential to understand birds as collective kin that are shared during different times of the year, handed off and returned again safely. Those Vultures can tie nations and cultures together in a kind of extended family.

Birds help to weave cities and metropolitan areas together as well. City and suburb, hinterland and urban edge share most of the same species; care and observation and love for birds can transcend these spatial and political boundaries. And as millions of birds flood the spaces and airways of our cities, especially during periods of peak migration, they also help us imagine our cities in new and fuller ways. We look up and see a bird perched in a tree or, perhaps, a Turkey Vulture soaring several thousand feet above the Earth—birds help us see and at least mentally occupy these three-dimensional spaces of cities.

Imagining how a bird sees a city can spark creative approaches to making urban areas safer for birds. This kind of change, aimed at protecting and benefiting birds, is graspable and possible. Big things matter, such as adopting a bird-safe building ordinance, but so do many small things, such as installing bird-safe window treatments for one's house or office.

Bird-Dangerous Buildings and Lights

Window and building strikes represent a major hazard for birds. It is one of the saddest and truly heartrending things to see in real time. It is almost as affecting to find a dead bird at the base of a building, the clear result of a deficiency of design and a moral indifference to the extreme and unfair outcome for birds.

The Golden-crowned Kinglet pictured in chapter 2 is not the only bird I have recovered from the base of a glass building, but it was one of the most startling and one of the saddest discoveries. It was one of the most emotional discoveries, to be sure, and a visceral demonstration of the danger posed by buildings and by clear glass facades especially.

Daniel Klem has studied bird-building collisions for more than forty years and has become one of the world's most cited authorities on how and why glass is so dangerous for birds. Klem sets up field experiments near his Muhlenberg College office in Pennsylvania. His findings were the first to generate a credible estimate of the annual number of birds killed by building strikes. His studies started with a crude estimate of birds killed per structure and resulted in the shocking estimate that as many as a billion birds may be killed each year in the United States alone. More sophisticated modeling by Scott Loss and colleagues yielded a similar estimate, of 365 million to 988 million deaths each year.[3] "Windows deceive the perceptual systems of birds," Klem wrote in 2015,[4] as they do for humans (something else we have in common). He suspects that these estimates are on the conservative side and that, certainly on a global level, many billions of bird lives are lost each year.

As an early advocate for addressing bird-building collisions, Klem is still shocked by the fact that more attention is not given to this threat. In a recent interview, he pointed out to me that even at the low end of his original estimate of one hundred million deaths, "you'd need 333 *Exxon Valdez*'s every year to equal that."[5] Klem wants to know, Why are we so complacent about bird-building strikes? The media tend to focus on such events as oil spills but miss this larger, more systemic threat. "We've got billions dying in windows, and no one is talking about windows."

For Klem, it is as much an animal welfare issue as a conservation issue. "They are vulnerable victims," he told me. "They have no voice, they're innocent, no one wants this to happen, but it's happening in huge numbers." He makes the point that windows are taking the healthiest members of the population as well as those less fit.

Klem's research has done much to identify which kinds of windows and window treatments work to reduce bird strikes, and slowly companies have started to offer new products. He told me that "applications of patterning, more visible to humans and birds, has become more acceptable." This includes ceramic fritted glass, in which a pattern is fired or baked into the glass, ideally onto the exterior layer (surface number one, as architects and builders refer to it). But there are other options, including exterior netting and even parachute cords (strips that hang down a building's facade), all things that will help birds see the glass as a hard facade.

Perhaps the most elegant solution, Klem believes, is the use of glass with built-in ultraviolet (UV) patterns, but his tests of leading products, such as the highly touted Ornilux bird protection glass, have not been very satisfactory. More work and better products remain a need. And especially in need are products to effectively retrofit existing buildings. There has emerged a healthy and largely friendly debate about the products that will be most effective and even the methods for testing these products (Klem has been critical of the tunnel tests used by the American Bird Conservancy).

Just a few decades ago, few Americans would have had any knowledge of the dangers of glass to birds. One individual who has done much to raise alarm bells about those dangers is Michael Mesure, founder of the nonprofit FLAP (Fatal Light Awareness Program), created in 1993 and based in Toronto, Ontario. Few groups have done as much to raise awareness of how birds are harmed by buildings.

Mesure told me the story of how he became involved in this pioneering work a quarter century ago.[6] An artist and gallery owner, he had always been fascinated with birds. In the late 1980s, someone told him about a teacher who was collecting injured birds from the bases of buildings in downtown Toronto. It was a completely new insight to him; he had never heard of migrating birds being drawn to and disoriented by the lights of buildings in downtown Toronto. Soon he and a friend went into the city to investigate for themselves and found many such birds, setting in motion a life's work to raise awareness about these dangers.

Awareness of the disorienting effects of lights at night has led to lights-out campaigns in many cities. Mesure told me that his nonprofit soon began to realize the problem of daytime bird strikes was even more serious than nighttime fatalities. "We found that when we hung around after daybreak we experienced this whole other wave of collisions, and in many cases twice as many birds as we found at night."

Glass is a major culprit: birds don't perceive glass as a barrier, and it frequently reflects the outside trees, vegetation, and clouds, fooling birds into flying into the glass, often fatally. Mesure told me an emotional story of a Common Yellowthroat hitting a building and dying in his hands. "Every time I think of it," he said, "it's one of the driving factors that keeps me going to this day." The dying bird seemed to be telling him something. Other volunteers have had similar personal and gut-wrenching experiences, not unlike my own discovery of the Golden-crowned Kinglet.

To raise awareness of the full impact of buildings on birds, Mesure and his FLAP volunteers have been engaged in a dramatic annual event—they take the dead birds collected over the past year and display them, usually at the Royal Ontario Museum. They started this visual layout of birds in the late 1990s, and in 2002 the layout image was published in *National Geographic*, gaining international attention and recognition.

It is a bittersweet but visually effective way of conveying the magnitude and seriousness of the bird strike issue. The precise number of birds that are killed in building strikes is unknown, but estimates put the number in North America at close to one billion, second only to the number killed by predation by cats (as discussed in chapter 3).

For some bird species, such as Swifts, changes in building design and construction and retrofitting of buildings have been taking away important nesting and roosting spaces within cities. Specifically, in many cities older buildings and homes with open chimneys are being replaced or their chimneys are being capped, gradually taking these important urban habitats away. Replacing these spaces, whether through erection of new Swift towers or through integration of Swift boxes into home and building exteriors, becomes an important response.

At the same time, some birds, such as Peregrine Falcons, can adapt well to urban environments. The 2018 annual report of New Jersey's Peregrine Falcon Research and Management Program noted an increase in the number of nesting pairs in that state, now up to forty. Half of these pairs nested on high-rise towers, and more than one-quarter nested on bridges.[7] This is a remarkable story of the comeback of a bird species, helped by the banning of DDT, and the ways in which spaces in the urban environment mimic the natural cliff habitats they prefer. Still, as more birds inhabit and nest in cities, there is a need to care for and manage elements of urban infrastructure, such as bridges, as habitats, clearly with birds in mind.

San Francisco: The First US City to Go Bird-Safe

San Francisco was the first US city to adopt mandatory bird-safe building requirements. In this famously contentious and highly politically engaged community (some have called it "hyperdemocratic"), demand for bird-safe buildings came to the fore through community protest. Two buildings in particular raised the public's ire, and created worries about impacts of buildings on birds, before there was even a bird-friendly ordinance. The first was the Exploratorium, a hands-on educational museum located on Pier 15 on the Embarcadero. This was a significant renovation and expansion of an existing structure located right on the edge of San Francisco Bay, a most dramatic setting but also one where birds were likely to be all around.

These concerns came up during the project review, and the Port Commission, which had approval authority, ultimately required the builder to include bird-friendly fritted glass. As a story in the *San Francisco Chronicle* noted near the opening of the building in April 2013, the bayfront location and water views are dramatic, with the exterior windows bringing "immense views of the city and bay into every gallery."[8] Visual connections to the bay would seem especially important to a facility such as the Exploratorium with the mission of connecting visitors and residents to the surrounding nature and ecosystems of that place. These energy-efficient windows were also part of a larger goal for the building to be net-zero, producing as much energy as it needs (a strategy that includes some 1.5 megawatts of peak production from rooftop solar panels and a unique heating and cooling system that utilizes salt water from the bay). The Exploratorium was an auspicious beginning for bird-friendly design in showing that expansive views of water and bird-safe windows could go together and that concerns about sustainability and bird-friendly design could indeed go hand in hand.

A second building of concern was, oddly enough, the new and highly touted design for the California Academy of Sciences (CAS). This structure has a number of green features and a dramatic green rooftop, but it also suffered from extensive reflective hazards. And there was already considerable evidence that the structure was killing birds.

Support for the city's Standards for Bird-Safe Buildings[9] was significantly buoyed by public support, much of it mustered by the Golden Gate Audubon Society. AnMarie Rodgers, senior planner with the city, who spearheaded the drafting of the code, told me the city received some two thousand letters of support, one of the largest such expressions of support for a proposed ordinance.

Rodgers described it as a "harm reduction" code: it seeks to reduce harm or threat to birds but does not eliminate it; it is not perfect and not as stringent as it could be. But it has done a good job of protecting birds, she thinks.

The city had few examples of codes to emulate and did seek the help of experts at the American Bird Conservancy. In the end, the Standards for Bird-Safe Buildings establishes requirements in two primary buckets: one set of requirements is imposed on development that lies in close proximity to parks and other bird habitats (construction within three hundred feet of a so-called urban bird refuge) and another set of standards that requires bird-friendly design for specific potentially hazardous building features, such as skywalks, greenhouses, and balconies.

For requirements in the first bucket, a key element in the code is the definition of an urban bird refuge: essentially any park or green space or open water, or even a green rooftop, of two acres in size or greater, believed to represent areas where birds are likely to be present. For new buildings, 90 percent of the windows must be bird-friendly (e.g., with fritting or other treatments) from grade up to sixty feet, what the ordinance describes as the "Bird Collision Zone." The code defines required bird-friendly glazing or facade treatments in this way:

> Glazing Treatment Specifications: Bird-safe glazing treatment may include fritting, netting, permanent stencils, frosted glass, exterior screens, physical grids placed on the exterior of glazing or UV patterns visible to birds. To qualify as Bird-Safe Glazing Treatment, vertical elements of the window patterns should be at least 1/4 inch wide at a maximum spacing of 4 inches, or have horizontal elements at least 1/8 inch wide at a maximum spacing of 2 inches.[10]

San Francisco has famously been in the midst of a construction boom, with notable new projects such as the Transbay Center and Salesforce Tower. It is a city where bird-safe design standards can make a big difference and are doing so. The issue of cost came up early, and the city hired a consultant to estimate how much additional cost the bird-friendly requirements could potentially add to the cost of new buildings. The answer: less than 0.5 percent. There were also early objections from local representatives of the American Institute of Architects who felt the standards might restrict the design choices and the aesthetics of new buildings in the city.

As mentioned earlier, one structure that predates the bird-friendly standards and helped raise awareness of threats to birds is the California Academy of Sciences. It represents an example of a building that has undertaken a retrofit to reduce the impact on birds as well as a long-term monitoring effort. Even during construction there were bird strike fatalities, and early in the life of the building it became clear that it was a dangerous building for birds. This was a clear outgrowth from the aesthetic goals and design concept behind the structure: it was intended to create the experience for the visitor of being in the middle of a park (it is in fact in the middle of Golden Gate Park) and thus surrounded with glass walls.

Moe Flannery is senior collections manager for ornithology and mammalogy at the CAS.[11] She explained to me how staff in her department took up the bird issue on their own and began training building staff how to collect dead birds. With the help of a high school intern, Flannery and her colleagues began to amass evidence of the dangers of the glass walls of the CAS and eventually published a paper in the journal *PLoS ONE* presenting these findings.[12]

The group was able to convince the operational higher-ups to take action. Initially, a series of exterior curtains were installed to cover the east and west exhibition areas during periods of bird migration; later, the curtains were kept in place all the time. These curtains stay down on the two upper levels. As Flannery said, they have significantly mitigated the hazard, though they have not completely solved the problem. These steps have made a huge difference and have significantly reduced the number of birds killed: "When the bird-safe building standards came out, we were able to convince [senior leadership] to address the bird-fatal flaws of the building." The amassed data and the cover provided by the San Francisco ordinance seemed to be key. The steps taken to retrofit also made sense given the building's emphasis on its green credentials and the importance given to reaching the platinum level under the US Green Building Council's LEED certification system.

The CAS's protocols for monitoring the building and collecting dead birds are still in place. As Flannery told me, the museum's custodial staff, guest services, and security personnel all know what to do and what to look for each day. There are a lot of eyes and ears on the alert for bird strikes. Dead birds become part of the museum's collection. Having a trained ornithologist means that more detailed information is collected about the birds than might usually be the case. Flannery told me that one thing they have learned is that birds that strike the building tend to be younger ones, just learning to navigate their way through the city.

One of the most visually distinctive buildings under construction in downtown San Francisco is the Mira, designed by Chicago-based architect and MacArthur Fellow Jeanne Gang. The structure is designed to combine high energy and environmental standards (including green roofs, greywater recycling system, and eventual gold-level LEED certification) with a distinct aesthetic form. A prominent design element is the San Francisco "classic bay window," but in this building assembled and rendered in a unique way, with windows that jut out from the surface and point in multiple directions. Its distinctive look and shape offer "platforms from which to view the city at all angles . . . the bays make every residence a corner unit," according to Studio Gang.[13]

This will be a striking structure when complete and one that competes with her Aqua Tower in Chicago for a unique look but also for its bird-friendly design. Several years ago, I spent the better part of a day circling the Aqua Tower and photographing it from every angle and direction. It is a building that puts birds front and center in its design, reflecting Gang's personal commitment to birds. The building shows persuasively that bird-friendly structures need not be boring and need not compromise on the strong design statements they might wish to make. This one has made a huge splash in the design world, and the Mira will, as well.

To date, the San Francisco code has been applied to thousands of buildings in the city, according to senior planner Rodgers. Andrew Perry, another planner involved in implementing the code, explained the city's preference for more permanent facade solutions. Some form of facade netting might be equally effective as fritted glass, but to ensure it remains in place and working would tax the city's inspection capacity.

One place where bird-friendly design has become controversial is

Figure 8-1 The visually distinctive Aqua Tower in Chicago, designed by Jeanne Gang, puts bird safety at the center of the design. Photo credit: Tim Beatley

in the building of new stadiums for sports teams. Minneapolis and Milwaukee offer some important contrasts in experience.

Bird-watching and professional football are two topics that rarely intersect. Yet in the land of the Minnesota Vikings, birders are unhappy about the design of the team's new stadium. At issue is the immense amount of clear glass in the design. For Minneapolis, it was a large new facility (two hundred thousand square feet of glass) for the Vikings, Minnesota's professional football team. In the end, cost and aesthetics appear to have doomed the bird-friendly glass. As Jim Sharpsteen of the Audubon Chapter of Minneapolis noted, "They said they wanted the aesthetic value of having transparent glass that would give the fans the effect of sitting in an outdoor stadium."[14] Despite early signs of encouragement, in the end no effort was made to design this large structure with birds in mind—a disappointing outcome, though there have been statements that the organizations would explore retrofitting some of the glass surfaces at a later time.

The best solution would have been to invest from the beginning in bird-friendly fritted glass. The Minnesota Sports Facility Authority, responsible for building and running the stadium, seemed to balk at the additional cost: by some estimates it would have added $1 million to the cost of the facility, a not insignificant amount, though a small proportion of the project's hefty total cost of $1 billion! Although supporters claim much of this would be recouped from the energy savings, it still became a major sticking point. There have been protests and petitions, with Minneapolis Audubon leading the way, providing an interesting window on how important birds are (or are not) to urbanites. We are in a period of transition toward a growing sense of the value of birds to urban life and the ways in which city design can help or hinder their thriving.

The story in Milwaukee has been dramatically different, making for a tale-of-two-cities moment. Here, the design of the city's new basketball arena—the Fiserv Forum—has indeed taken bird safety into account and included bird-friendly fritted glass; it is now proudly proclaimed to be the "world's first bird-friendly arena."[15] This more positive outcome seems primarily the result of the dogged efforts of bird advocate Bryan Lenz of the organization Bird City Wisconsin, who spent three years actively reaching out to educate and to "nudge" the

Milwaukee Bucks organization and the building's designers to include these features. A member of the design team was quoted as saying the extra costs were "inconsequential" but that the architectural firm, before hearing from Lenz, "didn't know the strategic treatment of glass could make the difference between a bird colliding into it or not."[16] This is a bit alarming and shows the extent to which a considerable part of the architecture and design world needs to be educated about birds and bird safety (and also suggests what we are teaching or not in schools of architecture).

Chicago, New York, and Other American Cities Not Far Behind

Other American cities, notably Chicago and New York City, have been moving toward adoption of their own bird-safe design ordinances. In Chicago, the opening of the Apple Store, a heavily glassed cube of a design, prompted much protest for its danger to birds. According to a recent study by the Cornell Lab of Ornithology, Chicago's lights and its key location on the Central Flyway make it the most dangerous American city for migrating birds, giving some extra impetus for such an ordinance.[17]

The Chicago Apple Store, designed by the famous architectural firm Foster and Partners, was opened in 2017 to fanfare and architectural praise that suggests some of the current problem with our design priorities. The architecture critic for the *Chicago Tribune* described the building as "thrillingly transparent, elegantly understated," with no apparent concern about or mention of birds.[18] Situated right on the Chicago River and designed with a facade of "huge sheets of floor-to-ceiling glass," the structure was soon seen to be a death trap for birds. The chief designer for the architectural firm Foster and Partners said that they thought about birds (how much?) but in the end "concluded that it would not be a problem."[19] Apple has agreed to dim its lights during periods of peak bird migration. It does seem as though the allure of glass is too great and the consideration given to birds and bird safety too minuscule.

Publicity over the Apple building and its hazardousness to birds (and apparently humans as well—there are various reports of people walking into these glass walls) has helped to elevate the importance of bird-safe design standards there. But equally important has been the release of the Cornell Lab's study of urban threats to migratory birds, placing Chicago at the top of the list for both fall and spring migrations. This has helped to educate and to create a sense of urgency about the standards, according to Judy Pollock, president of the Chicago Audubon Society and a member of a local coalition campaigning for an ordinance. As she told me in a recent interview, the timing of the Cornell study was serendipitous and helpful, in combination with the work of a collision monitoring group in the city.[20] The politics have been favorable, she said, and it was likely that an ordinance would see adoption in the months ahead. The biggest issue has been one of changing politicians: a recent election reduced the number of supportive alderman from five to two and added to the burden of educating new officials about bird safety.

Chicago's proposed bird-friendly design ordinance would mandate 95 percent bird-friendly facades on new buildings up to thirty-six feet. Pollock explained that although support was solid for the ordinance, there was a perceived need to phase it in over time, applying the standards first to buildings in the most bird-impacting districts in the city, the riverfront and waterfront districts. And the requirements would not apply to existing structures or to major renovations.

The Chicago ordinance would also mandate that buildings turn off nonessential lighting between 11:00 p.m. and sunrise. This is in line with Chicago's early leadership in controlling urban lights, specifically with its Lights Out Chicago program. Pollock explained that these efforts at moderating the negative impact of buildings' lights actually goes back to the 1970s and early iconic high-rise structures including the Sears Tower and the John Hancock Tower. The 1990s saw the emergence of a very effective lights-out effort with leadership from then mayor Richard Daley. Other cities, including San Francisco and New York, have lights-out programs, but Chicago's is unusual for its level of voluntary compliance, partly a function, Pollock believes, of the more top-down role taken by the city's Building Owners and Managers Association, which seems to have taken this issue to heart.

The issue of cost had emerged in Chicago, Pollock told me, but she believed it was not a major impediment. It is difficult for any organization to come out in favor of something that might raise the costs of construction, but on the other hand, she told me, "they're not actively opposing" the ordinance. "Nobody is really out there with a pitchfork," she said, and it is hard, frankly, to be against saving birds. The Building Owners and Managers Association and the design and construction firms, she told me, clearly understand that this is the right thing to do.

Some recent progress has been made in Chicago, Pollock told me in a recent email. In March 2020, the city council adopted an ordinance that elevates the priority given to bird protection in the city's Sustainable Development Policy.[21] "It is a positive step," she said, on the way to an ordinance. The city's Sustainable Development Policy is an interesting mechanism and may prove useful for bird safety in the short term. It is a kind of point system that requires all new development to reach a minimum number of points, with flexibility about which design elements to include. Inclusion of bird-safe glass is one option for getting some of those points.[22]

Although Chicago has stalled a bit, December 2019 brought the very good news that the New York City Council had adopted Bill 1482B, which mandates bird-safe facades. It is an amendment to the city's building code that mandates that bird-friendly glass be used for facades on new buildings and major renovations, up to the first seventy-five feet above grade, and also for facades facing and above green rooftops (up to twelve feet). Bird-friendly materials must also be used for "bird hazard installations" (glass awnings, handrails, acoustic barriers, for instance) and for "fly-through conditions" (e.g., parallel glass panels "creating the illusion of a void leading to the other side"). The new building requirements would not take effect until the end of 2020. Although there was some resistance from the building industry (and apparently a concern about the availability of bird-friendly glass), the council voted for the amendment by a whopping 43–3.

It was helpful to have had retrofits such as those at the Jacob K. Javits Convention Center, right there in New York, showing clearly the evidence of the effectiveness of bird-friendly windows. A New York City Audubon study has shown that the fritted glass led to a 90 percent reduction in bird fatalities but also a 26 percent reduction in the energy consumption of the building.[23] This half-billion-dollar renovation project not only replaced the deadly clear glass but also installed a nearly seven-acre green rooftop (which has served as a bird habitat and nesting site).

Much of the commentary after the vote seemed to highlight, appropriately, the ethical import of the city's actions. Rita McMahon, founder and director of the Wild Bird Fund, stated, "What the Council did today is going to save thousands of lives, and hopefully, other cities, builders, and architects will follow New York City's compassionate lead."[24] Indeed, it is quite significant that New York City has taken this step, and it does bode well for the attention and potential emulation we might expect in other cities.

The City of New York has also been a leader in sustainability more broadly, it should be noted, and has set some very ambitious carbon reduction goals. Some emphasis in the discussion has been given to the fact that rather than working against energy and climate change goals, bird-friendly design will actually help in reaching them. Chris Sheppard of the American Bird Conservancy points out that fritted glass is more energy efficient and will help to reduce the energy consumption of buildings in the city, "so that you spend less money on heating the building."

As Susan Elbin says, though, projects such as the Javits Center retrofit show it is possible to install bird-friendly glass with no additional cost. Such glass and facade treatments, moreover, are much more energy-efficient and are in fact likely to reduce costs for building owners.

Bird-friendly building facades can do much more than protect birds—they can make bold architectural and aesthetic statements. One good example of this is the new Interface headquarters building in Atlanta, Georgia, where biophilic and wellness features are prominent. There is abundant natural light, and there are wellness rooms and collaborative work spaces, for instance, in this unique design (actually a major remake of a 1960s-era four-story structure). But the most visually striking feature is the exterior facade. It is a black-and-white photograph of a piedmont forest that wraps around the outside of the structure.

The patterns used to create the image make the glass facade visible to birds, which was a key consideration, according to Chip DeGrace, vice president for customer engagement, but it also serves as a kind of natural billboard for the company, which produces sustainable and recyclable carpets.[25] And the metrics used to judge the performance of this green building are forest metrics—how much carbon would a native piedmont forest sequester, what about biodiversity, what about water? The visually distinctive facade saves the lives of birds but also reflects the corporate commitments of the company and the environmental aspirations of the building.

A similar story comes from Toronto, where Michael Mesure of FLAP has been saying for years that the shift to bird-friendly design can mean more visually interesting architecture. One great example of this is the new Ryerson Student Centre at Ryerson University, designed by Snøhetta. It has an exterior that would be difficult for birds to miss, made from a complex set of geographic shapes and patterns. Here is how Snøhetta describes the facade:

> The facades of the building are composed of a digitally-printed fritted glass that envelops the rugged armature and pared-down aesthetic of the exposed concrete structure. The varying façade pattern controls heat gain into the building and frames views of the city grid and nearby buildings from the interior, acting as a traditional framed window without actual frame constructions.[26]

Retrofitting structures to make them more bird-friendly need not be overly complicated, or expensive, and there are now many more options available and more products on the market. One I like a lot is marketed by a company in Pennsylvania. Called Acopian BirdSavers,

Figure 8-2 (opposite page) A key design element of the newly renovated Interface headquarters building in Atlanta, Georgia, is its unique facade—at once a large image of an eastern US forest and a fritted exterior that makes the structure bird-safe. Photo credit: Tim Beatley

Figure 8-3 (opposite page) The distinctive Student Centre at Ryerson University in Toronto, Ontario, shows that building design can be bird-safe and also aesthetically interesting. Photo credit: FLAP Canada

Figure 8-2

Figure 8-3

it is a relatively simple system of hanging parachute cords, or "para-cords." The cords hang down from the top of a building, spaced a little over four feet apart. There is a do-it-yourself option for this technique, and the company has an online guide for making a deterrence system. Some large applications have been made, including the retrofit of a large science building at the University of Chicago. The cords are dark olive green in color, though probably any darker color would work, and they are not fastened at the bottom, allowing them to move with the wind. The company's website says they are sometimes referred to as Zen Wind Curtains because of their movement in the wind.[27]

The Dangers of Urban Light

We are losing the night sky everywhere in the world with the expansion of urban population centers and the artificial lighting that accompanies it. In 2018, J. K. Garrett, P. F. Donald, and K. J. Gaston released a study that showed the extent of the planetary reach of what is referred to as skyglow, or light pollution. This study specifically looked at the spatial overlap of skyglow with the planet's key biodiversity areas (nearly fifteen thousand sites), including biodiversity hot spots rich in birdlife.[28] The study found that fewer than one-third of these sites have "pristine night-time skies, . . . and only about a fifth contain no area in which night-time skies are not polluted to the zenith." In other words, two-thirds of these areas of high biodiversity were found to be subject to light pollution, and this number is increasing. Dark night-time skies are in decline everywhere on the planet, with serious biological implications.

Nikki Belmonte of the Atlanta Audubon Society told me it is not just the lights of sprawling Atlanta but increasingly a larger lit-up landscape that crosses state boundaries: "If you look at the light maps, we're practically connected to Charlotte, up the 85 corridor." Most birds migrate at night, and they won't encounter only the lights of an occasional city or town but a much more expansive lightscape that includes highways like Interstate 85 and the associated sprawl and development that follows.

For animals such as birds and bats, such light pollution can be highly damaging. For birds, the intense lights of cities can be disorienting and can bring them into contact with glass facades. As Adam Betuel, conservation director for Atlanta Audubon, explained, birds are confused and attracted by the lights. The illuminated area "pulls them into the city," he told me. "They could be harmed at that point, but what's more likely to happen is that, as they've landed somewhere they [otherwise] wouldn't because of the attracted light, they then encounter reflective glass."[29] Birds disoriented by the lights of cities can become exhausted quickly, in turn becoming subject to predation or fatal window strikes. As Susan Elbin of New York City Audubon nicely put it, "The light lures them in and the glass finishes them off."[30]

Researchers with the Cornell Lab of Ornithology recently calculated the relative level of risk for 125 metropolitan areas in the continental United States by combining data on bird migration levels (using weather radar from 1995 to 2017) with the extent of radiance from artificial light at night. The authors developed a ranking of cities according to the level of exposure of migrating birds to nighttime light. Artificial light at night, they concluded, "continues to increase in many areas globally, presenting an ever-growing ecological threat to all nocturnally active animals, particularly migrating birds."[31]

For both spring and fall migrations, the Cornell study showed that three cities end up on top: Chicago, Houston, and Dallas. Box 8-1 presents the top ten cities for spring and fall migrations.

Of course, light pollution is a problem for other fauna, especially bats, and a problem for humans, both presenting health issues and interfering with urban residents' ability to see and enjoy the night sky.

What can cities do about artificial nighttime light? More stringent lighting codes and dark-sky ordinances are helpful. And, especially during peak bird migration times, building owners can turn off lights and minimize lighting both inside and out. A number of cities have developed and are implementing some form of lights-out program. One of the first cities to do this was Chicago, but today these efforts exist in a number of other cities, including Atlanta, New York, Toronto, and San Francisco.

A dramatic example of the highly damaging effects of city lights for migrating birds can be seen in the tribute to survivors and victims of

Box 8-1

Most Dangerous US Cities for Migrating Birds

Spring Migration	*Fall Migration*
1. Chicago	1. Chicago
2. Houston	2. Houston
3. Dallas	3. Dallas
4. Los Angeles	4. Atlanta
5. St. Louis	5. New York
6. Minneapolis	6. St. Louis
7. Kansas City	7. Minneapolis
8. New York	8. Kansas City
9. Atlanta	9. Washington, DC
10. San Antonio	10. Philadelphia

Source: Kyle G. Horton et al., "Bright Lights in the Big Cities: Migratory Birds' Exposure to Artificial Light," *Frontiers in Ecology and the Environment* 17, no. 4 (May 2019): 209–14, https://doi.org/10.1002/fee.2029.

the September 11, 2001, terrorist attacks in New York City. The *Tribute in Light* art installation began in 2002 and involves the shooting into the sky (some six kilometers, more than three and three-quarter miles) of two columns of blue light. The attraction of migrating birds was almost immediate. A study in 2017, carried out by some of the authors of the Cornell study, sought to quantify the impacts in terms of attraction and movement of birds and their flight calls, an indication of stress or disorientation. The authors found "large aggregations of circling birds above the installation under clear sky conditions during periods of illumination," affecting more than a million birds for that one night, for more than seven years.[32] "Removal of illumination," on the other hand, "resulted in rapid changes in nocturnal migration behaviors, with birds dispersing, increasing flight speeds, decreasing calling activity, and moving away from the site in a matter of minutes."[33] Thanks to the advocacy of New York City Audubon, an agreement was reached to turn off the lights for twenty minutes whenever volunteer monitors count one thousand or more birds around the lights.[34]

Beyond Glass

Glass facades and lighting are important dangers for birds that must be addressed, but there are other design elements that also can positively enhance the habitat value of buildings. The installation of a green roof on New York's Jacob K. Javits Convention Center, nearly seven acres in size, which now serves as bird habitat, is an important step in addition to installing bird-friendly glass.

The Javits Center's most recent annual report, to its credit, puts birds front and center, including in its "By the Numbers" summary page.[35] Some of the usual "numbers" are highlighted: the more than eighteen thousand jobs supported by the convention center and the $2 billion in economic activity generated. But there are also the thirty rooftop bird nests (identified in 2017). The number of nesting birds should be a development standard, a way to judge how well a building was designed and is functioning.

And according to the annual report, the monitoring work of New York City Audubon has confirmed the value of the roof for birds: twenty-six bird species have visited the roof and at least twelve birds have hatched there, in turn fanning out and being observed around the region and the country, "from Governor's Island and Roosevelt Island to Broussard Beach, LA and Farmdale, FL—1,000 to 1,500 miles away from New York."[36]

The rooftop is also home to five bat species and hosts several beehives, which produce a couple of hundred jars of "Jacob's Honey." A new addition to the center is underway that will carry forward the theme of green rooftops with a rooftop farm and orchard spanning forty-three thousand square feet.

A similar example, not quite as large, can be seen in the retrofit of the Vancouver Convention Centre West. This large green roof, hosting some four hundred thousand native plants, is managed as a meadow, irrigated by recycled blackwater from the toilets in the center.[37]

Cities' growing interest in installation of green and ecological rooftops is a positive sign and clearly an opportunity to expand bird habitat in already heavily developed cities.

Green rooftops can be installed on many different kinds of buildings. In Manhattan, not far from Washington Square Park, a green roof

Figure 8-4 Birds now nest on the green roof of the Jacob K. Javits Convention Center in New York, as evidenced by this camera-trap image. Photo credit: Dustin Partridge

has been installed on the roof of PS 41, Greenwich Village School. The roof park officially goes by its acronym, GELL (Greenroof Environmental Literacy Laboratory). As the school's website suggests, the roof plays an integral role in the life of the school:

> Since its opening, students have benefited from this outdoor learning space in all grade levels; from Kindergarten "listening walk" tours, to first-grade insect research projects, second-grade engineering investigations, skyline drawing in art, to upper-grade green roof STEM model-making projects. We also partner with The High Line for an after-school program.[38]

Vicki Sando, a teacher who had much to do with getting the green roof installed, recently surveyed the students about how they felt when they visited the roof. Responses included "calm," "happy," "free," "feeling good," "amazing," "excited," and "like I'm in the country."[39]

It was not easy to bring the green roof to fruition, Sando told me recently. The entire process took around six years, and it was not for the faint of heart.[40] The steps included getting all the necessary approvals (including from the New York City School Construction Authority), fundraising, and installation. The fourth-floor roof is visited by a number of different classes, with visits sometimes given as a reward for good behavior. But the roof is always integrated into a number of classes, and it's the location of an after-school class on green roofs, a collaboration with the city's High Line.

Of the 15,000-square-foot roof, about 9,000 square feet are planted in sedums and native plants. There are plenty of birds on this rooftop, Sando told me—a flock of Mourning Doves; Blue Jays; Mockingbirds; Kestrels; and Red-tailed Hawks. "It's this big, open space, so they come out."

And its proximity to and connections with nearby parks and green spaces, such as the Javits Center and the High Line, make it valuable to birds, creating "a pathway of connected habitats that allows wildlife to travel throughout the City,"[41] as the school's website notes. "Converting a fraction of the NYC DOE's 1,300 school building rooftops to green spaces would positively impact the surrounding community, reduce energy use for heating, cooling, and electricity, thereby mitigating the City's greenhouse gas emissions."[42]

How much education there is about birds is unclear, though students end up seeing many on the roof. Sando mentioned an incident witnessed by a class as a Red-tailed Hawk took a Mourning Dove. There have also been efforts to include birds in the curriculum of the school. Sando mentioned that she had developed her own special class unit on New York birds, something she had the flexibility to include when she taught first grade.

The roof has other benefits, of course, including stormwater retention. Sando also told me that energy consumption had decreased in the building by 20 percent, which is a helpful statistic when convincing leaders to invest in a green roof. The kids have come to think of it as essentially another park, which is good. Sando mentioned the interest of other schools in the city and estimated she had talked to perhaps fifty schools, with at least a few of these moving forward with a green roof.

Sando would like to see some kind of fast-tracking for green roofs

Figure 8-5 The green rooftop at PS 41 in Greenwich Village, New York, is bird habitat that also offers an important opportunity to engage students in learning about nature. Photo credit: Vicki Sando

like this one, where there are so many clear benefits from installing them.

Many European cities have mandated green rooftops and supported their installation through financial subsidies and technical assistance. North American cities have been slower to adopt mandates, though cities such as Portland, Oregon, have for many years implemented an eco-roof density bonus. Toronto became the first North American city to mandate green rooftops for certain kinds of roofs, and San Francisco and Portland recently became the first and second American cities, respectively, to have adopted a green roof mandate.

Even with a mandate, though, it is not clear that a typical extensive green rooftop will automatically serve as bird habitat.

Dustin Partridge and his colleagues at Fordham University have been monitoring green rooftops in New York City to see whether birds, and the insects that serve as the food for birds, are found on green rooftops in greater abundance than on nearby conventional roofs.

In a recent article published in *PLoS ONE*, Partridge and J. Alan Clark reported on pair-comparisons of green and conventional rooftops at four sites in New York: two in Manhattan, one in Brooklyn, and one in the Bronx. Bowl traps were used to collect arthropods, and the presence of birds was determined by recording bird vocalizations with automated acoustic recorders.

Partridge and Clark did indeed find more insects and more birds on the green roofs than on the nearby conventional rooftops. "Urban green roofs can increase connectivity between habitats in urban landscapes and can themselves provide usable wildlife habitat," they commented.[43] "Our study demonstrates the higher value of green roofs as arthropod habitat compared to conventional roofs. . . . We show that green roofs host a higher abundance and richness of arthropods." They found the number of birds on the green roofs during migration to be "higher than expected based on earlier studies in temperate environments," noting that "migrating birds that pass through urban landscapes can use urban green space to adequately refill fat stores during stopovers, and the birds we recorded during spring migration were likely using urban green roofs as stopover habitat." But by the same token, they concluded that "the abundance of such birds was limited, which could indicate that green roofs are insufficient habitat for prolonged stopovers."

One important variable in making a green roof attractive habitat for birds is the specific vegetation planted. More research is needed to better understand the factors that will influence how valuable the green roof will be for birds: "The influence of roof size, vegetation diversity, isolation, and elevation on bird abundance and diversity should be studied to more fully understand how green roofs can be used for bird conservation."

Are there ways in which green rooftops could be designed to make them better bird-friendly habitats? Partridge and Clark concluded yes.

> Most green roofs could be improved to increase their value to both arthropods and birds. For example, deeper substrate, increased vegetative diversity, and planting with native plants may benefit native fauna. We often observed birds using any available elevated platform as a perch (e.g., HVAC units, antennae, and weather stations), and installing bird perches within the vegetated areas of green roofs would likely benefit birds and increase bird use of green roofs. Planners should also consider connectivity to nearby green spaces. Finally, green roof planners and installers should attempt to keep green roofs safe for birds by using bird-friendly glass and planting vegetation in ways that reduce potential bird-window collisions.[44]

Can green roofs serve as important habitat stepping-stones in urban environments?

There is no doubt that we need to reimagine green rooftops as places of bird habitat and also, perhaps, as places more equivalent to the ground-level parks where most urban residents might be looking for birds.

Green architect Helena van Vliet, founder of the grassroots group BioPhilly, no longer likes to talk about these roofs as green roofs. She now calls them "roof meadows," words she thinks do a better job of conjuring up what they should be.

Parks and many other forms of green spaces in cities will also be important, and increasingly we will need to consider how these spaces connect ecologically.

I met with Nikki Belmonte and Adam Betuel, executive director and conservation director, respectively, for Atlanta Audubon, at what is perhaps that city's most famous park, Piedmont Park. On that day, when we were filming them for a short film, Betuel counted twenty-nine species near us, mostly from their songs. With joggers, bicyclists, and people swooshing by on scooters, the park also serves quite an important role for birds moving through the city. At least 175 species have been seen there. We stood near the rushing water of Clear Creek, and the presence of abundant birdlife was undeniable. "It's a great place for birds," Betuel said, "a green oasis" in the city.

In Chicago, one of the most impressive things done has been the gradual conversion of many lakefront parks to bird-friendly habitats. This is critical because, as Judy Pollock told me, especially during migration "you have lots of birds concentrating along the lakefront." As the sun rises, that's where they're heading and landing. She gives a lot of credit to the work of the Chicago Park District, which has over time converted sterile turfgrass shorefront parks and green spaces to places that provide important habitat. The district, she said, "really takes seriously its responsibility for providing habitat for migratory birds." One example is Montrose Point Bird Sanctuary, a ten-acre site that can support some three hundred different species of birds during migration and is home to the "Magic Hedge," more than four hundred feet of "trees and shrubs that are enormously (and inexplicably) popular for migratory birds."[45] The park juts out a bit into Lake Michigan and contains a variety of habitats, including a meadow, trees and shrubs, and dunes, that make it especially attractive as a stopping point.

The large number of birds killed in car and vehicle collisions suggests yet another way in which we will need to think beyond glass. In 2014, Scott Loss, Tom Will, and Peter Marra estimated annual bird fatalities of sixty-two million to almost four hundred million, placing such collisions higher in importance than many other threats to birds.[46] More research needs to be done in developing safer bird-friendly roads and roadway designs. There are likely more options than we know currently, and we are generally less likely to think about impacts on birds when designing roads. Loss, Will, and Marra suggested some options:

Following identification of mortality hotspots, potential options to reduce bird collision mortality along roads include placing flight deflectors along roadsides to force birds to fly above vehicle height, locally reducing speed limits and erecting signage to alert drivers, reducing or removing the amount of favorable bird habitat along roadsides, and using visual or auditory deterrents.[47]

The authors rightly noted that effective design responses will necessarily vary by many factors, including species and region. More research and accelerated design testing and piloting are needed to better understand both the magnitude of the problem for birds and what can be done quickly to reduce these kinds of roadway and highway impacts.

Putting Birds at the Design Table

There has been a positive trend in the direction of imposing new design standards in cities throughout North America. Toronto and San Francisco have been early leaders, followed by other cities such as Portland; Oakland, California; and most recently New York City.

And the issue has reemerged at the national level. Bird-friendly design is already an optional element (for which a point is available) under the US Green Building Council's LEED certification system.[48] Encouragingly, in July 2020, the US House of Representatives passed the Bird-Safe Buildings Act (HR 919). This bill would impose bird-friendly design standards on new federal buildings. Though it still has to pass in the US Senate, it shows that bird-safe design is gaining traction and attention at the national level.

Luckily, the view of architects also seems to be changing. Carl Elefante, then president of the American Institute of Architects, lectured at the University of Virginia in October 2018 and explicitly mentioned the need to design with birds in mind. This is a promising change. But it is also true that few if any design schools teach their students about birds and designing for birds. This is a lost opportunity and, in many ways, a kind of dereliction of duty.

There is now no doubt that buildings can and must be designed with birds in mind. This cannot be an afterthought but should be front and center in the design. And as buildings such as the Javits Center in New York and the California Academy of Sciences in San Francisco show, existing bird-dangerous buildings can be effectively retrofitted to reduce or nearly eliminate their hazards. There is no excuse not to do so.

Moe Flannery of the CAS feels that a mind shift is still needed in the architectural world and that more consideration should be given to the effects of buildings on birds and wildlife, as well as people, "versus just the way it looks." Many architects would disagree with this assessment, but there is no question that the aesthetic statement a structure makes, and its visual distinctiveness and splash, are viewed to be paramount.

The architectural world seems to be changing and more attention is being given to birds, thanks to the work and design advocacy of architects such as Jeanne Gang who have made this issue a priority.

Chapter 9

Birds in Ravine City
Toronto's Pioneering Work to Build Awareness and Design a Habitat City

As the seasons changed, so did the birds. And as the birds
changed, I changed. The land changed around me and
everything blended into a cycle of experience, in which
I'd built a connection. I'd developed what could be
described as a "sense of place."
—Joe Harkness[1]

In May, waves of migrant birds were passing through the
city's ravines, parks, and backyards. One morning after
breakfast my sons and I saw a delicate magnolia warbler in
our lilac tree. We huddled by the balcony door and watched
the tiny bird with its black-streaked yellow breast. I
imagined it weighed as much as a sharpie.
—Kyo Maclear[2]

Toronto, Ontario, has been described as a "migratory bird su-
perhighway" because millions of birds travel through this urban region during fall and spring migrations.

It is also the city with one of the earliest efforts at beginning to
think systematically about how birds are impacted by buildings and the

built environment of cities. This is largely through the early work of the nonprofit organization FLAP (Fatal Light Awareness Program). The group was founded by Michael Mesure, formally in 1993, though Mesure had begun working on urban bird issues as early as the late 1980s. An artist and gallery owner, Mesure had a lifelong fascination with birds and stumbled accidentally on the bird collision issue.

Mesure has made a career of raising awareness about the dangers of glass-walled buildings in Toronto, and in the process he has helped the city become a leader in bird-friendly design. Mesure told me his mission of making cities safer for birds was not exactly a professional or career choice but seems more of a calling. "It's like I'm listening to an inner voice," he told me in an interview in 2019.

FLAP was one of the first volunteer-based organizations to take on the bird strike problem. During periods of migration, a small army of volunteers patrol the base of certain buildings in the city. They look for birds, both dead and injured. It is emotionally draining work, Mesure told me, as many of the volunteers end up finding dead or severely injured birds, many of them species that one would be lucky to get a glimpse of in the wild. Mesure is proud of the retention rate of volunteers, turnover being a problem for many nonprofits, but he does recognize this is emotionally difficult work and is not for everyone.

FLAP deserves credit both for putting bird-building collisions on the popular and public radar in a way they simply weren't before and for pioneering a systematic approach to collecting and counting the birds impacted by glass and buildings.

These techniques have been learned by and are now in use in other cities. FLAP has become an inspiration and a model for bird groups; for instance, a group called Safe Wings Ottawa has employed similar techniques for raising awareness.

The work of FLAP would simply be impossible without its volunteers. The organization has only three full-time employees, including Mesure, but during migration periods one hundred or more volunteers patrol portions of the city. The financial district is an especially important place for birds affected by the lights of buildings at night, but mortality from building strikes during the day is an even more serious problem, and it seems there are not enough volunteers to be in every place that needs patrolling.

Dead birds are tagged and eventually make their way to a freezer. At the end of each migration season, FLAP displays all the birds that have died and been collected, often at the Royal Ontario Museum, where the birds become part of the museum's collection. The display usually takes place at the end of spring. Mesure said, "It's proven to be one of our most valuable ways to educate the public on the magnitude of the problem, because when you lay those birds out, it really is an eye-opener for the vast majority of people. Most people have never seen so many birds in one spot, and not only that, the array of species is quite astonishing."[3]

Press coverage of these events has also gotten the word out. The annual display of dead birds is dramatic and is a compelling way to visually demonstrate the diversity and sheer number of birds killed by building strikes. No one had ever done this before. For Mesure, the idea was appealing because it sought to educate on a large scale but was not a shrill protest that would turn off those in the city he needed to convince, such as building owners and developers. His philosophy has always been one of developing working relationships with these groups.

> Instead of taking all those birds and dropping them on a doorstep, we found a neutral territory, we lay them all out, and we invite all those buildings [and building owners] to come in and look at them. We invite members of the public, the media. . . . It's turned out to be one of the most effective ways of keeping the story alive in the eyes of the public, without getting people's backs up.[4]

Thanks in large part to the advocacy work of Mesure and FLAP, Toronto has done more than any other city to reduce bird-building strikes. In 2007, Toronto adopted its Bird-Friendly Development Guidelines, part of the city's larger Green Development Standard. It was the first city in North America to institute a mandatory bird-safe building standard. Under these provisions, all new construction in the city must meet the minimum standards, including the use of bird-friendly glass.

According to Mesure, window strikes during the day are more frequent than those at night, as learned through years of collecting data, and most of these strikes take place at relatively low levels, mostly

Figure 9-1 Each year, FLAP publicly displays the birds that have been killed by building strikes in Toronto. Photo credit: FLAP Canada

between one and six stories (about 90 percent of bird-window strikes happen at or below sixteen meters, more than fifty feet). The emergence of glass as a preferred architectural material and look is a major part of the problem, but Mesure notes this is changing. He points to new buildings in Toronto that promote a different aesthetic, one he finds more interesting. He points to the Snøhetta-designed Ryerson Student Centre as a case in point, a visually dramatic building "clad in digitally printed fritted glass, which minimises solar heat gain and results in varying light conditions within the building."[5] Such a building is "far more pleasing to look at," he said.

Over twenty-five years of work, Mesure has become encouraged that the mind-set is changing and that bird-friendly design is gaining momentum. He describes the feeling of being patronized over much of the time he has worked on this issue. He notes with pride how over these years he and his group have been able to shift public opinion. This he describes as a huge victory. "We were seen as a bunch of crazy people running around buildings before daybreak with nets in our hands." Today that has changed—citizens and public officials

Box 9-1
Mandatory Bird-Friendly Glazing: Toronto Green Standard for Mid- to High-Rise Buildings

Tier 1
EC 4.1 Bird-Friendly Glazing

Use a combination of the following strategies to treat a minimum of 85 percent of all exterior glazing within the greater of first 16 m of the building above grade or the height of the mature tree canopy (including balcony railings, clear glass corners, parallel glass, and glazing surrounding interior courtyards and other glass surfaces):

- Low reflectance, opaque materials
- Visual markers applied to glass with a maximum spacing of 50 mm × 50 mm
- Building-integrated structures to mute reflections on glass surfaces.

Balcony railings: Treat all glass balcony railings within the first 12 m of the building above grade with visual markers provided with a spacing of no greater than 100 mm × 100 mm.

Fly-through conditions: Treat glazing at all heights resulting in a fly-through condition with visual markers at a spacing of no greater than 100 mm × 100 mm. Fly-through conditions that require treatment include:

- Glass corners
- Parallel glass
- Building-integrated or free-standing vertical glass
- At-grade glass guardrails
- Glass parapets

EC 4.2 Rooftop Vegetation
Treat the first 4 m of glazing above the feature and a buffer width of at least 2.5 m on either side of the feature using strategies from EC 4.1.

(continued)

Box 9-1 *(continued)*

BIRD COLLISION DETERRENCE
Tier 1

EC 4.3 Grate Porosity
Ensure ground level ventilation grates have a porosity of less than
20 mm × 20 mm (or 40 mm × 10 mm).

LIGHT POLLUTION
Tier 1
EC 5.1 Exterior Lighting

All exterior fixtures must be Dark Sky compliant.

Source: City of Toronto, Ontario, "Toronto Green Standard, Version 3: Ecology for Mid to High-Rise Residential and All Non-Residential," accessed April 1, 2019, https://www.toronto.ca/city-government/planning-development /official-plan-guidelines/toronto-green-standard/toronto-green-standard -version-3/mid-to-high-rise-residential-all-non-residential-version-3/ecology -for-mid-to-high-rise-residential-all-non-residential/.

listen, and FLAP has credibility. "Finally we've gained the attention of an audience [in Toronto] and that audience is quite determined to reverse the problem."

Mesure's work, along with efforts of others in the city, has helped to create some of the earliest bird-friendly development standards. Now part of the city's quite comprehensive Toronto Green Standard, they stipulate, among other things, a stringent set of mandatory bird-friendly window glazing requirements (see box 9-1), standards that have inspired and guided some of the other cities discussed in this book.

Two high-profile lawsuits against bird-fatal buildings helped to solidify the legal and regulatory basis for bird-friendly design. Mesure and FLAP did not initiate these lawsuits, but they supplied most of the bird collision data. Consequently, Mesure was demonized and threatened by the developers and their lawyers. His usual approach is what he described to me as "honey versus vinegar," wanting to work together with developers and builders to reduce hazards for birds.

One thing the lawsuits did was establish a legal obligation under the Ontario Environmental Protection Act, which places restrictions on the discharge of contaminants. The law specifically includes radiation as a contaminant, and through the lawsuits the court concluded that reflected daylight, inasmuch as it is harming birds, is covered under the act. The court opinion was powerful indeed and essentially turned the city's building owners into violators of the law. This has provided a "tremendous amount of leverage" on behalf of birds, Mesure told me, but has also made enforcement difficult for Ontario's Ministry of the Environment, Conservation and Parks.

Despite lack of enforcement of the law, one very positive outcome of the lawsuits has been a significant increase in the number of bird collision avoidance products on the market. "Even though a lot of these glass fabricators and window film companies were intrigued, they weren't prepared to invest their resources in developing products that they felt weren't in great enough demand," he said. The court opinions have served to nudge these companies, and many new products are now on the market.

Mesure estimates that there are a million or more buildings in the city of Toronto alone that could represent bird strike hazards. It is easy to see how this would be an overwhelming enforcement challenge. For Mesure and FLAP (back to his philosophy of honey versus vinegar) the right approach is to look to other mechanisms to bring about change. One current approach is the work of the Canadian Standards Association, which has developed voluntary bird-friendly standards (Mesure sits on the technical committee). If these standards are adopted, it is likely they will make their way into provincial building codes.

But, as Mesure told me, the bigger challenge is what to do about the existing building stock. The city's Bird-Friendly Guidelines will largely take care of new construction and require it to be bird-friendly, but what about existing structures? He said that 99.9 percent of bird deaths were happening on existing buildings. "That's just an insurmountable number of buildings." FLAP has sought to help reduce this to a manageable number by helping to identify the most dangerous buildings, and it has developed a special methodology for doing this.

Funding remains a continuing challenge. Over the years, FLAP has partnered with and received significant funding from Environment and Climate Change Canada. New sources of funding have included the soap company Lush.

One building that recently met the city's standards is the Daniels Building, on Bloor Street, across from the city's iconic High Park. I met with Susan Krajnc, one of FLAP's other two full-time employees, at a café on the ground level of this complex to talk about her experiences with FLAP.[6] She described her first experience as a volunteer, finding an Indigo Bunting that had just struck a building. "You could just see the confusion in his eyes," she told me, relating her sense of helplessness as the bird died in her hands.

The Daniels development is sometimes offered as an example of the difference the bird-friendly standards can make. The fritted glass is obvious in this multistory complex, baked into a ten-by-ten-centimeter (about four-by-four-inch) grid, a density mandated in the code. Krajnc pointed out that the code needs to be stronger, and in fact more stringent revisions will go into effect for private buildings in 2020. The fritting density will increase to five by five centimeters, the standard now applied to new public buildings, such as city hall, where new windows have recently been installed.

Another issue has been the precise layer of a window on which the fritting is found. FLAP has determined that for multilayered windows, having the fritting baked into interior layers makes the windows more difficult for birds to see. Ideally, the fritting should be on the outer layer of the window to maximize visibility to birds. There are now so many local window manufacturers and window companies, and increasingly so much product selection, that satisfying this design requirement should not be difficult.

Public education has certainly been another plank of the work that FLAP does. This includes installing signage in building lobbies. To address what individual homeowners can do, FLAP has developed a wonderful foldout brochure titled "Homes Safe for Birds," printed in both English and French.[7] It's concise but highly informative: What do I do with an injured bird? How do I make my home bird-safe? How do I position my bird feeder to reduce window strikes? It includes a perforated pop-out square showing the dimensions of fritting recommended (five by five centimeters, or two by two inches). "Pop out this

Figure 9-2 FLAP volunteers monitor downtown Toronto during spring and fall migrations, rescuing injured birds and collecting dead birds. Photo credit: FLAP Canada

box," the brochure says, "and hold it against your treated window. The spacing of the markers [as through the use of Feather Friendly fritting tape] should be no more than the height and width of this box." Citizens are also encouraged to take the BirdSafe Homes Pledge and to use the Global Bird Collision Mapper, an online tool for reporting the location of a dead or injured bird in Toronto (and now in other cities around the world).[8] FLAP also sends out migration alerts to building owners during periods of peak bird migration as part of its Lights Out program.

Krajnc also pointed out the limitations apparent in the example of the Daniels Building, which she knows quite a lot about as a former resident of the neighborhood. One controversial issue is the massing and density of the building and the sense among residents that the structure is just too big for the location. Krajnc supports the need for more density in the city but believes this should be accommodated more through mid-rise structures and less through high-rise developments.

The loss of trees in the construction process has been another hot-button issue. The developer was permitted to cut down some of the last remaining black oak trees, something that even took place during the nesting season (more on that later). Part of the structure contains a green roof, which Krajnc sees as positive, but she wonders why there wasn't a better attempt to integrate this development into the larger environment and especially an attempt to connect with High Park. This is a common theme I found in my visits and discussions with people in Toronto. High Park is a part of Toronto's ravine network and home to one of the last remnants of black oak savanna habitat in the city. Perhaps maintaining and even expanding the tentacles of black oaks along neighborhood streets and nearby spaces would create more ecological connectivity and amplify the positive power of High Park.

But also clear is that much of the mortality from bird strikes is happening not at larger commercial or residential structures but rather in more suburban neighborhoods. For this reason, FLAP started its homeowner campaign.

Birds in Ravine City

Toronto is sometimes called Ravine City because of the profound way in which its physical setting is defined by its ravines. Ravines represent a major geologic and ecological feature of Toronto. They are its forested river valleys and, as it turns out, are especially important movement and migration corridors for birds. The ravines define the city, really, making up about 17 percent of its land area. Some 60 percent of this land is publicly owned; the rest is in private hands. Efforts to protect the ravines and to steer development away from them go back Hurricane Hazel, which struck the city in 1954.

There has in recent years been a renewed interest in the ravines and a renewed sense of their importance in defining Toronto. The city recently drafted a new ravine strategy,[9] which lays out an ambitious vision: "a ravine system that is a natural, connected sanctuary essential for the health and well-being of the city, where use and enjoyment support protection, education and stewardship."[10]

On the first of my visits to Toronto in October 2019, I had the chance to become reacquainted with one prominent ravine in the Don River Valley. I began with a visit to Evergreen Brick Works, a wonderful example of adaptive reuse and a staging ground for some amazing initiatives. My tour guides that day were Nina-Marie Lister, a planning professor at Ryerson University, and Cam Collyer, executive lead for Evergreen.[11]

As you walk into the Brick Works, one of the first things you catch sight of is a wall-size sculpture, essentially a living map of Toronto, vividly depicting its system of ravines as the growing elements of a green wall. The work of local artist Ferruccio Sardella, it is a prominent feature and a common meeting place for those rendezvousing at the Brick Works.

Evergreen Brick Works is a wonderful place to begin telling the story of Toronto's ravines. Now a terrific example of adaptive reuse, it was for one hundred years the site of a brick factory that helped to build much of the city. Many of the city's important historic buildings, including the Old City Hall and Massey Hall, were built with bricks made there.

Running out of local sand, the factory closed down, and it was vacant for some twenty years before Evergreen helped bring it back to life. It has since emerged as a hub of local environmental activity (Evergreen already had a positive reputation for its long history of work in habitat restoration) and a public gathering spot. The former quarry is now a lake and public park, and the site has a very popular farmers market and restaurant. School groups come frequently to the Brick Works for events and, now, to visit a unique children's water park. Most impressive is the chance to see some of the remaining kilns and factory structures, which are being restored and repurposed. It is possible to stand and take in the production logic of the longish conveyor system for heating and cooling the bricks and to glean a little sense of what it must have been like at the height of production.

Although the Brick Works operated until 1989, much of what else existed within the ravines was largely cleared out when, as mentioned earlier, Hurricane Hazel hit the city in 1954. The ravines are the location of the city's main rivers and thus flooded extensively. This became (literally) the watershed moment for Toronto to recognize the hazards of occupying the ravines, and they were set off limits from that year on. Most of the land fell under ownership of the Toronto and Region Conservation Authority (TRCA), a creature of the province. The TRCA continues to own most of the ravines.

To get a sense of the beauty and extent of the ravines, I had to do some walking. After touring the Brick Works, I headed out for a hike along the Lower Don Valley, stopping at various points along the way to take pictures of blooming wildflowers and eventually ending up in downtown Toronto. This ravine is the most developed of the city's ravines, and as you walk along, it is clear that although there is solitude and privacy, there are also the sounds of a nearby highway, the presence of utilities and flood control, and other human alterations. Where the Queens Bridge crosses the ravine, I climbed some very steep stairs and ended up in a more urban setting as I made my way toward city hall.

That the city's ravines are essential bird habitat and major corridors as birds move through the city is not doubted. But there is evidence that not all is well in the ravines and that a history of limited ecological management is beginning to take its toll. Jane Weninger, senior planner with Toronto's City Planning Division and the agency's lead on environment, explained the importance of the ravines for birds. "They're our flyways," she said. They are important habitats, of course, and help to safely guide and funnel birds through the city.

Weninger explained the way activities and proposed uses in or near the ravines are regulated, for instance, the requirement that new structures be set back from the edge of a ravine.

But just setting the land aside may prove to be an inadequate strategy, as impressive as the acreage might be. Recent work by a doctoral student, Eric Davies, has raised serious questions about the ecological health of the ravines, pointing out the way non-native trees such as invasive Norway maples have taken over, as well as the absence of native conifers and larger trees of all kinds, such as hickories, which provide such important habitat for birds. Davies noted that the Norway maples are "driving out everything."

The past forty years, this study suggests, have seen a significant decline in biodiversity and ecological function.[12] Landscape architect Walter Kehm agrees with this assessment, though he is critical of this work for its failure to take account of the deeper causes of ecological dysfunction in the ravines. I asked Kehm about the importance of the city's ravine system. The ravines are key, he told me, but he offered some cautionary observations. One is a concern about the declining biodiversity and habitat value of the ravines for birds. The ravines, he pointed out, increasingly "have no sublayers of vegetation, only isolated pockets.

"One of the big missing pieces in the puzzle isn't really the trees so much as it is the second-story shrubs," or, more accurately, the lack of them, he said. "As soon as you establish the shrubs, my gosh, the spring migration of warblers, and thrushes, and ovenbirds, it's unbelievable." More active management of the ravines is what is needed, Kehm believes, to restore the shrubs and understory so important for birds and many other creatures in the city. Dust and debris and other detritus is smothering the soil in the ravines, he says.

Although Kehm is somewhat critical of the way the ravines are being managed (or not), he is highly complimentary of some of the city's newer parks, which have created some impressive new habitats for birds. One impressive example is Tommy Thompson Park, along the Lake Ontario shoreline, essentially formed by dredging the lake. It is a park he had a personal hand in designing, and so one close to his heart. A hundred years ago it did not exist, but today it boasts 500 hectares, about 1,200 acres. It has been designated an Environmentally Significant Area and an Important Bird Area by the organization BirdLife International. It is part of a national network of twenty-six Bird Research Stations. The research station is run jointly by the TRCA and the Toronto and Region Conservation Foundation (TRCF, known as the Living City Foundation before November 2018).

Tommy Thompson Park has lots of lessons for the protection of urban birds, Kehm believes. "The most important thing we have to do here is [preserve] the variety of ecosystems, from wetland edges to the next level of semi-wet areas to areas that are a bit dryer.

"Do not plant a thing," he told me, but try to understand prevailing winds. Take advantage of these and of the role that birds and other animals will play in natural seed dispersal.

"Tommy Thompson now has evolved into a layered landscape," Kehm said. The birds it is attracting are impressive, he noted, mentioning the Canvasback Ducks that came for the first time three years earlier and were now returning and nesting. That is a very good sign, he thinks.

The lessons are important for cities. We need to bring a diversity of landscapes directly into the city. "Cities have been plagued with monoculture plantings," Kehm pointed out. "How do we bring a diverse ecology into a backyard, into a street, into a sidewalk, into a bikeway, into a parkette, into a baseball diamond?" We need to rethink all these kinds of spaces.

Another concern of Kehm's is the need to think beyond the ravines. They might be the green superstructure for the city, but we need to extend and expand nature beyond these main green corridors. "It's as if they put a line around the ravines." We need to "see the city as a silvi-cultural network rather than just the ravines," he said, arguing that the key task will be to expand and extend out from the ravines tentacles of trees, greenery, and habitat.

And that brings us back to the Daniels development, where I had coffee during that October visit. It is a site and project that illustrates how the city is seeking to accommodate and increase density in designated areas of the city. Bloor is considered an "avenue" in the city's growth plan, a place where additional growth can and should be fitted in. In Toronto, this is called "gentle density," emphasizing mid-rise buildings. The Daniels development, Jane Weninger told me, is on the upper end of mid-rise and is rather large and bulky. It does have the requisite bird-friendly glass, and part of the rooftop is a green roof, but there is the sense that more could have been done.

And there has been criticism about the loss of trees during construction, even black oaks. Local columnist Joe Fiorito wrote about this scathingly in a commentary in the *Toronto Star* after visiting the construction site with forester Eric Davies:

> Never mind that the trees are important for the genetic diversity of the black oak savannah in the park. Never mind that the black oak savannah in the park is a wonder of nature on the continent.
>
> Never mind that this is nesting season. . . .
>
> The saddest thing?
>
> A songbird landed on a nearby wire, with a caterpillar dangling from its beak. Eric said, "See that? Birds tend not to fly with food in their beaks unless they are feeding their young."
>
> This, of course, is nesting season. The songbird was on its way to feed its young. It was looking for a tree, and for a nest that was no longer there.
>
> The nestlings would have been too young to fly from the chain-saws; dead now, crushed.

There was no study or inventory done of the diversity of bird, animal and insect life in and among those trees.

And the songbird with the caterpillar in its beak flew above the site as if, by flying, its tree and its young would somehow reappear.

There is a sign on boarding around the site of the condos: "Love Where You Live."

Yeah, whatever.[13]

Losing any large trees in the development process is unfortunate, but in Toronto the loss of black oaks especially so.

I asked Jane Weninger whether there had been any thinking about how the beautiful qualities of High Park across the street might be extended into this urban neighborhood. A green extension, including some black oak savanna, or at least an urban version of it?

Yes, Weninger said, that idea was indeed in the area plan for this neighborhood. It was hard to visualize in the present, and I thought it could be a wonderful design outcome both for humans and for birds.

The Daniels complex lies just north of Toronto's magical High Park, and the need and opportunity for an ecological connection and extension would seem obvious. It is in the so-called High Park Apartment Neighborhood, a place where residents have not always been happy with the changes there, including the growth along Bloor Street and the loss of older trees, including the prized black oak. Indeed, High Park is known for its remnants of black oak savanna, the last in the city, one of the things that makes this park so special. Each year, the city organizes controlled burns within the park to maintain and rejuvenate this habitat.

High Park is a jewel in the natural spaces Torontonians get to enjoy, and it is another key place to see birds. One popular birding site in the park is Hawk Hill, one of three sites participating in the Greater Toronto Raptor Watch. Here, one can see eighteen species of raptors as they migrate through. It is also a prime spot to see Nighthawks. Citizens can help count these birds as part of High Park Nighthawk-Watch, a monitoring program run by Bird Studies Canada.[14] Watchers come to Hawk Hill around six o'clock in the evenings from mid-August through early September.

On my fall visit to Toronto, I had the unexpected opportunity to join a medicine walk in High Park led by Irish Canadian botanist and tree activist Diana Beresford-Kroeger. It was an enchanting and unusual view of the forest. Beresford-Kroeger grew up thinking of trees as people and learning from her elders the ancient secrets and medicinal uses of trees. As a trained scientist as well, she blends the sacred with the scientific in a way few tree advocates can. On that day, she told many stories about the magic of trees, those in High Park that we touched (and at several points hugged) but also trees in the boreal forest and other parts of the world. She told us about how healthy forests on land are the cornerstone of the food web in the marine world (the fulvic acid from tree leaves providing an essential source of iron for marine phytoplankton). These were stories of profound interconnectedness of life, and of the mystery and wonder and sacredness of trees and all the life, including birds, that they support. In her wonderful memoir *To Speak for the Trees*,[15] she describes an oak tree as a kind of biological metropolis "for insects, butterflies and pollinators." Her voice is but one of many that we would be wise to listen to, that will instill a sense of the magic of the trees, birds, and other life around us for which we should make room in our urban neighborhoods.

Toronto never seems to rest long on its laurels, innovating new and interesting kinds of parks and urban spaces. These include the proposed Rail Deck Park, which would create a park on top of a stretch of rail corridor running through downtown, and the newly opened Bentway, a 1.75-kilometer (1-mile) park and skate trail below the Gardiner Expressway.

Another exemplary bit of nature and habitat for birds is the Rouge National Urban Park. Described as "Canada's first national urban park," it lies in another of the city's ravines. It is quite large, being nearly eighty square kilometers (more than thirty square miles), and very close to where many urbanites live, offering a variety of habitats for birds and humans alike, including one unique experience for Torontonians—it is the only place in the city to camp. Kids and families can learn how to camp through workshops offered in the park. With 247 species found there, the park is considered one of the city's birding hot spots.

An example of a green tentacle connecting other parks and green spaces is the Meadoway. This is a project of the TRCA, an effort to reimagine as habitat and public amenity a large transmission line utility corridor. Although the project was underway at the time of this writing, only about 40 percent of the cost (estimated at $85 million) had been secured, which included $25 million from the W. Garfield Weston Foundation.[16] When finished, it will constitute a 16-kilometer (10-mile) linear park of about 500 hectares, or 1,200 acres, that will run from downtown Toronto to Rouge National Urban Park, connecting many neighborhoods and parks and at least four ravines. It will also include a multipurpose trail. Already some 40 hectares (almost 100 acres) of native meadows have been restored. Through this effort, a heavily mowed low-biodiversity area of land planted in non-native fescue will be replaced with high-amenity, high-biodiversity land that is available to many residents and neighborhoods in the city.

This is a creative way of finding new connections and new places in the city to rewild. These ravine extensions and connections could be magnified further, as blogger Trevor Heywood noted in his blog *Metroscapes*. He identified other similar hydro (transmission) corridors, existing and former, amounting to some 160 kilometers (100 miles) in length and 1,400 hectares (3,500 acres) in area.[17]

A Cautionary Pioneer

Toronto has been a leader and a pioneer in raising awareness about the threats to birds in cities, especially through the work of Michael Mesure and his volunteers at FLAP. As a bird advocacy group, its efforts and methods have been inspirational for many other cities. FLAP was the first group, and Toronto the first city, to engage in the kind of bird collision monitoring that has become common in a number of cities. Equally true, Toronto (thanks in no small part to FLAP's advocacy) has become the first city to adopt mandatory bird-friendly design standards. Its new and creative ways to approach parks and green spaces in the city, and especially the ravine system that forms the bones of Toronto's green infrastructure, are impressive indeed.

But Toronto serves also as a cautionary tale, as do all the cities in this book. These have led the way on mandatory bird-friendly design, but is it, or will it be, enough? Susan Krajnc told me that at FLAP they have noticed fewer birds, and of course there are more buildings.

She mentioned the lakefront, where a lot of growth has been happening. "It's another wall," she said. "We worry so much, honestly." She tracks birds by radar as they make their way south. "You're holding your breath." Maybe the birds are fine in Toronto, but they must travel great distances and through and around cities far less committed to birds.

And Toronto's efforts and commitment to birds are partial and incomplete in some important ways. Although important habitats and green spaces are being conserved for birds and humans alike, especially though the city's ravines, there are questions about the declining biodiversity and the lack of adequate management of these urban spaces. Toronto seems up to the challenge, however. Through its work on a ravine strategy and in establishing new parks such as Rouge National Urban Park and the Meadoway, Toronto will continue to be among the cities most committed to making a safe place for birds.

Chapter 10

Black Cockatoo Rising

The Struggle to Save Birds and Bush from a Proposed Highway

A flock of birds
Hovering above
Just a flock of birds
That's how you think of love.
—Coldplay[1]

Protecting remnant swaths of nature is not easy, but it is essential for ensuring urban habitat for birds and biodiversity. There are many threats, the most common of which seem to be highways and development, and they are often backed by considerable financial resources and lots of momentum. So one takes notice when something unusual happens and a community effectively and doggedly organizes itself to protect something dear, and actually succeeds in doing so.[2]

I became aware of one inspiring example of a community coming together to save a remnant stretch of bush, and the birds and animals that depended upon it, through my colleague Peter Newman at Curtin University in Perth, Western Australia. There, in a place I had lived in and visited multiple times and had strong affection for, a conservation drama had been unfolding. Over the course of several years, a conservative state government and premier (Colin Barnett) sought to push through a highway expansion and new freight link connection to the Fremantle port. Ill-conceived and costly from the beginning, the Roe 8 highway expansion seemed unfortunate and unnecessary. And standing in the way, inconveniently for the Barnett administration, were remnant bushlands, remnant swaths of banksia hardwoods, and some very rare wetlands. The highway would have eliminated most of this land.

I had the glorious chance to visit and spend time in these remaining bushlands and to interview and film some of the key players in this urban conservation drama. Peter Newman, filmmaker Linda Blagg—assisted by my daughter Carolena, whose photographs convey some of the magical quality of this nature—and I came together to make a documentary film telling this story. It is a saga that takes place over several years. Partly battled in the courts, it is mostly a story of how a community rallied and never gave up. It involved thousands of residents, many of whom put their personal safety at risk and many of whom were arrested. Two of the most important voices were Kate Kelly, who ran the group Save Beeliar Wetlands, and Kim Dravnieks of Rethink the Link. It has been noted that the majority of the leaders of this campaign were women, and Kate and Kim were two of the most steadfast and passionate.

We had the chance to see firsthand the majesty of these surviving bushlands when we interviewed Kate Kelly. She spoke of her experiences in leading people through these spaces, watching how the land affected them. She spoke of the majesty of these trees and wetlands, which have become her church. She spoke of the many guided walks she has given and the magical effects the wetlands and woodlands have on people. People "soften and they talk slowly and they engage more carefully in their relationships." These spaces, in short, help to make us better citizens and people.

The Perth region is a biodiversity hot spot with a remarkable variety of endemics, especially plants. Much of this is found even in these small remnants, from orchids to bandicoots and blue-tongue lizards and, of course, the majestic trees—paperbarks and swamp banksias—where we filmed Kate Kelly. And the birdlife and animal life there are wonderful. As I walked through the bush on one visit, I saw and heard Rainbow Lorikeets, Red Wattlebirds, New Holland Honeyeaters, and

Figure 10-1 Kate Kelly, shown here standing in a stretch of ancient banksia forest, was one of the key leaders in a fight to save this important bird and wildlife habitat. Photo credit: Tim Beatley

Australian Ravens (which have one of my favorite calls). A lucky visitor may be treated to the raucous sounds of a Forest Red-tailed Black Cockatoo or, even rarer, a Carnaby's Cockatoo, both of them species that inhabit the greater Perth area. A third species of Black Cockatoo, Baudin's Cockatoo, is also found in the South West region of Western Australia, but, smaller in number, this species is restricted to forested habitats there. All three species are in trouble: Carnaby's Cockatoo is classified as endangered, and the Forest Red-tailed Black Cockatoo and Baudin's Cockatoo are classified as vulnerable, under Western Australia's Biodiversity Conservation Act.[3] Gradual loss of habitats such as these ancient banksia forests is a major cause of these birds' decline in number, and as such they made a compelling mascot for the campaign to stop the highway.

In the end, through a multiyear community campaign, the highway and freight link were beaten back and the remaining bush was saved, with a new state administration in power. However, in the months running up to the election, the premier accelerated land clearance, tragically resulting in the loss of some half of these ancient woodlands. The Western Australia state government's response to what was a peaceful protest was vigorous, and some would say mean-spirited, starting with the decision to accelerate bush clearance in the face of clear opposition from the community. Police officers on horseback treated the protesters harshly and arrested many of them, raising unresolved questions about the legal and ethical extent of peaceful protest and when those rights should ever be thwarted.

Many community forums were held and many guided walks led through the bush to allow people to see firsthand what was about to be lost. There were marches in which protesters carried beautiful color photos of what was about to be lost. One campaigner used a drone to capture a bird's-eye view of what was at risk, providing an unusually powerful vantage on the beauty and extent of these bushlands and the extent of deforestation about to take place.

Kim Dravnieks spoke of the philosophy of nonviolent direct action taken during the protests. In so many ways, she said, people "stepped out of their comfort zones" and did whatever was necessary to help. Hundreds would appear on-site to protest, often having been alerted by text messages late the night before. On one day, there was a call to show up in the garb of one's profession or job—doctors came with stethoscopes around their necks. Young people came and occupied trees for days.

The campaign was a lesson in the many creative tools and strategies available for peaceful protest. There was music, with musicians often on-site (a music CD was even recorded on behalf of the bushlands), and poetry was written and recited. Humor played a key role, something that Dravnieks said "really resonated with a lot of people." There were the protesters dressed up in Black Cockatoo costumes, one of whom approached the premier in a shopping center and asked, "Which way to my offsets?"—a reference to the absurd idea that the state government could in fact replace or compensate for these irreplaceable lands. And there were the protesters in bikinis who, cozying up to the premier on a beach, cleverly displayed protest messages written down their arms, something the premier did not notice but photographers did.

Figure 10-2 Protests over the Roe 8 highway extension project were emotional for residents and often ended in violent clashes with police. Photo credit: Nancye Miles-Tweedie

"This has been the whole campaign," Dravnieks said. "People would just come up with ideas and do things." One of the most creative was an hour-long "silent stand." A thousand people showed up in downtown Perth to protest in silence. One person had the idea of using small patches of blue fabric to symbolize the remnant bushlands, and these become a common sight pinned on clothing. Even today, many supporters continue to wear these small pieces of blue fabric pinned to their shirts or coats, showing solidarity and meant to indicate the value of saving "remnant pieces" of bushland.

Dravnieks speaks about the longer legacy of protesting and of a community that learned the virtues and values of collectively standing up for something they strongly believed in. "It showed people that civil disobedience is today," not just something suffragettes had to engage in a hundred years ago. And she speaks of the sense of being able to do something, to stand up and oppose something profoundly wrong, and of pride that she saw from taking a stand. "I watched children who were so very proud of their parents for the stand that they were taking."

The power of nature, especially in a city, is an important point of hope in this story. The protest campaign was in the end a massive awareness-raising exercise, an epiphany for many about the beauty and wildness close by and the ability to engage in a process of standing up in defense of something dear. It was a chance to cultivate a spirit of concern for a larger world, beyond short-term thinking and beyond self-interest.

The clearance that occurred marked moments of shared violence as many watched bulldozers in minutes knock down trees hundreds of years old. Residents and protesters witnessed firsthand when bandicoots, Frogmouth Owls, and other animals were displaced or killed by the deforestation. Most often the pain and suffering of wild fauna is not experienced or seen. Professor Hugh Finn of the Curtin Law School, who was also involved in the campaign to oppose the Roe 8 project, has studied with others the magnitude of these impacts and referred to them as the "invisible harm" in a recent article in *Wildlife Research*. He and his colleague Nahiid Stephens estimated that deforestation in Queensland and New South Wales likely results in more than fifty million animals being killed each year.[4]

It remains to be seen what the long-term implications of the Beeliar campaign and victory will be. There is now an especially well informed constituency, emboldened by this political victory and perhaps a force for future conservation good. It will be interesting (and maybe a good research project) to monitor how the cultivating of this stronger civic environmentalism plays out and shapes conflicts and planning in the future. And one wonders how the emotional connections with and deep caring for nature might be harnessed on behalf of larger global threats of deforestation and habitat destruction. Could Save the Beeliar Wetlands become a force for stopping land clearance in Borneo or sub-Saharan Africa or perhaps even in other parts of Australia? There is little doubt in my mind that cultivating awareness and practicing conservation activism can and must carry over to other places, though the precise mechanisms and processes to allow this to happen are unclear. Similar public and grassroots challenges to the loss of urban trees and forests, and the birds and wildlife that depend upon them, is happening throughout the world, from India to the United States to the United Kingdom. From Sheffield, England, to Mumbai, there is a new and optimistic kind of activism that is saying enough is enough and questioning the loss of these critical and beloved elements of urban nature.

There are some important postcampaign tasks in Perth, including formal transfer of these bushlands from ownership by the state roads department to its parks department. And there is major restoration and revegetation work to be done for those areas that were cleared, much of which has already begun. Sadly, some off-road vehicle use has already trammeled newly sprouting vegetation, but in the longer run the prospect for regeneration is quite good.

And there is a lot of momentum around the idea of connecting these remnant bushlands into a larger ecological corridor—a concept being called Wetlands to Waves, given that the corridor will extend from the Beeliar Wetlands all the way to the coast. This is a promising initiative, though one wonders whether an even larger ecological concept could weave together parks and green spaces of various kinds into a much larger "bushland green grid," one that might extend well into the Indian Ocean, perhaps more fully encompassing nature protection to include marine protection as well.

Peter Newman told me that the state government has stood firm on its highway decision. And regeneration of the vegetation has been taking place. "It certainly looks impressive at the spot where we filmed," Newman said.[5] I am anxious to see for myself and hope to be able to do so on a return visit in upcoming months. It will undoubtedly take many years for the cleared areas to return to any real semblance of what they were, ecologically and in terms of their deep beauty.

The story of the Black Cockatoos extends well beyond the remnant habitats of the Roe 8 highway corridor, with both discouraging and optimistic elements of how vulnerable bird species can coexist with a rapidly developing metropolitan population, one that is predicted to reach 3.5 million by 2050. Forest Red-tailed Black Cockatoos and Carnaby's Cockatoos face a variety of urban threats including, again, habitat loss from urbanization, loss of trees and nesting cavities and important nest sites throughout the area, the danger of being hit by cars, and even the risk of being shot.

When injured Cockatoos are found, they benefit from an effective partnership between Perth Zoo, where they receive veterinary treatment, and the Kaarakin Black Cockatoo Conservation Centre in Perth, where they are rehabilitated and healed and, it is hoped, later released.[6]

In April 2018, the five hundredth rehabilitated Cockatoo was released back to the wild. This impressive number shows the importance of rescue and treatment of injured birds, something that depended in no small part on the commitment and good graces of the residents of Perth.[7] The Cockatoos benefit from a recovery facility that includes a 64-meter (210-foot) flight aviary for strengthening the birds' flight muscles, "like a lap pool for recovering cockatoos."[8]

Consider the plight of Sweetie, a Carnaby's Cockatoo who had been shot in the head. She was treated at Perth Zoo, spent a year in rehabilitation at Kaarakin, and was eventually released.[9] Or Handsome, who was struck by a car and endured a broken wing.[10]

Interestingly, and inspiringly, while at Kaarakin, Black Cockatoos may have some interaction with inmates from nearby Karnet Prison Farm who work at the center, building and repairing fences and enclosures and caring for the birds.[11] It is a partnership that has been going on for about a decade, and it seems to deliver as much benefit, perhaps more, for the prisoners as for the birds.[12]

The state of Carnaby's Cockatoos in the South West region of Western Australia, which have seen a 35 percent reduction in number in just the past ten years, shines a light on another form of habitat loss there. This species has grown to depend on nuts from pine plantations as a main source of food, a response to a decline in native banksia forests. Decisions about when and how much these pine plantations are allowed to cut their trees have major implications for Cockatoos and have led the state government to place some restrictions on harvesting, though not enough, conservationists believe.

Conservation of these wonderful birds is complex, but it is clearly achievable in Perth and is increasingly a priority for residents. The need to protect remnant banksia forests and ancient wetlands, as in the case of the Roe 8 highway victory, is beyond doubt, and it influences the ability of residents to see, hear, and experience on a daily basis these colorful birds. We can only hope that the resolve to protect what is there, and to recover and grow back what has been lost, will hold firm.

One of the most powerful voices in this story was that of Noel

Nannup, a Noongar elder, who we had the chance to interview and film. Along with my colleague Peter Newman and filmmaker Linda Blagg, I met with him at a most hopeful site—Telegraph Hill, a park in Fremantle that has itself gone through regeneration, though it took 120 years from the time it was denuded. Nannup spoke of the aboriginal heritage and deep history of the bushland sites in jeopardy and how the government ignored this heritage (and structured the project in a way that allowed it to ignore or skirt the requirements of the Aboriginal Heritage Act). "They pushed us aside," he said, "treated us with contempt." For the Noongar people, these sites were sacred, and they have been continuously visited and occupied, likely for more than sixty thousand years. "There's a spiritual energy line," Nannup told me, "a flow through there that our people have followed for thousands of years. Our people are buried along it. A lot of people were born along it and lived their complete lives traveling around in a six-season cycle. Being born there, every year you went back to visit your birth site."

Despite the tragedy of half of these sacred lands succumbing to the bulldozer, Nannup remains optimistic. It was the spirit at work, through people, that saved the land. And he sees the key to the future as continuing what he calls this "social investment in the environment." For the Noongar people, this is a natural thing and the result of long-standing traditions that foster deep social and emotional investment in the natural world.

"For us, our social investment is that for millennia our people have buried placentas under certain trees," Nannup said. "So our DNA is in our trees. So when we say 'that tree is me and I am that tree,' we mean it." That unity with environment, that sense of oneness, is perhaps the best way to guard against its destruction. How we can fully cultivate that in the non-aboriginal world, though, remains an open question.

The Perth story is a hopeful one for campaigners and organizations in other cities and countries where highway projects threaten nature. Perth shows it is possible to mount a compelling campaign to bring the community together around a different vision of the future and to win elections and change direction. And there are other planning and policy dimensions.

From the violence of bushland clearance and pursuit of a flawed highway came a renewed sense of the shared value these bushlands have in the lives of Western Australians and the special role they play, indeed must play, in urban life. That is one of the hopeful messages. *Never Again* is the title of a recently published book about the campaign written by a group of professors (they call themselves "the Angry Academics") and edited by Peter Newman. There is the sense that the broader community simply will not allow a similar loss to take place in the future. Without land transfer, in the case of the Roe 8 lands, and better, stronger environmental laws and land protection standards more generally, it's not entirely clear that this collective admonition will stand up, but I certainly hope it will.

Although ultimately this is a hopeful story of how a community can successfully oppose a project such as this and can come to the defense of nature, it has many cautionary elements. One is just how flimsy the legal protections were (and are) for such lands and how pliable the existing environmental laws and regulations were. The highway was allowed to move forward in part as a result of the provision of compensatory "offsets" for the habitats that would be lost, yet almost all agreed that these bushlands, and especially the wetlands, were simply irreplaceable.

I asked Nannup whether he saw any chance that the non-indigenous population of Western Australia might learn from and embrace some of the deep connections to nature and place held by the Noongar people. Indeed, the larger world would benefit. Nannup described the sense of oneness with the bush the Noongar have, something that would make the kind of destruction set in motion by the state government pretty unimaginable.

A Practice for Our Time: Adopting a Bird Totem

One Noongar practice that I'm especially fond of and believe might have some practical conservation effect is that of adopting one or more totems. Nannup told me about this deep tradition and explained the importance of the Bronzewing Pigeon, his own totem. Nannup said that when you are given a totem, you are expected to learn everything you can about that animal or plant. He went on to explain, in remarkable detail, how the Bronzewing Pigeon cools itself and how it digs

Figure 10-3 In Noongar culture, children are given one or more totems (animals or plants in nature) to learn about and protect. Shown here is the Bronzewing Pigeon, which is Noel Nannup's totem. Photo credit: "File:Common Bronzewing (Phaps chalcoptera) (30554138873).jpg" by Dominic Sherony is licensed under CC BY-SA 2.0.

small holes that later become important receptacles for wattle tree seeds.

I have been thinking a lot about what ought to be my own totem. In my recent time in Perth, I encountered many different plants and animals that fascinated me. Shortly after arriving, we were visited by a pair of Black Cockatoos, which hung around to watch us. I've been enamored of Black Cockatoos, and I had the pleasure of seeing flocks of them at several points during this recent visit. I don't know enough about them but will endeavor to learn more, and since my own deep home is Virginia, I will be selecting some local totems more appropriate to where I live.

Chapter 11

Birdicity

What Makes for a Deeply Bird-Friendly City, and How Do We Measure It?

"Hope" is the thing with feathers —
—Emily Dickinson[1]

A truly bird-friendly and bird-loving city, a city high in "birdicity," is a city working to reduce the physical risks for birds in urban areas—taking steps to enhance habitat, providing guidance about better building and urban design. But it must do much, much more—making changes that are less tangible too.

Partly this is a recognition that cities represent a remarkable opportunity to ignite in their residents a lifelong love of birds, upon which everything else in this book would seem to depend.

Many cities have now developed biodiversity strategies, a good step toward becoming places that merge human and natural habitat. These strategies address birds to some degree, since birds benefit from many of the key steps for conserving local biodiversity, whether establishing more greenbelts and land conservation or rewilding parks and backyards. But more cities need to follow the lead of Vancouver, British Columbia, in preparing a stand-alone bird strategy. This has many advantages, including the ability to focus in detail on ways to make a city more bird-friendly and raise awareness for bird conservation issues in local government.

Vancouver aspires to be the "greenest city in the world." Its Greenest City Action Plan sets out goals and targets for connecting residents with nature. The plan includes targets for access to nature (a park or green space within a five-minute walk for all residents), for habitat restoration and annual tree planting (150,000 per year), and for tree canopy (22 percent by 2050), among others—all specific actions that also help birds. Vancouver's Greenest City vision is an exemplary effort to imagine a more natureful city.

Perhaps most impressive, the city has prepared the Vancouver Bird Strategy, part of a set of additional plans and strategies for implementing its Greenest City vision. Released in January 2015, the plan lays out arguments for why the city should strive to be bird-friendly and specifically identifies objectives, key opportunities, key challenges, and action areas. Many of these overarching ideas can be adopted by cities regardless of size or geography.

The strategy begins with this vision: "By 2020, Vancouver will be a world leader in supporting a year-round rich and diverse assemblage of native birds, accessible to Vancouver residents in every neighbourhood and park in the city, and attracting visitors from all corners of the globe."[2]

The strategy states a key premise, that birds enhance city life: "The high visibility and auditory presence of birds creates an experiential link with nature that can foster stewardship of the natural environment and enrich the lives of Vancouver's citizens." Key opportunities identified in the strategy include protection and restoration of habitat, bird-friendly development, bird-watching, and tourism. Key challenges include habitat loss from urbanization (a drastic reduction in urban forest cover), invasive species, predation by domestic pets, and building strikes.

The strategy also identifies current actions and future recommendations. One key recommendation is to adopt and voluntarily apply bird-friendly landscape design and bird-friendly building design guidelines for private and public development, and bird-friendly landscape operational guidelines for public parks and land. There are also recommendations for expanding citywide research and monitoring and for arts, awareness, and education. Finally, the strategy calls for the expansion of economic development and tourism around birds.

The strategy was prepared by a standing bird advisory committee consisting of volunteers. The committee meets nearly monthly and includes representatives of many local and national bird groups. According to Alan Duncan, who has served as city staff to the committee, the committee has given birds "a higher profile" in the city.[3]

One bird species of particular interest in Vancouver is the Pacific Great Blue Heron. The Herons have been returning to Stanley Park to nest since 2001, and there are around eighty-five active nests. A Heron management plan was prepared in 2006, and this colony offers the chance for monitoring and surveys conducted from nearby rooftops. According to the 2018 monitoring report, ninety-eight fledglings were produced by these nests. Bald Eagle predation has been a significant threat in the past, along with predation by raccoons. To respond to the raccoon threat, colony trees were fitted with special raccoon-proof metal shields placed at the base of the trees, which have been reported to work well.

On-site talks educate residents about the Herons, and there is even a Heron cam, which allows residents to watch them remotely. The cam is accessible day and night from March through the end of July, the end of the nesting season. More than 180,000 people have watched the Heron cam since it was set up in 2015.

One of the city's accomplishments has been the attraction of the International Ornithological Congress to Vancouver in August 2018. This brought some 1,600 ornithologists and bird lovers from seventy-four countries. There were paper and poster presentations, guided bird walks, lots of participatory bird art, and an opening parade put on by members of local First Nations.

The art included a collaborative one-hundred-foot-long mural called *Silent Skies*, providing a composite of small portraits of all 678 endangered bird species. Some 160 artists worked together on this project, organized by a nonprofit called Artists for Conservation. The resulting mural, along with a set of vinyl reproductions, has been making its way around the world.

Designation of a city bird is another way a city raises awareness about birds. As Alan Duncan with the City of Vancouver explained, the first vote in 2014 (corresponding to Bird Week) generated remarkable community interest; more than seven hundred thousand residents voted. Citizens could vote online, but the city came up with some other creative ways to vote, including the placement of cardboard birdhouses in libraries and community centers with paper ballots to slip into them. The result was the choice of Black-capped Chickadee.

In 2017, the city chose to select a permanent city bird instead of having an annual vote. This process began by querying Vancouverites about the qualities of people who live in the city (a process called "Words for Birds").[4] A set of experts used this list to identify four bird species reflecting these qualities and put them up for a vote. Anna's Hummingbird won, with 42 percent of the more than 8,200 votes (Duncan explained that fewer votes were cast than in the first contest, as the novelty wore off). So now the city has a permanent city bird as well as three other bird designees (earlier choices for city bird): the Northwestern Crow, the Black-capped Chickadee, and the Peregrine Falcon.

Recently, Houston Audubon chose an official bird using a similar process, creatively structured as a series of "bracket rounds" of voting that began with some sixty nominated species. In the end, the Yellow-crowned Night-Heron was the winner, beating out the Attwater's Prairie-Chicken in the final round. The announcement garnered considerable public attention, culminating with a ceremony at city hall and coordinated with Houston Bird Week.[5]

Every City a Bird City

Increasingly there are efforts to establish and apply some sort of minimal certification system for cities and towns that take actions to make themselves bird-friendly. Modeled after Tree City USA, Bird City Wisconsin seeks to stimulate local bird conservation by recognizing cities that take steps to meet certain minimum criteria. Cities have considerable leeway in what they do, but they must satisfy at least seven criteria from a list of twenty-two across five main categories, from habitat protection to public education. One criterion (its own category, actually) requires that all participating cities acknowledge and celebrate in some way International Migratory Bird Day.

Once the minimum criteria are reached, the participating city is given an eye-catching road sign to display. Participating cities also receive a Bird City flag, suitable for flying outside city hall. Cities must be recertified each year, and there is a special High Flyers recognition program for cities that go above and beyond the basic criteria.

Carl Schwartz, then executive director of the program, told me it has two main catchphrases: one is "the power of partnerships," and the other is "making our communities healthy for birds and people." Together they reflect much about the approach of this program. The assumption in the first case is that a lot can be accomplished when groups in communities work together, each perhaps doing a little. The second phrase reflects the value in understanding that we are in fact in this together and that when birds decline or are under threat, humans are at risk as well.

Does such a program actually make a difference? Are cities taking steps in support of birds that they otherwise would not be taking? Is the ability to call one's city a Bird City a meaningful form of recognition? It is hard to say, but Schwartz believes it does support and encourage cities and provides meaningful incentive to think about birds. It has also created a peer group of cities in Wisconsin in which cities might learn from one another about steps to conserve and protect birds. Schwartz noted that while the program is designed to provide flexibility in reaching the criteria, many cities end up doing more over time, in part because of the prodding and encouragement of the Bird City organization. Review of a Bird City application may result in a favorable decision, but often it is also an opportunity to point out additional steps a city can take to protect birds. The Bird City approval letter is a chance to make positive suggestions for the future, many of which are pursued by participating cities.

The program might be judged a success on participation alone. There are now fifty-four participating communities, with a number of them reaching the designation of High Flyer.

The program has some important educational benefits and may get people talking about birds and what needs to take place to ensure their protection. Not a day goes by, it seems, that someone doesn't ask Schwartz, looking at his baseball cap and T-shirt, what "Bird City Wisconsin" is. Presumably the prominent placement of signs and flying

---

Box 11-1
A City High in "Birdicity"

Is a City With . . .
A city bird strategy
Mandatory bird-safe building standards
A comprehensive or general plan that includes birds
Designation of one or more official city birds
A standing bird advisory committee
One or more bird and wildlife rehabilitation centers
Parks, trees, and green spaces planted with bird-friendly plants
Many places to watch birds and many urban bird hot spots
Many bird walks and venues for bird walking (e.g., trails,
    tree-lined streets)
Many opportunities to connect with birds in real time (including
    bird cams)

Where . . .
Citizens can identify and recognize many local species of birds
Many residents are engaged in watching and caring about birds
Many organized bird walks are available, as well as other events
    that make enjoyment of birds easy
There are diverse ways to engage with and enjoy birds (from Falcon
    cams to bird walks)
A large number of homeowners seek bird-friendly certified gardens
There are abundant citizen science opportunities

---

of the Bird City flag will raise the visibility and local awareness of birds in a community and ignite some needed conversations.

A City That Thinks Like a Bird

I vividly recall hearing architect Bill McDonough describe the undulating green roof on the Gap Headquarters in San Bruno, California, in terms of how birds might experience it. It made me imagine what a bird might see when flying above it. McDonough's idea was that birds would not detect the building; from above, there would be no sign it was a human structure. Some of the bird-friendly buildings described in this book take the idea even further, with eco-roofs designed and planted to be significant forms of bird habitat.

In a similar way, I wonder if we might attempt to understand what high birdicity means by trying to put ourselves in the position of birds. Of course, we can never truly experience this, but there is nevertheless utility and certainly value in this design metaphor, something close to what Aldo Leopold meant when he spoke of "thinking like a mountain": could we think like a bird-friendly city, or look closely at our city from the perspective of a bird? What are the dangers, and what are the obstacles to flight and movement? Where are the stopover points, where is the habitat, where are the places of respite and nourishment that will permit a migratory songbird to successfully move through the city?

As the stories in this book illustrate, there are many places in cities where new bird habitat can be inserted, from green rooftops to backyard habitats to urban tree planting.

These areas of nature in the city perform many functions for us in addition to providing habitat for birds. They retain floodwater, moderate urban heat, capture carbon, and moderate air pollution, among other ecosystem services. And they provide important areas for respite, recreation, urban hiking, and of course bird-watching. The mental health benefits of such various forms of nature in cities are considerable.

These are also investments that make economic sense. A recent study commissioned by the Friends of the Chicago River estimated the economic benefit of improving and restoring blue-green corridors and found annual benefits of $192 million (increased value of property along the river), and more than 1,600 full-time jobs, generated from these investments.[6] One segment of river restoration, called Wild Mile Chicago, has already been undertaken and aspires to be "the first-ever mile-long floating eco-park in the world."[7]

One major challenge for cities will be to reimagine the many smaller spaces—turfgrass lawns, side yards, and spaces adjacent to urban buildings and development—as opportunities for birds and for bird habitat. And they are places to bird-watch. I am heartened by stories of how in cities such as St. Louis they have preserved one of the last remaining native prairies, in Calvary Cemetery, no less. A controlled burn was undertaken in this remnant prairie, necessary to germinate prairie plants and to ensure this unusual oasis is beneficial for birds and insects, according to Erin Shank with the Missouri Department of Conservation.[8] There is only 1 percent of this natural prairie left, and it offers an unusual opportunity to save and appreciate this biodiversity in the city. I don't know whether any residents of St. Louis go to Calvary to see birds, but the active work of habitat management there suggests it would be an excellent place to explore with birds in mind.

A city high in birdicity is also a city where there are abundant and interesting places for walking, hiking, and strolling. Cities such as Singapore and Wellington, New Zealand, have extensive networks of urban trails with unusual and often dramatic vistas and views of the city and beyond.

Bird-friendly cities must provide extensive places for bird hikes, but they must also help to organize these events, as a helpful nudge for residents. This can be undertaken by local parks departments and nature centers or private organizations and nonprofits. An example of the former can be seen in the Cleveland Metroparks spring migration bird walks, a long-standing tradition in that city. An example of the latter can be seen in the bird walks organized by the Urban Ecology Center in Milwaukee, a nonprofit with a focus on birds.

Investing in a trail network can be transformative in many ways. San Francisco is an inspiring example. The city is currently celebrating the thirtieth anniversary of adopting a plan to build the San Francisco Bay Trail—a public trail at water's edge, circling San Francisco Bay, traveling through nine counties and forty-seven cities, and providing unusual connections to and contact with this watery habitat and the many shorebirds that can be found there. The trail is not yet complete—it will eventually be 500 miles long, an impressive 350 miles of which have already been completed. I recently spoke with Laura Thompson, who has run the program for the Association of Bay Area Governments for the past fifteen years.[9] The benefits of the trail in providing access to birds and bird-watching are especially important. "The Bay Trail is really a kind of vehicle for birders to come out," she told me. Birders from all over the country attend the San Francisco Bay Flyway Festival, much of it at sites along the trail.

In an era of unprecedented levels of mental illness and depression, biking and walking in nature offer an unusually potent tool. A recent study from the United Kingdom of group nature walks found strong support for their ability to moderate or reduce mental illness and depression. This large study of more than 1,500 participants found that "nature group walks—and frequent nature group walking—were associated with a reduction in perceived stress, depression, and negative affect, and an increase in positive affect and mental well-being."[10]

Walking in nature, then, has a strong beneficial effect on mental health, and it would be wise of elected officials, planners, and citizen advocates to work to increase the availability of such opportunities in a city. Individuals and families today experience a variety of often debilitating stressful events, from natural disasters to divorce to the loss of a job, and this study and others provide evidence that such nature walks can help to "undo" or "dampen the impact of stressful events on mental health."

Parks in cities provide extremely important habitat for birds as well as places and amenities essential for a high quality of life for humans. Piedmont Park in Atlanta, Georgia, is an excellent case in point. Recently, I stood with Nikki Belmonte and Adam Betuel near the park's Swift tower, and on the banks of Clear Creek that day the sounds of birds were everywhere. Betuel counted twenty-nine species in just the short time we were there. The value of two hundred acres in the center of a sprawling metropolis of Atlanta cannot be underestimated.

We need these kinds of larger urban parks. They are important stopover points for birds and offer wonderful opportunities for residents to see and experience birds. We also need to look carefully at the ecological changes that have taken place in larger green spaces, such as the ravines in Toronto, and do a better job of controlling invasive plants and restoring the native trees and understory plants that provide the best habitat for birds. As Betuel explained to me, we need to ensure there are berry-rich plants to provide the fatty berries my Wood Thrushes will need as they continue south from Atlanta on their fall migration. Urban parks can help immensely.

Figure 11-1 A ceremony celebrates the new Swift tower at Piedmont Park in Atlanta, Georgia. Photo credit: Jessie Parks for Atlanta Audubon

Every city will have opportunities to restore and repair habitats for birds, often through creative reuse and recycling of urban infrastructure and landscapes. The Walthamstow Wetlands in London is a good example. This former industrial site and waterworks is now a popular birding site and important habitat, one close to the city and easily reached via the London Tube. San Francisco's efforts to convert thousands of industrial salt ponds back to natural tidal wetlands is another good example.[11]

The hazards of building facades and glass, and urban lighting, have never been more prominent in the popular press, and it is extremely encouraging that cities such as San Francisco and Chicago have adopted or are considering mandatory bird-safe building standards. The design of new structures such as sports arenas incorporating bird-safe glass is encouraging; the Milwaukee Bucks Fiserv Forum is a significant success story. There is strong momentum around this issue now, thanks in no small part to the years of advocacy by groups such as the National Audubon Society. Federal legislation has been introduced that would create requirements for bird-safe design for all federal and federally funded structures; if this comes to pass, it will make a huge positive impact.

Representative Mike Quigley (a Democrat from Illinois) and Representative Morgan Griffith (a Republican from Virginia) are cosponsors of HR 919, the federal Bird-Safe Buildings Act of 2019. Assessed to be budget-neutral, the bill would make bird-safe materials and design mandatory for all new construction or substantial rehabilitation procured by the General Services Administration, exempting historic structures. The bill requires at least 90 percent of the glass facade below forty feet to be treated with bird-safe material (e.g., netting or patterned or ultraviolet light–reflective glass), along with a minimum of 60 percent of the glass above forty feet.[12] There are also provisions that address outside lighting and monitoring. In July 2020, HR 919 passed in the US House of Representatives, a remarkable accomplishment and a cause to be hopeful that momentum is finally building. A similar bill passed one chamber of the New York state legislature, suggesting that reform of state building regulations is another promising direction.

Protecting birds from dangerous buildings and glass is essential, but cities must do much more. Green rooftops are growing in importance and popularity. The bird-friendly cities Toronto, Ontario; San Francisco; Portland, Oregon; and, most recently, New York have adopted mandatory green roof requirements. This is a positive step, but efforts must ensure that the design of these roofs and the plants selected for them will maximize habitat value for birds. We need to continue to reimagine where bird habitat can be inserted in a city. As we've seen with large facilities such as the Jacob K. Javits Convention Center in New York and the Vancouver Convention Centre, wildflower meadows can be successfully planted on these large rooftop spaces.

Although much of this book has focused on the important role that cities can play, it is also important to recognize that homeowners (and apartment renters) can do many things as individuals to help birds, actions that can have clear, direct, and often fairly immediate impact. Wonderful programs such as Portland's Catio Tour show, for instance, what is possible and how an individual can make an important and tangible contribution to reducing threats to birds.

As Daniel Klem, Michael Mesure, and others are quick to point out, all structures, especially suburban homes, represent a building strike hazard for birds, and so every homeowner or flat occupant has the chance to do many, often small, things to retrofit windows and glass doors so that birds can adequately see them. The cost is minimal, and the potential cumulative effect is great.

It is promising that we have seen a movement, albeit still small, to consider the habitat value of public infrastructure such as bridges, which are now being designed from the start to accommodate bats, and building facades, which can host a variety of other forms of life. I am especially taken by architect Joyce Hwang's work in "habitecture" and reimagining building facades as habitat facades, and Terreform One's prototype of a butterfly wall for a new office building in Manhattan is exciting.[13] But of course we still often have a hard time accommodating and living with the wildlife that already finds a way into our homes, such as Chimney Swifts. "We lack a tolerance for harmless things," said Edward Mayer of Swift Conservation. But it is more than that—it is a lost opportunity for a daily dose of joy, wonder, delight.

Cities will need to work hard in the future to ensure that parks and green spaces of all kinds are planted and maintained to maximize benefits for birds. Rewilding of spaces in parks will be important, and creating no-mow zones will help increase some of the insect food sources in decline. It will be important to actively manage parks and green areas to ensure the presence of native species of plants and trees. Recent research suggests, encouragingly, that when invasives are actively controlled, native understory plants rebound relatively quickly.[14] A recent study of Pileated Woodpeckers in suburban communities recommends maintaining a minimum tree cover (20 percent) and "retaining large deciduous trees and snags in public green spaces and yards."[15] Homeowners should do their part as well, and their efforts can be successfully supported by backyard habitat certification programs such as the one run by Portland.

Every open and available space in a city or suburb, whether a park or a green rooftop, can and should be planted with native plants and trees, which will significantly help the habitat and food web needs of birds. Few individuals have been as active or outspoken in advocating for native plants as University of Delaware professor Doug Tallamy.[16] He makes a convincing case that if we love birds, we must plant the

Figure 11-2 Two Portland, Oregon, homeowners stand in front of their catio. Their backyard has also been certified through Portland Audubon's Backyard Habitat Certification Program. Photo credit: Tim Beatley

trees and plants that will sustain the food sources—the native berries and especially the caterpillars—that fuel the raising of young birds. Trees that are not native to North America, such as ginkgoes, may be lovely to see, but they provide almost no value to birds, supporting zero species of caterpillars. Evolution has resulted in specialized relationships and interdependences between native plants and wildlife; almost all butterflies and moths, for example, rely on specific host plants. In contrast, the white oaks native to the eastern United States support more than five hundred species and remarkable amounts of biomass and food for growing bird chicks. Tallamy argues that we must plant natives, but we must be sure to plant the 5–7 percent of natives that are productive ecologically—what he calls keystone species—and that produce, he told me, more than 75 percent of the food for birds. "Not all natives are equal," he points out. Online databases, such as Audubon's Native Plants Database, can help homeowners and cities select plant and tree species that are native to their particular regions.[17]

We must do more, Tallamy says. Because caterpillar pupae depend for some of their life cycle on the soil below trees, we must manage our yards and parks in ways that allow these spaces to be wilder and more biodiverse. Around the bases of trees would be excellent places for native ground cover, such as wild ginger, and for those spaces, some of the layered landscapes will be best. "City parks are designed for easy maintenance," Tallamy told me, "not for biodiversity." No need to plant grass right to the edge of that oak, he warns.

Our notions of the suburban lawn continue to evolve as we recognize ways in which we can plant bird-friendly landscapes and curtail unnecessary mowing. This uses fewer resources and helps create ecological hot spots where bees and insects and birds find a home. Tallamy believes that homeowners should reimagine their yards as important habitat spaces, and he suggests the target of converting at least half the yard to natives. That, he says, would result in the addition of some twenty million acres of native habitat, something that would really help birds and that he labels a "homegrown national park." These new yard-habitats can provide important habitat for birds and serve as biological corridors for many different kinds of species.

Invasive plants represent a serious problem for birds, and there are some 3,300 species in North America. As a result, parks like the one a block from my home are covered with non-native species such as lesser celandine. Producing a beautiful yellow flower, it is inedible and poisonous for native wildlife and serves little ecological value to birds. Invasives squeeze out essential natives. Although birds eat berries from some non-native plants, these often lack the fat and the nutritional value of berries from natives.

Tallamy emphasizes the need also to address the proliferation of artificial lights and makes the point that even where parks and urban spaces contain native trees and plants, they will remain biologically empty when they are heavily lighted. We need dark-sky lights, just as much for insects and birds here on Earth as for maintaining our connections to the night sky. "Lighting is key," Tallamy argues. "Those keystone plants work really well in a natural area, but when you surround them with lights, like we do everywhere, they don't work anymore because the moths come in and they're killed in the lights. You don't have a thriving population of moths for those birds when you have the light on all the time." For homeowners, and presumably for cities as well, the choice of outside lights is important—Tallamy recommends yellow LED lights, which are the least attractive for insects. "Immediately you've stopped the slaughter at your lights all summer long."

I find it interesting that in many cities in the United States and around the world there are renewed efforts to protect trees, often through protest and activism, but birds are rarely thought about or mentioned, even though in terms of the habitat and enjoyment of trees, it is birds that are the animating force.

As the climate continues to change, cities will continue to become hotter, and as we recommit to protection of birdlife in cities, we will also need to think about design and planning solutions that help birds and other urban wildlife sustain themselves in these new levels of heat. Protecting and expanding a city's tree canopy is certainly one important part of this. We need to design for maximal natural air-conditioning and heat reduction, including ways to better understand and take advantage of natural breezes and wind patterns, as is common in German cities.[18]

Dallas, Texas, offers a useful example in the United States. One of the top three cities most dangerous for migrating birds according to researchers at the Cornell Lab of Ornithology,[19] Dallas is beginning to map out an impressive strategy for trees that will help birds as well. One of the first American cities to conduct a comprehensive urban heat study, Dallas has plans to plant 250,000 new trees. This strategy was chosen because modeling shows that trees are the most effective way to battle urban heat (compared, for instance, with reflective building materials).[20] The models seem to indicate that abundant tree canopy can result in summer environments that are as much as fifteen degrees Fahrenheit cooler, better for birds and for humans. And even better if they are native tree species.

Ensuring the presence of water in cities will also be essential for birds, and this could take many forms, including the restoration of rivers running through cities and the bringing back to the surface (or "daylighting," in the common design parlance) of streams and waterways that have been placed in pipes underground. There are many good reasons to do this, but it is also part of what will make cities more hospitable to birds.

Cities also have a long history of engaging water through public fountains and various kinds of urban design that incorporate water features. These are often not designed with birds in mind at all, or other kinds of urban wildlife, and that is a missed opportunity. In fact, they may often become a danger to birds. When I discussed with Ed Mayer the hazards faced by Common Swifts in London, he mentioned that in England, any water feature that sprays water must be treated with the chemical bromine, a precaution against Legionnaires' disease. "Public fountains are effectively poisonous," he told me. And even if they aren't, edges are not designed to make it easy for a bird to reach the water.

In downtown Perth, in Western Australia, a traditional urban water feature—sterile, highly chlorinated, and energy-intensive—was transformed into a natural wetland. The result is truly remarkable, bringing living nature and the biodiversity of a native wetland to the heart of this city. Its clever design includes native species of fish, such as the pygmy perch, that naturally control mosquitoes. It also has a public stage that has become a popular setting for concerts and events. The designer, Josh Byrne, describes the space as "quite magical." It has been

Figure 11-3 An urban wetland in downtown Perth, Western Australia. Here, a sterile water feature was converted into a native habitat wetland supporting birds and other native wildlife. Photo credit: Tim Beatley

a great success and represents a much better approach for birds and humans alike.

Getting Architects and Designers on Board

As a member of the teaching faculty in a school of architecture for more than thirty years, I have been startled sometimes at how little information is given to design students about bird-friendly design principles and practice and the needs of birds. Architects, landscape architects, and urban planners have a special opportunity to influence the design of urban and built environments that could better take into account the needs of birds. Aside from my own Cities + Nature class, I don't know of another course in my school that addresses birds.

This is changing, however, both within the professions and within academia. Carl Elefante, president of the American Institute of Architects (AIA) from 2017 to 2018, has regularly spoken of birds. In a guest lecture and taped interview at the University of Virginia, he was asked about the idea of designing for multiple species. His answers were thoughtful and eloquent; he said we must first plan and design well for the human species, understanding that we are biological creatures, a part of the natural world rather than apart from it. In his words:

> The second species that's really being thought about is birds. Because our cities today are annihilating birds by the millions. And it's a totally unintended consequence. No one said, Let's figure out how to maximize how many birds we can kill by the way we're designing our buildings. But it's out of absolute ignorance that we're building buildings that are literally killing millions of birds every year.[21]

This is a telling admission and a call to action. We must make sure that every aspiring architect or designer is challenged early in their career to think about birds and how their designs impact birds, positively or negatively. Design for birds must be seen as a primary goal, not a peripheral consideration or an afterthought.

On a positive note, things are changing in the architectural world thanks to the work of design leaders such as Jeanne Gang and Bruce Fowle. Susan Elbin, science and research director for New York Audubon, related to me how supportive the AIA has been in efforts to develop and adopt the bird-safe ordinance.

Perhaps a part of what must happen is the development and promotion of a new set of design aesthetics—one that questions the feverish admiration of sealed, shiny, glass-enshrined buildings, which are not only bird-killing machines but also energy hogs and heavy emitters of greenhouse gases.

Some of the most interesting and exciting new buildings put protection of birds front and center. Examples include the Aqua Tower in Chicago (a Studio Gang design) and the Interface headquarters retrofit in Atlanta, Georgia (Perkins and Will). I find them beautiful, visually distinct, and remarkable in ways most bird-fatal structures are not. Birds are good for design, I would argue. Designing buildings and neighborhoods with birds in mind results in more interesting buildings and more distinctive places. Bird-friendly cities are more interesting and nourishing places.

There are, as well, positive signs that developers and the development world are more interested in birds. One of the best examples, but certainly not the only one, is Kingsbrook, in Aylesbury, United Kingdom (discussed in some detail in chapter 4), where as a result of a unique partnership between Barratt Homes and the Royal Society for the Protection of Birds, thousands of bird- and wildlife-friendly homes will be constructed. We need to actively explore more of these kinds of partnerships between the real estate and development communities and those advocating for bird and wildlife conservation.

But too often it seems that birds are used only to adorn the colorful renderings of building and project designs. Almost every rendering I have seen lately has birds flying nearby, in the foreground or background or both. But using images of birds to sell a design is simply not acceptable—it is time to commit to designs that genuinely protect and make spaces for birds, that lead to a more, not less, secure future for them in cities.

Judging a City by the Presence of Birds and Birdsong?

I like the idea of using the metric of birdsong to judge the long-term progress and success of cities. For a lot of us, it is the remarkable songs and sounds that birds make that uplift and brighten our days. We look forward to the dawn chorus but also to the sweet and subtle sounds that the birds around us deliver.

All residents, wherever they live, ought to be able to hear native birdsong. They ought to be able to enjoy as I do the remarkable singing of a Wood Thrush or one of their many local species. A positive case in point is Zealandia, a unique conservation effort in Wellington, New Zealand (discussed in chapter 3), aimed at creating a predator-free space for native birds to rebound. Zealandia's tagline is "Bringing bird song back to Wellington." It is an appropriate and inspiring goal, and that is exactly what has been happening in that city, adding immensely to the quality of life there.

In addition to Wellington, leaders in other cities around the world recognize the need to protect these audible connections to the avian world. Samir Shukla, a newspaper commentator in Ahmedabad, India, has been writing for years about the unfortunate loss of birds in that city and the importance of birdsong. In an essay titled "Birdsongs and

Urban Planning" he argued for the importance of a different kind of standard.

> As I stare out of my window looking at what should be a winter morning, the architect in me trained at School of Architecture, Ahmedabad makes me feel that all urban planning norms should be replaced by a simple test.
>
> Walk into a garden or an academic campus of any city. Close your eyes and listen to birds. If you can figure out which season is going on from the birdsongs, it is a city worth living in.[22]

This kind of goal will require more focused work around sound in cities and planning for soundscapes. We tend in planning and de-sign to think almost exclusively about the negatives of sound—that is, noise, which we now understand has more a negative impact on health than previously realized. We need to continue to work to reduce urban exposure to high levels of noise while cultivating sounds of nature. Cities such as New York have taken important steps, such as mandat-ing use of newer, quieter electric jackhammers and other construction equipment. Many cities are identifying quiet zones with public parks, thinking more systematically about zones of quiet and solitude in the city, and identifying parks, urban spaces, and walks that permit con-templation. These will be helpful in allowing us to hear the wondrous birdsong, such as that of my Wood Thrush, that would otherwise be masked by urban noises.

We have not quite yet, however, evolved to the point that we also understand the natural soundscape, birds included, as positive place qualities and assets that should be monitored, tracked, and, where pos-sible, fostered. Much of the work of enhancing bird habitat in cities and suburbs discussed here will, of course, also enhance the natural soundscape. No-mow zones in urban parks will increase the inver-tebrate life of these spaces, which will in turn enhance their natural sound qualities.

Recently the citizen group BioPhilly organized a conference in Philadelphia around the need for natural forms of air-conditioning. We know that the planet is poised to see a dramatic growth in air-conditioning; a recent International Energy Agency report predicted a rise in global air-conditioning units from 1.6 billion today to 3.7 billion in 2050.[23] During this conference I had the chance to reflect on my childhood home in Alexandria, Virginia, a place I lived from birth until I departed for college. We had no air-conditioning. Instead we were surrounded by trees, benefiting from the natural cooling provided by shading and evapotranspiration. We had operable windows (with screens) that we cranked open when it got hot, delivering breezes but also the sounds of birds and the wonderful night sounds of crickets, katydids, and tree frogs. Enjoying birdsong in our communities may in part depend on ways we can rediscover these older time-honored design strategies, as well as the needed investments in natural air-conditioning (e.g., through urban tree planting) at the neighborhood and city level.

The popular power and appeal of birdsong was recently demonstrated in the United Kingdom. In April 2019, the Royal Society for the Protection of Birds released a single of composite birdsong called "Let Nature Sing." The two-and-one-half-minute recording reached number 18 on the UK singles chart. Adrian Thomas, who recorded all twenty-five of the bird species featured in the single, explained to me that the goal was to raise awareness about the plight of birds as a run-up to the environmental summit in Beijing in 2020. Using facts and standard arguments is one thing, he said, but there was a sense that "you need [also] to touch people emotionally," which these sounds indeed do. Using the power of its 1.2 million membership to drive presale of the single, and knowing it was going to reach the singles charts, made it an important news story and indeed has helped to raise awareness there.

In recent years, a growing body of experience and research has demonstrated the therapeutic and stress-reducing benefits of birdsong, and it is increasingly being used in hospitals, schools, and elsewhere to enhance these settings. Eleanor Ratcliffe and her colleagues at the University of Surrey in the United Kingdom have explored the importance of bird songs and sounds through different methods. In a series of semi-structured interviews, they found that "bird songs and calls were . . . the type of natural sound most commonly associated with perceived stress recovery and attention restoration."[24]

Precisely why birdsong is so therapeutic is not clear, but Ratcliffe and her colleagues believe it is a combination of the sounds themselves (some sounds, such as squawking and screeching, are viewed less positively) and the associations and memories that go along with those sounds. My own personal experiences bear this out; I grew up listening to Wood Thrushes and Northern Mockingbirds and understand the importance of their songs and vocalizations. For many of us, birdsong is the soundtrack of our lives, and we miss it sorely when we can't enjoy it.

Sound expert Julian Treasure of the consulting firm The Sound Agency has worked on several projects including introducing birdsong in gas station restrooms. Treasure has even developed a smartphone app called Study that will deliver soothing birdsong wherever one happens to be.

Airports, such as Amsterdam's Schiphol, have for many years employed birdsong to create restful areas. Airports seem especially to be prime candidates for this kind of therapeutic intervention. One of the most impressive examples can be seen in a large public art and sound installation in Hartsfield-Jackson Atlanta International Airport, the busiest airport in the United States. I was pleasantly surprised to have discovered this installation as I passed through on my way to a connecting flight, and I have gone out of my way to visit it again. It is otherwise a subterranean environment with no natural light or connection to the outside world.

Located on a walkway corridor between the A and B terminals, it is a remarkable 450-foot-long digital immersion in a Georgia forest, with native birds flying above and birdsong along with sounds of thunder and rain. Every visitor knows it is not the real thing, but it is remarkably realistic, and the laser projectors produce a real sense of connection to birds and the natural world. Flocks of birds flying over you as you traverse the walking sidewalk is a genuine nature experience. A trade journal article about the technology used in the installation points out that a key element in why it works is the synchronizing of images and sound: "the pitter-pat of raindrops increases as the rainfall intensifies and mini triggers match birdcalls to the species flying overhead."[25] The only problem (at least for me) is that you may end up missing your flight as you walk back and forth enjoying this unexpected visual and audible treat.

Figure 11-4 An innovative art installation at the Hartsfield-Jackson Atlanta International Airport, *Flight Paths*, includes virtual birds flying above as passengers walk to their gates. Photo credit: Tim Beatley

Flight Paths is the creation of artist Steve Waldeck and is funded through the city's 1% for Art"program and its public art master plan, with most of the funds coming from airport lease payments and parking revenues. The installation's price tag of around $4 million meant that it was not without controversy. One hope is that such installations, and other forms of public art, will entice travelers to do more walking to and from their gates—most travelers passing through the airport (an estimated 80 percent) take the train that connects the terminals rather than walk.

An important demonstration of the power of birdsong can also be seen in how these sounds are being used in the Alder Hey Children's Hospital in Liverpool. Here, in a project organized by sound artist Chris Watson, birdsong is recorded in local parks and delivered to young patients at especially stressful times, such as when they are receiving an inoculation or before surgery.

Actual birds, delivering actual birdsong in real time, is a feature some hospitals have discovered. In Atlanta, Georgia, Emory University Hospital Midtown has two small aviaries housing around fifty birds. These are favorite places for visitors and patients who look forward to hearing and watching the birds, all non-native species such as Finches and Parakeets. A description of the aviaries on the hospital's website quoted one regular patient, Wendy Darling, who looked forward to seeing the birds on her regular visits to the hospital: "At times, it's unpleasant" [visiting the hospital for weekly allergy shots], "but in the end, I know that the birds will be there. Whether I get to watch them for a minute or a half an hour, I always enjoy my time with them."

Connecting with the Birds in the Neighborhoods Where We Live

Several of the site visits and sets of interviews conducted for this book demonstrate the value and power of thinking about how we can more effectively connect residents to the birds they will see around them in their neighborhoods. The inspiring emerging examples of wildlife- and bird-friendly developments such as Kingsbrook in the United Kingdom and the new urbanist development Aldea in Santa Fe, New Mexico, suggest that birds are a largely ignored asset and resource for enhancing quality of life. In Kingsbrook, developers are beginning to see prospective residents drawn to the neighborhood because of the promise of seeing and being around Swifts and other birds. They actually want to have a house that accommodates birds, that includes built-in Swift boxes, bat boxes, hedgehog highways, and wildlife-friendly gardens. The experience at Kingsbrook is showing, moreover, that connections with birds and nature can enhance salability of the housing units, a strong argument that can then be made to other builders and developers.

At Aldea, a new urbanist community outside Santa Fe, a small number of enthusiastic residents launched their own efforts to enhance bird habitat, installing seventy bird boxes built by local high school students for the threatened Juniper Titmouse. A bird group and a permaculture committee engage residents in a variety of ways, including by organizing lectures, working on native landscaping and water management projects in the community, and installing bird boxes and monitoring

Figure 11-5 Residents of Aldea, near Santa Fe, New Mexico, have adopted the threatened Juniper Titmouse and have been installing nest boxes for these birds. Photo credit: Tim Beatley

them during the nesting season through the NestWatch program. This work has enabled birds to become a way to deepen connections to landscape and place and to foster new friendships and social activities. Monitoring the nest boxes has become a way to be outside and to engage in walking and exercise. One resident told me that the NestWatch boxes are arrayed along a nearly two-mile-long walking loop, getting her out and into nature.

And harnessing the labor and volunteer power of residents on behalf of birds is not to be overlooked. During my meeting with NestWatch volunteers at Aldea, they were quick to point out how important their work was, especially to understanding the biology of the Juniper Titmouse. As leader Don Wilson explained, their observations about nesting constituted (according to the Cornell Lab of Ornithology) some 92 percent of all the information submitted about this species.[26] Neighborhood efforts such as this one can indeed provide important scientific and management data and can make a biologically meaningful difference in enhancing habitat conditions.

It is also a cliché, but with considerable truth, that we are most likely to care about and take active steps to protect the spaces and places around us. At Aldea, this has manifested in the form of installing bird- and wildlife-friendly gardens—more than forty residents have had their gardens certified through the National Wildlife Federation's Certified Wildlife Habitat program—and in discussing how stormwater is managed (with a push to install Zuni bowls and rain gardens that would keep more of the water on-site) and how residents could and should avoid using rodenticides to control mice and rats. The latter concern was a primary motivation behind the installation of Aldea's five Screech Owl boxes. These are discussions that can be effectively had at a smaller neighborhood level. What better way to convince someone to shift away from pesticide use than through a discussion with a neighbor?

Engaging the Urban Public with Birds

Bird feeders could be one way to overcome the sense of disconnect from nature, the fact that many residents of cities don't see these environments as places of nature at all. Daniel Cox and Kevin Gaston, in their UK study of the self-reported benefits of feeding birds, asked why more people don't do it. "A bird feeder has the potential to be a powerful tool for people to make this connection, because it provides a focal location where people both expect to and are able to observe birds and their behaviours."[27]

There is a major challenge in getting residents, especially those in larger cities, to realize the extent of the abundance of the rich nature all around them, including birds. Perhaps it is one of the negatives of a hectic urban life that many things around us often go unnoticed.

Cities such as Vancouver, British Columbia, have done an excellent job of helping to raise the visibility of birds and to encourage a new view of cities as bird habitats as well as human habitats. The annual Vancouver Bird Week involves organized bird walks throughout the city. The city publishes a guide to common birds and a series of maps that help guide citizens to bird-viewing hot spots.

Photographing birds is a significant and rewarding hobby for many people and is an art form in itself. Bird photography can be encouraged

Figure 11-6 A nest box for the threatened Juniper Titmouse built by local high school students. Photo credit: Tim Beatley

in many ways, through workshops, classes, and mentoring. Contests are one way to stimulate interest, and each year, a variety of bird photography contests are held. These include the Audubon Photography Awards, with a top prize of $5,000 and a Youth Prize award of a six-day summer camp at the Audubon Nature Center on Hog Island.[28]

There are also many local bird photography contests. One example is the contest in my own part of Central Virginia, a collaboration between the Monticello Bird Club and the Charlottesville Camera Club. Photographers are encouraged to submit photographs in one of four categories: backyard birds, birds up close, birds in their habitat, and birds in motion. The photography that results from this annual contest is striking for its beauty and artistry focusing on the particular species near to where we live.[29]

There are many ways in which art and the work of artists in cities can help connect us to birds and to deliver some of the same sense of beauty and wonder that actual living birds provide. And these various forms of art may allow us to think about birds in a different way, or to appreciate an aspect of birds—their shapes and plumage and behaviors—that we may not have noticed. Given the love and fascination we have for birds, it is little wonder that they figure so prominently in our urban art.

One of the most impressive urban art initiatives is the Audubon Mural Project. Growing out of an idea to celebrate birds in the Harlem neighborhood where John James Audubon lived in the latter years of his life, this is a collaboration between the National Audubon Society and the Gitler &_____ gallery. Small stipends have been given to artists to create beautiful and colorful birds on the sides of buildings. There are now 110 of these bird murals, specifically of species that are climate threatened (of which there are 314, so there are many more to paint!). All of the murals can be seen online, and there is a printable map for those who would like to visit them in situ. A recent editorial in the *New York Times* described some of these images and the joy they bring to this urban setting.

> A tour of the Washington Heights and Harlem neighborhoods with the aid of an Audubon map amounts to a new sort of bird-watching. It takes a search to track down the Williamson's sapsucker, bigger than life, down by the West Side Highway. The black-billed magpie is visible all day now on the Broadway gates of the defunct New Happiness Chinese Restaurant. Elsewhere, Audubon himself is rendered in flesh tones and with mutton-chop sideburns, staring curiously at a cerulean warbler on his shoulder with neither his rifle nor palette at hand.[30]

Bird art can take many other forms. Some of the most striking examples are the *Ornitographies* of Spanish artist and photographer Xavi Bou. Inspired by early bird walks with his grandfather, Bou undertakes a creative process through Photoshop of compressing photos of birds into dramatic single frames. These visually striking photos show the flight paths of single birds or flocks of birds across the sky. Some viewers have likened them to ribbons or double helixes. Bou photographs a variety of bird species, from Flamingos to White Storks to Herring

Figure 11-7 Shown here is one of the 110 beautiful bird murals in the Harlem neighborhood of New York City, a result of the Audubon Mural Project. Photo credit: Mike Fernandez/Audubon

Gulls. For me, it is as if birds gave off smoky contrails showing the elegant and beautiful strokes of winged flight. Bou describes his artistic quest as one of "making visible the invisible."[31] The goal with this work is, he says, "to capture a moment that is past, present and future, all at once."[32]

Photography of plight or peril faced by birds is another important exercise in similarly making something visible that is mostly invisible. The annual display by FLAP in Toronto, Ontario, of all the birds killed in building and window strikes is certainly an example. Minnesota photographer Miranda Brandon has taken a similar approach but focuses on one bird at a time, depicting and photographing birds in the moment of impact. The series, called *Impact*, was inspired by her time as a volunteer for Audubon, and the birds photographed were collected from the bases of buildings. Here is how she describes the work:

> *Impact* literally and figuratively enlarges the issues faced by birds when moving through built spaces, giving visual voice to their

plight. Birds appear 6 to 12 times their natural size, depicted as if at the moment of impact or just after: falling through the air, or posed in quiet portraiture with heads drawn at eerily unnatural angles. At such a large scale the birds cannot be easily tidied up and discarded. The photographs demand physical and contemplative space for their subjects, offering in return an intimate view of each bird and allowing minute details to be revealed. The beauty of the birds coupled with their abnormal postures provokes viewers to consider how humans impact the spaces we occupy. . . .

Designed to generate new awareness and knowledge of the presence of birds in our everyday lives *Impact* expands our capacity to care more about them, and about other non-human animals.[33]

There remains the need to shift the mind-set of most urban residents so they see their cities as places of co-occupation, of cohabitation with and celebration of those many cohabitants. In a city such as Vancouver, with its diversity of natural habitats, there are likely many different bird-human encounters. Alan Duncan, who staffs Vancouver's Bird Advisory Committee, mentioned to me that there are eleven Bald Eagle nests within the city boundaries. One exists just fifty-five yards from his patio. As I write this, in April 2020, a Bald Eagle pair is nesting in a park in the center of Pittsburgh, Pennsylvania, with young chicks that are being watched intently by residents through an Eagle cam—a remarkable seven million people have watched this Eagle cam.

There is no doubt that urban residents need some help and need some nudging. In Vancouver, largely as an outcome of the work of its standing Vancouver Bird Advisory Committee, bird-viewing hot spots have been identified, and several guides have been produced to different bird species and the parks and places in the city where they can be seen.[34]

Bird walks and other educational offerings that teach but also insert an element of fun are key. In Vancouver, there are Owl Prowls in Stanley Park, for instance. "There is a huge interest" in such events, Duncan told me, with some eighty people showing up for the first of these events. "I think it's really untapped," he told me.

Matt Knittel, a naturalist with Cleveland Metroparks, described the value of the bird walks organized during spring migration. These occur over six Sundays at thirteen different locations, and they date back to 1956.[35] They also manage NestWatch and FeederWatch programs that enlist and engage citizens to help observe closely the successes and challenges faced by species such as Bluebirds in urban settings.

Designing for the Future

There are some new threats to birds on the horizon that have not been fully considered or thought through. One has to do with the likely proliferation of drones in the future. We already know that birds of prey can react in a territorial way to drones, actually attacking them; the Dutch have already been utilizing Falcons as a tool for neutralizing drones around Amsterdam Airport Schiphol. With home delivery of goods via drone, could this congested neighborhood airspace lead to collisions and death for songbirds? It is unclear, but Australian architecture professor Peter Fisher wondered in a recent op-ed article whether steps should be taken to ensure drones are designed and used in ways that minimize bird mortality (similar to what we are now asking of wind parks).[36] This might take the form of color schemes that would make drones more visible, perhaps, or restrictions on how fast they can travel, or the use of blades that are softer and less likely to injure birds.

There remain important questions about what physical investments in cities would deliver the most positive and powerful impacts in terms of birds. We know what we need to do to design bird-friendly buildings, but what about bird-friendly roads and highways?

This includes work to reduce vehicle-bird collisions, which are much more significant than we realize. Road ecology has emerged as a growing area of research and practice, leading in many places to productive investments in wildlife overpasses and underpasses and in the growing view that ecological connections and connectedness are essential. What this agenda means for birds is less clear. Wildlife passages are less evident as a solution to birds flying over and alongside roads. Some of the answer is to slow down car and truck traffic, but perhaps connected forest canopy and other strategies involving landscape design and vegetation patterns could create skipping-over opportunities, or "micro urban flyways," that would steer and funnel flying birds out of harm's way. More research, testing, experimentation, and pilot projects are needed here.

And we need to rethink (again) how we use and treat the spaces around us—our yards and courtyards where we live and our parks and green spaces in our cities. We must plant them with native plants and trees, grow them and care for them without harmful pesticides, and integrate spaces for nesting into our building facades. We must work to reduce light pollution, turn lights off, and shift to dark-sky lighting, which is less disruptive to nature (and to humans who seek a connection to the night sky) and increasingly important to ensuring the food web essential for birds.

In designing cities and metropolitan areas, we know much of what we need to in glass and building design. But what will be the most effective mix of green spaces, parks, tree cover and green rooftops, and other designed green features for birds, both resident birds and those migrating through the city? Through a combination of research, collaboration, and new design approaches, we can begin to transform our cities into better bird habitat.

The Richness of Life in a Bird-Friendly City

What many of the stories in this chapter show is just how improved our lives are when we have birds around us. We benefit immensely when we design for them, when we reimagine our neighborhoods as places where our avian friends are welcome and where we are likely to encounter them daily, if not hourly. There is joy in having them around. The chance to see a Burrowing Owl, or a soaring Vulture, or a darting Swift at sunset adds immensely to the quality of our lives. There are also important elements of meaning and purpose when we take personal steps to work on their behalf, to repair habitat, to grow the plants they need, to retrofit dangerous windows. It is a positive sign that in many parts of the country there is an impulse to give back and to engage in some form of "conservation actions" on behalf of birds, as Cathy Wise of Audubon Arizona describes them.

There is often an element of awe that comes with this coexistence. Awe, according to Richard Louv in his wonderful book *Our Wild Calling*, "is what we feel during or after an encounter with something unexpected, which stimulates a sense of vastness and possibility, such as hearing thunder, listening to a moving piece of music, sensing the infinite during prayer or meditation."[37] There are many other wild animals and elements of wildness that might stimulate this sense of awe and wonder, but birds are the most likely subjects of our gaze, most likely to be what we see, notice, and hear. And the awe they inspire is manifold: whether the physics-defying upside-down walking of Nuthatches or the drumming of Woodpeckers or the impossible flights and flying skills of (you name it . . .) Vultures, Swifts, and Pelicans. These times when birds are all around are often the periods of our lives when we are more likely to be happy and content with the world, more at home where we live and work. And in the moments when we focus on these magical winged creatures, we break free from our narrow and self-interested human selves.

Chapter 12

Cultivating a Bird-Caring Citizenry

Make a little birdhouse in your soul . . .
—They Might Be Giants[1]

As we've seen throughout this book, there are so many physical changes to make in cities that can benefit birds. These are much more likely to happen if more people are aware of and excited about the birdlife around us. How do we cultivate a lifelong love of birds?

At a time when we are worried about the public health epidemics of our inactive, sedentary lives and growing loneliness, lifelong birding holds the potential to address all of these concerns. It challenges us to meet other people (and other species), to see the world beyond our own self-interest, to exercise and engage in an outdoor life, and to forge new social connections. Learning to identify the birds about you where you live is an essential skill that will help set you off on a productive, stimulating, magical life.

Every young person should learn about birds at an early age. After all, they are all around us, and many kids express an early curiosity about birds. This early exposure and learning can happen in many different ways, and ideally a parent or grandparent or a sibling can stimulate interest. But more formal bird education and conservation programs can and should be included in public schools.

Schools can be much more engaged with birds and bird conservation. One recent example is Team Wood Thrush, a school-based program started by then Audubon staffer Mary Elfner. For about five years, with a very small budget, Elfner worked with teachers in several middle schools in the area of Richmond, Virginia (and several schools outside of Richmond, including one high school), to introduce the subject of Wood Thrushes. The program included in-class lectures on Wood Thrush birdsong and biology (connected to the state's Science Standards of Learning) and at least one field visit to look and listen for Wood Thrushes later in the spring, when the birds arrived. Elfner told me recently that she may have been able to reach two or three hundred students, but that there was interest, though no funding, to significantly expand the program to cover more schools and more students.[2] (Funding is often a challenge for programs such as this, another thing that needs to change.)

One of the places Elfner took her students was Dutch Gap, a natural area of woodlands and wetlands just outside the city. Here the local news channel captured the students' enthusiasm. They seemed to know Wood Thrushes well and could describe their unique song and the habitat fragmentation challenges the species faces. "We need birds," one child declared, and "I think that we should save the Wood Thrush."[3] I expect this experience has shaped these kids in deep ways and, perhaps for some, ignited a lifelong interest in birds. Elfner told me about hearing several years later from one of her students who had heard (and recognized) a Wood Thrush in another part of the state and wanted to let her know. These programs can make a huge difference and can change the course of kids' lives.

Elfner told me the Team Wood Thrush initiative was modeled after an earlier example called Team Warbler, another program she was involved in at Audubon with a focus on the Prothonotary Warbler, "which serves as [a] link between Virginia and Panama."[4] This is another species that migrates for the summer to the Richmond area, spending its winters in mangrove forests in Panama. Elfner and I agreed that it would be a wonderful idea to arrange to connect schoolkids in Richmond with their counterparts in Panama (Panama City is now a member of the global Biophilic Cities Network), to collaborate in learning about and working together to conserve this species.

Atlanta Audubon has several important school programs. One, called Connecting Students with STEM through Birds, works with six schools in the city of Atlanta or Fulton County. For participating schools, Audubon helps install a bird-friendly garden and trains the teachers to educate their students about birds. Audubon volunteers and staff take the kids birding and supply the binoculars; most of the kids have never used binoculars before. The conservation and education directors converge on the school for some events, including a day when mist nets are used to temporarily capture birds, allowing at least some kids to have the experience of holding and releasing a real bird.[5]

These kinds of experiences can be transformative; Atlanta Audubon's director, Nikki Belmonte, told me about her own so-called spark experience when, as an eight-year-old summer camper, she got to hold a bird from a mist net. "I've been a birder ever since," she said.

Atlanta Audubon's teacher education program, called Taking Wing, assists teachers in using birds as a lens for teaching other subjects. "What we have found is that teachers are very interested in utilizing anything that is in their schoolyard as a subject to teach," said Belmonte. Teachers learn to identify birds and learn about their biology. In addition to its school-focused work, Atlanta Audubon operates a number of other community engagement and education programs. These include field trips throughout the region, bird walks (in places such as Piedmont Park), and workshops for adults.

Engaging kids and young adults directly in the actual retrofit of buildings to make them safer for birds is an excellent way to both educate people and address the underlying problem. One great example is the Frick Environmental Center in Pittsburgh, Pennsylvania. A certified Living Building (an ambitious green building certification level)[6] with many impressive biophilic design features, including the mimicking of forest patterns in its interior and exterior windows and facades, it nonetheless had significant large windows on the building dangerous to birds. As the center's director of education, Camila Tinsley, explained in an interview, they enlisted participants in their Young Naturalists program (kids of high school age exploring careers in environmental sciences) to design and construct a bird-safe retrofit

Figure 12-1 The Atlanta Audubon Society has been working with elementary schools in the area to teach students about birds and to support STEM (science, technology, engineering, and mathematics) education. Here, Adam Betuel, Atlanta Audubon's director of conservation, gives kids a chance to see native birds up close through mist-net capture and release. Photo credit: Atlanta Audubon

Figure 12-2 Participants in the Young Naturalists program at the Frick Environmental Center in Pittsburgh, Pennsylvania, designed and installed these paracords, which make the windows more bird-safe. Photo credit: Tim Beatley

of the large windows in the front of the building. Working with the local group BirdSafe Pittsburgh, the students designed and constructed (with purchased materials) a paracord system, which has proven to work quite well in alerting the birds to the glass. As Tinsley explained, the students learned as they built it and were able to see the impact of their efforts right away. "That's peak education right there," she said.

The Power of eBird

eBird is an online global database of bird sightings also maintained and managed by the Cornell Lab of Ornithology. It is described as the "world's largest biodiversity-related citizen science project, with more than 100 million bird sightings contributed each year."[7] It is essentially a web-based platform for reporting on birds that users have seen or heard, including their location, during the normal course of bird-watching. It is free and open-access, and there is an eBird app that makes the reporting even easier. It also allows users to maintain and manage their personal life lists of birds. Through the database, it is also possible for users to see where there are birding hot spots and find their favorite birding spot.

There are also regional portals, which provide more localized information and facilitate connections with birders and bird events in one's area. For my home state of Virginia, for example, there is an element of friendly competition in that there is a running list of jurisdictions according to the number of species identified and the number of checklists. The global database of bird sightings has also generated important scientific and conservation insights. A recent paper published in *Nature Communications* showed the power of this crowdsourced bird species data. Here, the authors developed a "robust multi-species planning tool to estimate the land area needed to conserve 117 Nearctic-Neotropical migratory songbirds throughout the annual cycle."[8]

On the Cornell Lab's annual Global Big Day, birders around the world are encouraged to submit eBird observations. The 2018 event broke records, with some thirty thousand participants identifying seven thousand species of birds around the world. There is also an important yearly event called the Great Backyard Bird Count, held for four days in February. Jointly sponsored by the Cornell Lab and the National Audubon Society, it has been underway since 1998. Some 160,000 individuals participated in February 2019.

A Need for Greater Diversity in Birding

There is little doubt that birding as a hobby has been dominated by those who are affluent and white. If birds are to be fully appreciated, and if the joy and wonder they deliver are to be fully enjoyed by the larger world, much more work must be done to expand the diversity of the birding community. Urban birding offers at least the hope that this can happen.

J. Drew Lanham is an African American birder and scientist, a professor of wildlife ecology at Clemson University. He has been one of the most vocal in helping others to understand the challenges of being a minority in the birding world. In his book *The Home Place*, Lanham specifically talks about "birding while black" (the title of a chapter). He describes what it feels like to be out birding along the backroads of South Carolina, the anxiety and fear, trying to focus on the birds he is seeing and hearing but also aware of the potential danger nearby, made evident by the occasional glimpsing of a Confederate flag. "I am a black man and therefore a birding anomaly. The chances of seeing someone who looks like me while on the trail are only slightly greater than those of sighting an ivory-billed woodpecker. In my lifetime I've encountered fewer than ten black birders. We're true rarities in our own right."[9]

What to do and how to change this circumstance? Lanham advises of the need to work to get more folks of color, more kids, into birding. More kids need to see and learn from more black birders.

The wild things and places belong to all of us. So while I can't fix the bigger problems of race in the United States—can't suggest a means by which I, and others like me, will always feel safe—I can prescribe a solution in my own small corner. Get more people of color "out there." Turn oddities into commonplace. The presence of more black birders, wildlife biologists, hunters, hikers, and fisherfolk will say to others that we, too, appreciate the warble of a summer tanager, the incredible instincts of a whitetail buck, and the sound of wind in the tall pines. Our responsibility is to pass something on to those coming after. As young people of color reconnect with what so many of their ancestors knew—that our connections to the land run deep, like the taproots of mighty oaks; that the land renews and sustains us—maybe things will begin to change.

I'm hoping that soon a black birder won't be a rare sighting. I'm hoping that at some point I'll see color sprinkled throughout a birding-festival crowd. I'm hoping for the day when young hotshot birders just happen to be black like me.[10]

In April 2019 I traveled to Warren Wilson College, near Asheville, to hear Lanham give the Power of Place annual lecture. It was an inspiring talk, though I found myself thinking a lot about the two large Confederate flags I had seen along the highway. They were a reminder of the kind of America people of color must live in and navigate. Why add to the dangers of life, I wondered, by doing what Lanham does, following his heart outside and in pursuit of feathered sights.

Black birders face a host of challenges and even risk to life and limb when they simply engage in the casual bird-watching that most of us who are not of color don't understand. Working to overcome prejudice and racial injustice in our larger society is, of course, part of the answer. But specific things can be done in cities to expand the diversity of those who watch, and feel empowered to advocate on behalf of, birds.

The perils of bird-watching while black became national news on Memorial Day 2020, when a white woman walking her dog called the police on black birder Christian Cooper, who had only asked that she place her dog on a leash. For many African Americans, it was an all-too-familiar experience of feeling threatened and unwelcome in public spaces like Central Park; for those of us who are not black or brown, it was a small window into how difficult, and often dangerous, it is simply to watch birds in the United States. On that same day, George Floyd, another black man, was killed by Minneapolis police, setting off protests in cities around the country mourning his loss and the underlying racism and police brutality that led to his death (and the deaths of countless other people of color). In these ways, the desire to study and enjoy birds became inextricably intertwined with racism and discrimination.

One response was the creation of Black Birders Week, a chance to celebrate and learn about the remarkable scientists and activists of color working on behalf of birds. Co-organizer of the week's event, Corina Newsome, a graduate student at Georgia Southern University doing research on the Seaside Sparrow, spoke of the hope she gains from birds and the need to "change the narrative" about birds and nature. The prevailing narrative says that people of color don't watch birds, don't care about nature, and are not to be found in the outdoors engaged in these activities. The undergirding of this narrative is structural racism and spatial inequality that says, essentially, these are spaces and activities reserved for whites. More inclusive birding is a step in the right direction, of course, but deeper and harder work will be necessary to overcome underlying racism and to make our society profoundly more just and equitable. Working to make the birding and bird conservation world more ethnically diverse and inclusive will in some important ways help to advance this larger cause.

There are many other ways that birding and bird conservation could be more diverse. Including more of the voices and perspectives of women, and ensuring women equal and safe access to the joys of birding, would be one important way. It has been observed that male voices dominate in birding circles and in bird science and conservation. Olivia Gentile, in a perceptive essay titled "A Feminist Revolution in Birding," observed that it is men who write the bird guides and are the leading bird scientists, and that male approaches, even to the way we watch birds (with an emphasis on "fast-paced listing" of the species seen), tend to dominate.[11] She wrote that "women birders are too often overlooked, underestimated, and belittled," which partly helps to explain the creation of all-woman birding clubs. Misogyny and violence toward women in the larger society necessarily carry over into birding. Street harassment and worse are facts of daily life for women, something that necessarily limits their ability to watch, enjoy, and study birds in the wild (and in parks and forests of cities). Atlanta Audubon has formed an Equity, Diversity, and Inclusion Task Force, partnering with National Audubon. One thing that has already come out of it is the creation of an apprenticeship program providing opportunities for young people of color to find positions within the birding world. Atlanta Audubon has hired Jason Ward, a young black birder who now regularly leads the bird walks at Piedmont Park. Such programs are a step in the right direction, to be sure, but birding organizations must be careful not to settle for a kind of tokenism or partial representation of minority communities. There must be a more wholesale opening up of the birding world to people and communities of color. And to a broader definition of diversity that includes more women and more LGBQT members and participants.

Changing Perceptions of Birding

To some degree, birding needs a public relations makeover. For many Americans, it suffers from a level of either "creepiness" or "nerdiness" or perhaps both. I had not fully appreciated these perceptions until I read a 2016 *Washington Post* article titled "Sorry, Birdwatchers: People Think You're Creepy."[12] It is largely based on an academic study by two Knox College researchers. Their paper, "On the Nature of Creepiness," published in the journal *New Ideas in Psychology*, attempted to gauge

Figure 12-3 Organized bird walks are one way to engage urban residents. Here, a group of the author's students participate in an annual bird walk through the University of Virginia grounds. Photo credit: Tim Beatley

through an online survey which professions, hobbies, and personal traits people find creepy. The second-creepiest hobbies were those that involved watching, including bird-watching. It may be because of the prevalence of binoculars and suspicions about where those binoculars are being aimed.

While average middle schoolers or high schoolers might not necessarily believe bird-watching to be creepy, they also aren't likely to volunteer it as a "cool" hobby. For most young people, I suspect it is not even on their radar; nevertheless, it's something they might get a lot of joy from.

One especially important point is the need to acknowledge that there are many of us (myself included) who love birds immensely, are affected by them deeply, are awestruck, and are motivated to do whatever we can to help them. Yet we would be hesitant to refer to ourselves as "birders" in that we do not, perhaps, maintain bird lists, do not observe and report bird observations via birding tools such as eBird, and may generally struggle to identify birds by sight or call. "Bird lovers" is how I would describe this quite large and growing bird constituency, and we must remember that not everyone will aspire to being a birder but can nevertheless play an important part in bird conservation and can make birds a no less important or less central part of their lives.

Avian Citizenship: Birds as Conservation Gateways

Considerable evidence shows that modest steps in ecological stewardship, such as being involved in a local tree-planting initiative, can lead to other forms of civic engagement. Dana Fisher, Erika Svendsen, and James Connolly studied the MillionTreesNYC initiative and the role that participating as a volunteer steward has on stimulating other forms of civic engagement. They scheduled a series of follow-up phone interviews with people who had been involved in tree planting, seeking to gauge whether their involvement with trees continued (it did) and in what other ways they had been democratically engaged. They concluded, "Overall, our sample shows that, other than the activities that are built into people's lives at an early age, such as voting and religious participation, environmental stewardship precedes other forms of civic engagement."[13]

There seems little doubt, and the MillionTreesNYC research demonstrates this, that there is a healthy synergy between democracy and engagement with nature of all kinds, including birding. If we care about, watch, and work on behalf of birds in our communities, we are also more likely to want to vote, show up at a public meeting, and participate in a protest march. These values are reinforcing. As Fisher, Svendsen, and Connolly said, "In the absence of structured institutional motivations, stewardship drives people to become more involved democratic citizens. As membership in groups such as religious organizations and unions continues to decline, this less structured path toward democratic citizenship is becoming ever more essential."[14]

This research also demonstrates the importance of social connectedness and networks of social connection and trust, which I believe we know to be true intuitively and through our life experiences. As the authors suggested, this is a counternarrative to observations by

Harvard University professor Robert Putnam (author of the famous book *Bowling Alone*)[15] about the phenomenon of (and worry about) a growing individualism. Volunteer tree stewards "were not disconnected individuals who bowl alone; they were digging together."[16]

While much bird-watching is an individual activity, it can often occur in groups and social settings. We can "dig together" in the collective creation of new bird habitat in cities. We can also watch together and ooh and aah together, as the appreciation of birds is something that lends itself to shared enjoyment and the building of new friendships through birding.

Many of the projects and programs profiled in this book rely heavily on volunteers. As Adam Betuel told me, Atlanta Audubon certainly falls into this category, and there is always the need for more volunteers, especially in smaller Audubon units. "We have a great pool [of volunteers]," he said; "we're doing well, but we need to grow our volunteer base." This is a wonderful opportunity to engage the larger public, to educate about birds, and also to foster a sense of the importance of contributing to something larger than ourselves. It is also true that the wonder of birds helps us to break out of our self-absorption, to celebrate a larger whole.

As mentioned several times in this book, birds offer us the chance to overcome our sense of despair. In the midst of climate change and our global extinction crisis, it is easy to slip into thinking that there is nothing meaningful to be done. The stories in this book tell otherwise. There are many things within our reach at the individual and community levels. Actions can be as simple as a homeowner changing out windows so that birds can see them or planting a habitat garden and getting it certified, an option in cities such as Portland, Oregon. But there are other things you can do within your community, including standing up for the birds that visit and migrate through your city and demanding that your city council adopt and implement bird-safe building standards.

New York Times writer Margaret Renkl pointed out that "there's a difference between doing something and doing nothing. That 'something,' small as it might seem, is not 'nothing.' The space between them is far apart, limitless stretching distances apart. It's the difference between a heartbeat and silence."[17]

Need to Think about the Bigger Conservation Picture

People must also confront the ways in which their consumption patterns and their large ecological footprints impact birds both close by and far away.

Jeff Wells of the Boreal Songbird Initiative told me, "Cities have this undue heavy influence in different ways." He posed the example of the White-throated Sparrow that you might see in your backyard, which is dependent on the boreal forest. Yet do we choose to purchase recycled paper products to support that forest and those birds we love? We may not even make the connection, unfortunately. If you choose to purchase paper towels made from virgin boreal forest, he said, "you're helping to destroy the birds you love."

Buying recycled paper products is one of the things Wells does. Purchasing products certified by the Forest Stewardship Council (FSC) more generally is a positive step. Despite concerns about the stringency of FSC certification (concerns that as applied in some countries it may allow too much logging and be too loosely enforced), he is very skeptical of the newer competing certification scheme called the Sustainable Forestry Initiative (SFI), which is backed by the forest industry and, he believes, is less rigorous. The SFI has been reaching out and enlisting support from the birding organizations, something Wells is quite critical of.

Many bird conservation organizations, Wells says, are too content with small acts, which are not unimportant, but there is also a need to confront larger questions about climate change and transitioning quickly to renewable energy. "They oppose wind turbines, but they say nothing about coal." Any threat a wind turbine might have for birds pales in comparison with strip mining, Wells believes, which is "destroying habitat for millions of birds."

Another essential part of the bigger picture that the birding world must address is the rampant and highly destructive forms of agriculture, especially the monocultural and highly chemical-intensive approach to food production. The startling and dramatic decline in insects globally represents one of the most pressing dangers to birdlife and suggests the need to rapidly transition to more sustainable forms of agriculture. The rapid rise in insecticides, especially friponil and neonicotinoids ("neonics"), has been especially damaging. Their water-soluble nature has meant that they have contaminated many water bodies as well as soil. Rachel Carson's warnings are even more dire and relevant today, and with crashing insect populations, there is real possibility that we will experience the silent spring she warned so passionately about.

What to do? Francisco Sánchez-Bayo, coauthor of a recent study published in *Biological Conservation* (cited in chapter 2), speaks of the need to shift agriculture away from monocultures and to integrate trees and habitat that insects will need. Eliminating the use of insecticides seems an essential step, he says, as does shifting to the techniques of integrated pest management (IPM). "If we took the time to educate farmers and put sensible practices into place to produce food without dependence on chemicals, the whole thing would change overnight."[18] There are serious political challenges here, of course, and a strong pesticide industry and corporate agriculture interests that will resist change, often with well-funded campaigns. But to save birdlife, we must begin to see the connections to how we grow food and what we purchase in the grocery store.

Cities that care about birds will need to increasingly think about the actions and policies they can take to advance global biodiversity conservation. How can cities show global leadership?

Working to reduce the size of their ecological footprints and the extent of their global resource demands would be good steps. Many cities are taking steps to divest from fossil fuels—New York City, for example, is taking steps to divest its pension funds from fossil fuel companies.[19] Cities of the global North especially can assume leadership roles in expanding protected areas and in advancing global conservation visions, such as Half-Earth, the idea of setting aside at least half the area of the Earth for nature.[20] Another important step would be like-minded cities working together to sustain and protect bird species they have in common (species that because of migration depend on safe habitat in multiple cities and regions). City-to-city treaties and agreements to work together must become more common; they can be a wonderful way to leverage resources on behalf of birds and global nature more broadly.

As cities make room for birds within their city boundaries and work to rewild parks and urban landscapes, they must also look beyond their borders to ensure that sufficient habitat and movement corridors exist at regional and even continental scales. Support for innovative efforts such as the Eastern Wildway, developed and advocated by the Wildlands Network, is also key, as well as working to fit local land use policies and decisions into such larger landscape visions. The Eastern Wildway is a vision for a biologically connected network of parks and green spaces from Canada to Florida.[21] Ron Sutherland, who directs the initiative, told me this is less a blueprint for what land needs to be purchased than a map meant to inspire and to show what is possible.[22] Together, the map and vision would protect about half of the eastern United States but an even higher percentage of existing biodiversity. Largely by connecting existing national parks and other protected areas, cities could in tangible ways help to implement this vision. Cities such as Edmonton, Alberta, and San Francisco have already sought to implement strategies that advance ecological connections and connectivity (e.g., extensive use of wildlife passages in Edmonton; the Green Connections plan in San Francisco). In the future, cities will need to ensure that these important local strategies connect with, and help to advance, even largely landscape-oriented conservation efforts.

Politics and Birds: How Do Birds Become Political Constituents?

There is a need to continue to expand advocacy for birds in cities, and this could happen in many different ways. It is clear that while many in cities actively watch and enjoy birds, the numbers who actively work on behalf of birds is relatively few. We need more advocates for birds and more urban residents willing to stand up and voice support for birds and to actively work on behalf of bird-friendly urban design and urban policies.

The National Audubon Society is a major resource in many cities. John Rowden of Audubon told me that although there are some 460 chapters around the country—impressive—most of them are heavily staffed by volunteers. "About 80 percent of our chapters are completely volunteer-run," Rowden said. Chapters such as those in Portland, San Francisco, and New York, what Rowden referred to as chapters with "powerhouse staff," are relatively few.

Do politicians care about birds? Not much, I am afraid, although there is hope that with more public support, this can change. There are a few hopeful examples: former Australian prime minister Bob Hawke famously said, "Penguins Can't Vote," as part of his explanation for spearheading what became a prohibition on mining in Antarctica, a prohibition that exists to this day.[23]

We need to find more creative ways to make support for birds and bird conservation more politically palatable and to give political voice and power to birds. Obviously, this already happens through the surrogate voices of advocacy groups such as city Audubon chapters. Notable examples profiled in this book include the work of Portland Audubon and the Golden Gate Audubon Society in San Francisco. The latter, as we saw, very effectively mobilized the community of birders to support the adoption of the country's first bird-safe design standards. Portland Audubon has been similarly engaged in effective lobbying for bird-friendly standards in that city.

Might there be other ways? Can we imagine changing the very nature of our political system to acknowledge the right and need to represent all of the living things that exist within an elected official's electoral district? In other words, aren't birds constituents as well? Although they are unable to vote, they are affected by the many decisions a city council might make—from the siting of a highway (as we saw with the Burrowing Owls in Phoenix, Arizona) to the clearance of land and cutting of trees (as we saw in Western Australia) or perhaps the management of the roosts of Turkey Vultures.

Deborah Tabart, the founder and director of the Australian Koala Foundation, has sought to change the way we think about and talk about animals. She has been a tireless defender of koalas, a species that is struggling as a result of land clearance and loss of habitat to coal mines and housing projects (which equally impact bird species). "If you lose this species, you might as well say goodbye to this country," she told me.[24] It is shocking, unthinkable, really, that the koala, such an iconic species, could become extinct. But it will not be without a fight on Tabart's part. "The koala army is strengthening up," she said, describing herself as "commander in chief."

She has worked hard to highlight the amount of koala habitat and estimate the number of koalas located within different electoral zones. "Act or Axe" is how she labels this challenge to elected officials. On her website, for instance, there is a map of "Koala Numbers in Your Electorate." For the district of Luke Howarth, member of the Liberal National Party of Queensland, there are an estimated two hundred to four hundred koalas.[25] The map also shows the amount of remaining habitat and the pre-1750 koala habitat, noting that only 15 percent of the original habitat remains. Will such an electoral map make a difference? Perhaps not on its own, but it is a good strategy to begin to count the "koala constituents," giving them visibility and, through Tabart's organization, something closer to a political voice.

We should think of ways to do this with birds. They are not the only elements of the natural world that deserve representation, of course, but they are obvious and important members of our ecological community, and they in turn stand in for many other living creatures.

Another idea of Tabart's: if you use an image of a koala, such as in the sale or rental of cars or a facial care product, you should be expected to share some of the profit with them. This idea has found expression in an initiative championed by UK naturalist David Attenborough called The Lion's Share. It is a joint initiative between the United Nations Development Programme and several advertising and production companies. The goal is to generate $100 million over three years, to be invested in conservation projects. Participating companies will agree to donate 0.5 percent of any advertising campaign that utilizes an image of an animal.[26]

We use the images of birds in many commercial ways, of course. How about if every time we sent a Twitter message—which takes the bird as an icon and birdsong as its model—a small amount of money went into a global bird conservation fund? Recently, the shoe company Allbirds sold a limited edition set of its running shoes with the proceeds going to the Audubon Society. We need to find ways to elevate the political and economic commitments we make to birds and to tap into and steer some of the immense collective wealth and assets in support of bird conservation.

Caring for Non-native Birds

One issue of ongoing debate is the status of non-native bird species. Rachel Carson addressed this issue early in her career in her 1939 essay "How About Citizenship Papers for the Starling?," wondering how

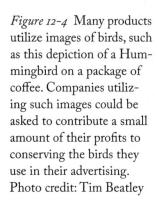

Figure 12-4 Many products utilize images of birds, such as this depiction of a Hummingbird on a package of coffee. Companies utilizing such images could be asked to contribute a small amount of their profits to conserving the birds they use in their advertising. Photo credit: Tim Beatley

long a bird must live among us before we consider it a part of our biological community.

It is not an academic question, of course. In a number of cities, non-native populations of some species, parrots especially, have become ensconced and reached a kind of beloved status among residents. One notable example are the Parrots of Telegraph Hill in San Francisco. As a result of Mark Bittner's popular book and movie, these birds have developed quite a local (and international) following.[27]

Similarly, in Southern California there are an estimated twenty species of Parrots, including several thousand Red-crowned Parrots. There are parks in Pasadena where at the end of the day they roost in a spectacular and loud way.

What is the status of such birds in our framework of bird-friendly cities?[28] They are not native, but they are present and by most accounts thriving. Professor Ursula Heise, who loves these parrots, believes that this story opens up the possibility of cities serving as "biological arks" for endangered birds and other species staging a comeback. The Red-crowned Parrot is originally from Mexico and has largely been extirpated from its original home, so it may be an especially good test case. Moreover, it eats berries and plants that are non-native, so its presence in Los Angeles does not appreciably harm native bird species. As Heise said, the Red-crowned Parrots have become "naturalized citizens in a way," in that they have been added to the state's official list of birds.[29] "The raucous calls of the Red-crowned Parrot remind us that we live in a cosmopolitan city of many different beings. A city that can be sanctuary for humans and non-humans alike."[30]

At the broadest level, how cities commit to international cooperation on behalf of birds also remains an important question. Is there room for a set of real city-to-city bird treaties that might bind cities (perhaps along a migratory route) to conservation targets or tangible actions to reduce bird mortality? The emerging Biophilic Cities Network might be one platform to instigate such cooperation, and there are other groups of cities, from ICLEI—Local Governments for Sustainability to C40 Cities. Regardless of the implementation approach, there is little doubt that we need to direct the growing political and economic clout of cities behind bird conservation, and global biodiversity conservation more generally.

A Final Note. On the Unique Moment of Time We Are in and Why Birds Are Key

As I bring this book to a close, it is appropriate to reflect candidly about the daunting tasks ahead. The release of the Cornell Lab of Ornithology's study of the remarkable loss of birds—some two billion—since 1970 was startling and deeply saddened many of us. It was a stark and gut-wrenching reminder of the extent to which our single species has so profoundly altered the collective ecosystem upon which millions of other species rely. But perhaps the shock induced by these findings can be guided and steered for good. We are clearly at a moment in time unlike any other. The actions we take, or don't take, in the next decade especially, will have profound and lasting impact on the future world, and certainly on the quality of future existence for our children and descendants.

Birds represent hope in an age of extinction and help us overcome despair. What can we possibly do to address the immense global

Figure 12-5 The return each year of Ruby-throated Hummingbirds is a source of hope, delight, and constancy in the author's life. Photo credit: Tim Beatley

problems of climate change and habitat loss? There are simple and significant things we can do by the day, hour, and minute to notice and help the birdlife around us.

We might do many things, from eating less meat to recycling, but does any of it add up to meaningful change? "What's the point? How will any of this matter?" asked *New York Times* writer Margaret Renkl, who recounted watching a nest of bluebird chicks and being concerned that for some reason the parents were missing in action.[31] She went on to observe that such concerns (about the conditions and fate of the birds around us) are within our reach in ways that larger and more distant environmental matters may not be. We may not be able to convince a distant country's leaders to protect its rain forest, but there are so many things that can be done locally that are directly within our grasp. "I can put up boxes for cavity-nesting birds and roosting boxes for bats," she concluded. "I can cultivate the host plants of butterflies, knowing that some of their caterpillars will feed baby birds. I can make my yard a haven for insects, including the red wasp, an important pollinator which is too quickly maligned. I can keep my yard free from chemicals and let the wildflowers go to seed."

The good news is that, as the stories and initiatives reviewed in this book show, there are many tangible steps we can take at both individual and collective levels. Birds can help us pivot from despair to hope and purpose. They are especially positioned to serve as sentinels of change, returning in a grander way to their role of "canaries in the coal mines."

Birds can help us be better human beings and can serve as (sometimes noisy) witnesses to what we know we are duty-bound to do. They are also the angels of our collective salvation. I know life on planet Earth would be much less interesting, joyful, and meaningful without them. Birds keep us tethered to the present moment and offer experiences of brief elation as we interact with them throughout our lives. There are innumerable ways that individual and collective actions, especially in cities, can make a huge and lasting difference. There's time, but not much—let's get to work.

Notes

Chapter 1: The Benefits of Birds in a World Shaped by Humans

1. Viscount Grey of Fallodon, *The Charm of Birds* (New York: Frederick A. Stokes, 1927), 198.

2. Grey, *Charm of Birds*.

3. Grey, *Charm of Birds*, 198.

4. Grey, *Charm of Birds*, 210.

5. Rachel Carson, "Help Your Child to Wonder," *Woman's Home Companion*, July 1956.

6. See Julian Treasure, "The 4 Ways Sound Affects Us," TED video, 5:46, recorded July 2009, https://www.ted.com/talks/julian_treasure_the_4_ways_sound_affects_us? language=en.

7. Rachel Clarke, "In Life's Last Moments, Open a Window," *New York Times*, September 8, 2018, https://www.nytimes.com/2018/09/08/opinion/sunday/nhs-hospice .html.

8. For example, see Julia Jacobs, "The Hot Duck That Won't Go Away," *New York Times*, December 3, 2018, https://www.nytimes.com/2018/12/03/nyregion/hot-duck -mandarin-central-park.html?searchResultPosition=1.

9. "Robin Causes a Stir in Beijing," BirdGuides, December 1, 2019, https://www .birdguides.com/news/robin-causes-a-stir-in-beijing/.

10. Çağan H. Şekercioğlu, Daniel G. Wenny, and Christopher J. Whelan, *Why Birds Matter: Avian Ecological Function and Ecosystem Services* (Chicago: University of Chicago Press, 2016).

11. Anil Markandya et al., "Counting the Cost of Vulture Decline: An Appraisal of the Human Health and Other Benefits of Vultures in India," *Ecological Economics* 67, no. 2 (September 15, 2008): 194–204, https://doi.org/10.1016/j.ecolecon.2008.04.020.

12. Şekercioğlu, Wenny, and Whelan, *Why Birds Matter*, viii.

13. Gustave Axelson, "Birds Put Billions into U.S. Economy: Latest U.S. Fish and Wildlife Report," Cornell Lab of Ornithology, September 19, 2018, https://www.allaboutbirds .org/news/birds-put-billions-into-u-s-economy-latest-u-s-fish-and-wildlife-report/.

14. Şekercioğlu, Wenny, and Whelan, *Why Birds Matter*, vii.

15. As Plumwood said, "Human/nature dualism conceives the human as not only superior to but as different in kind from the non-human, which is conceived as a lower non-conscious and non-communicative purely physical sphere that exists as a mere resource or instrument for the higher human one. The human essence is not the ecologically-embodied 'animal' side of self, which is best neglected, but the higher disembodied element of mind, reason, culture and soul or spirit." Val Plumwood, "Nature in the Active Voice," *Australian Humanities Review* 46 (2009), http://doi.org/10.22459 /AHR.46.2009.

16. Jeffrey Gordon, foreword to Şekercioğlu, Wenny, and Whelan, *Why Birds Matter*.

17. Jim Bonner, executive director, Audubon Society of Western Pennsylvania, interview with the author, April 22, 2019.

18. Susan Elbin, director of conservation and science, New York City Audubon, interview with the author, January 31, 2019.

19. Elbin, interview.

Chapter 2: Birds in a Changing World

1. Terry Tempest Williams, *Refuge: An Unnatural History of Family and Place* (New York: Vintage Books, 1992), 149.

2. Kenneth V. Rosenberg et al., "Decline of the North American Avifauna," *Science* 366, no. 6461 (October 4, 2019): 120–24, https://doi.org/10.1126/science.aaw1313.

3. Elizabeth Pennisi, "Three Billion North American Birds Have Vanished since 1970, Surveys Show," *Science*, September 19, 2019, https://doi.org/10.1126/science.aaz 5646.

4. BirdLife International, "State of the World's Birds: Taking the Pulse of the Planet," 2018, https://www.birdlife.org/sites/default/files/attachments/BL_Report ENG_Vꜰꜰ_spreads.pdf.

5. Caspar A. Hallmann et al., "More than 75 Percent Decline over 27 Years in Total Flying Insect Biomass in Protected Areas," *PLoS ONE* 12, no. 10 (October 2017): e0185809, https://journals.plos.org/plosone/article?id=10.1371/journal.pone.0185809.

6. Bradford C. Lister and Andres Garcia, "Climate-Driven Declines in Arthropod Abundance Restructure a Rainforest Food Web," *Proceedings of the National Academy of Sciences* 115, no. 44 (October 2018): E10397–405, https://doi.org/10.1073/pnas.1722477115.

7. Francisco Sánchez-Bayo and Kris A. G. Wyckhuys, "Worldwide Decline of the Entomofauna: A Review of Its Drivers," *Biological Conservation* 232 (April 2019): 22, https://doi.org/10.1016/j.biocon.2019.01.020.

8. Michael DiBartolomeis et al., "An Assessment of Acute Insecticide Toxicity Loading (AITL) of Chemical Pesticides Used on Agricultural Land in the United States," *PLoS ONE* 14, no. 8 (August 6, 2019): e0220029, https://doi.org/10.1371/jour nal.pone.0220029; the authors found a forty-eight-fold increase for oral contact and a fourfold increase for contact toxicity between 1992 and 2014.

9. Center for Food Safety, "Hidden Costs of Toxic Seed Coatings: Insecticide Use on the Rise," Fact Sheet, June 2015, https://www.centerforfoodsafety.org/files/neonic -factsheet_75083.pdf.

10. Avalon C. S. Owens et al., "Light Pollution Is a Driver of Insect Declines," *Biological Conservation* 241 (August 2019): 108259, https://doi.org/10.1016/j .biocon.2019.108259.

11. Douglas Tallamy, interview with the author, March 13, 2020.

12. Scott R. Loss, Tom Will, and Peter P. Marra, "Estimation of Bird-Vehicle Collision Mortality on U.S. Roads," *Journal of Wildlife Management* 78, no. 5 (July 2014): 763–71, https://doi.org/10.1002/jwmg.721.

13. National Audubon Society, "Audubon's Birds and Climate Change Report," 2017, http://climate.audubon.org/.

14. Boreal Songbird Initiative, "Conserving North America's Bird Nursery in

the Face of Climate Change," 2018, https://www.borealbirds.org/sites/default/files/publications/report-boreal-birds-climate.pdf.

15. Interview with Jeff Wells, Boreal Songbird Initiative, February 27, 2019.

16. Boreal Songbird Initiative, "Conserving North America's Bird Nursery."

17. National Audubon Society, "Survival by Degrees: 389 Bird Species on the Brink," 2019, https://www.audubon.org/climate/survivalbydegrees.

18. Brad Plumer, "These State Birds May Be Forced Out of Their States as the World Warms," *New York Times*, October 10, 2019, https://www.nytimes.com/2019/10/10/climate/state-birds-climate-change.html.

19. Boreal Songbird Initiative, "Conserving North America's Bird Nursery," 5.

20. Eric A. Riddell et al., "Cooling Requirements Fueled the Collapse of a Desert Bird Community from Climate Change," *Proceedings of the National Academy of Sciences* 116, no. 43 (October 22, 2019): 21609–15, https://doi.org/10.1073/pnas.1908791116.

21. Robert Sanders, "Collapse of Desert Birds Due to Heat Stress from Climate Change," Berkeley News, September 30, 2019, https://news.berkeley.edu/2019/09/30/collapse-of-desert-birds-due-to-heat-stress-from-climate-change/.

22. Jonathan L. Bamber et al., "Ice Sheet Contributions to Future Sea-Level Rise from Structured Expert Judgment," *Proceedings of the National Academy of Sciences* 116, no. 23 (2019): 11195–1200, https://dx.doi.org/10.1073%2Fpnas.1817205116.

Chapter 3: Protecting the Birds around Us: How Cities Such as Portland Are Nurturing Unlikely Alliances of Bird and Cat Lovers

1. Kyo Maclear, *Birds Art Life Death: The Art of Noticing the Small and Significant* (London: 4th Estate Books, 2017), 127.

2. Heidy Kikillus et al., "Cat Tracker New Zealand: Understanding Pet Cats through Citizen Science," Public Report (Wellington, New Zealand: Victoria University of Wellington, November 2017), http://cattracker.nz/wp-content/uploads/2017/12/Cat-Tracker-New-Zealand_report_Dec2017.pdf.

3. Scott R. Loss, Tom Will, and Peter P. Marra, "The Impact of Free-Ranging Domestic Cats on Wildlife of the United States," *Nature Communications* 4, no. 1396 (January 29, 2013): 2, https://doi.org/10.1038/ncomms2380.

4. See *Catio Tour, Portland, Oregon*, https://www.youtube.com/watch?time_continue=22&v=TMlvtZnYrcw&feature=emb_logo.

5. Kikillus et al., "Cat Tracker," 20.

6. Kikillus et al., "Cat Tracker," 20.

7. Kurt Knebusch, "Feral Cats Avoid Urban Coyotes, Are Surprisingly Healthy," Ohio State University College of Food, Agricultural, and Environmental Sciences, November 14, 2013, https://cfaes.osu.edu/news/articles/feral-cats-avoid-urban-coyotes-are-surprisingly-healthy.

8. Catherine M. Hall et al., "Assessing the Effectiveness of the Birdsbesafe Antipredation Collar Cover in Reducing Predation on Wildlife by Pet Cats in Western Australia," *Applied Animal Behaviour Science* 173 (December 2015): 40–51, https://doi.org/10.1016/j.applanim.2015.01.004.

9. Cat Goods, "Frequent Answered Questions," https://catgoods.com/faq/.

10. Murdoch University, "Protecting Wildlife from Cats," n.d., accessed June 11, 2020, http://www.murdoch.edu.au/News/Protecting-wildlife-from-cats/.

11. ACCT Philly, "ACCT Philly Community Cat Program," n.d., accessed June 11, 2020, http://www.acctphilly.org/programs/community-cats/.

12. For example, there is the case of Newburyport, Massachusetts, where over time and through attrition a feral cat colony essentially disappeared. See Daniel D. Spehar and Peter J. Wolf, "An Examination of an Iconic Trap-Neuter-Return Program: The Newburyport, Massachusetts Case Study," *Animals* 7, no. 11 (November 2017): 81, https://dx.doi.org/10.3390/ani7110081.

13. R. J. Kilgour et al., "Estimating Free-Roaming Cat Populations and the Effects of One Year Trap-Neuter-Return Management Effort in a Highly Urban Area," *Urban Ecosystems* 20 (2017): 207–16, https://doi.org/10.1007/s11252-016-0583-8.

14. I have written about several koala-friendly communities in Queensland and New South Wales, Australia, where cats and dogs are prohibited entirely. See Timothy Beatley and Peter Newman, *Green Urbanism Down Under: Learning from Sustainable Communities in Australia* (Washington, DC: Island Press, 2009).

15. Charles Daugherty, professor of ecology, Victoria University, video interview in *Wellington: A Biophilic City*, https://www.youtube.com/watch?v=7HqCfyjstyo.

16. Tim Park, presentation to the Biophilic Cities Network, October 2018.

17. Daugherty, video interview.

18. Wild Bird Fund, "About Us: Location and Hours," https://www.wildbirdfund.org/about-us/location/.

19. Wild Bird Fund, "Humane Education," https://www.wildbirdfund.org/education/.

20. Meryl Greenblatt, "Rita McMahon: Rehabilitating Injured Birds in New York City," *Urban Audubon* 38, no. 3 (Fall 2017): 6, http://www.nycaudubon.org/images/UA_Fall_2017_UA_final_reduced.pdf.

Chapter 4: Returning Home: Inspiring Work from London to Pittsburgh to Make Space for Migrating Swifts

1. From Anne Stevenson, "Swifts." The full poem can be found here: https://www.poetryfoundation.org/poems/49866/swifts-56d22c67c55eb.

2. Kyo Maclear, *Birds Art Life Death: The Art of Noticing the Small and Significant* (London: 4th Estate Books, 2017), 132.

3. Caroline Van Hemert, "Birds and Humans Can't Resist Zugunruhe—the Urge to Be Gone," *Los Angeles Times*, March 10, 2019, https://www.latimes.com/opinion/op-ed/la-oe-van-hemert-migration-birds-spring-20190310-story.html.

4. National Audubon Society, "Arctic Tern: *Sterna paradisaea*," n.d., accessed June 11, 2020, https://www.audubon.org/field-guide/bird/arctic-tern.

5. Christina Holvey, "Record-Breaking Arctic Tern Migration Secrets Revealed," BBC Earth, June 7, 2016, http://www.bbc.com/earth/story/20160603-mystery-migration-solved.

6. Van Hemert, "Birds and Humans."

7. Helen Glenny, "Humans May Have an Ancient Ability to Sense Magnetic Fields," *Science Focus*, March 23, 2019, https://www.sciencefocus.com/news/humans-may-have-an-ancient-ability-to-sense-magnetic-fields/.

8. Including "inert moth caterpillars" from the needles of pine trees.

9. Val Cunningham, "Birding: Golden-Crowned Kinglets Are Little Kings of the Forest," *Minneapolis Star Tribune*, January 27, 2015, https://www.startribune.com/birding-golden-crowned-kinglets-are-little-kings-of-the-forest/289846351/.

10. "RSPB Helps Develop Brick That Gives Swifts a Home," *Construction Index*, August 16, 2018, https://www.theconstructionindex.co.uk/news/view/rspb-helps-develop-brick-that-gives-swifts-a-home.

11. Sarah Knapton, "Welcome to Kingsbrook, Britain's Most Wildlife-Friendly Housing Development," *Telegraph* (London), November 12, 2017, https://www.telegraph.co.uk/science/2017/11/12/welcome-kingsbrook-britains-wildlife-friendly-housing-development/.

12. Several boroughs in London are now including Swift policies in their plans and codes. The City of London's Draft City Plan 2036, for example, contains provisions aimed at conserving biodiversity including Swifts and other birds: "6.6.26. Measures to enhance biodiversity should address the need to provide habitats that benefit the City's target species (house sparrows, peregrine falcons, swifts, black redstarts, bats, bumblebees and stag beetles) and by extension a wider range of insects and birds."

13. Adrian Thomas and Paul Stephen, Royal Society for the Protection of Birds, interview with the author at the offices of Kingsbrook, June 10, 2019.

14. Ketley Brick, "Walthamstow Wetlands," https://www.ketley-brick.co.uk/Walthamstow_Wetlands.html.

15. The Convention on Wetlands of International Importance; see The Ramsar Convention Secretariat, "The Ramsar Convention: What's It All About?," Fact Sheet 6, https://www.ramsar.org/sites/default/files/fs_6_ramsar_convention.pdf.

16. The short documentary that resulted can be found here: https://vimeo.com/311286706.

17. Although on the night we visited and watched, it was estimated that around four thousand Swifts roosted.

18. Nikki Belmonte, executive director, Atlanta Audubon Society, interview with the author, April 11, 2019.

19. Jim Bonner, executive director, Audubon Society of Western Pennsylvania, interview with the author, April 22, 2019.

Chapter 5: Replacing Habitats Lost: The Story of the Burrowing Owls of Phoenix and Efforts at Urban Relocation

1. Monica Gokey, "Burrowing Owls: Howdy Birds," BirdNote, July 2019, https://www.birdnote.org/show/burrowing-owls-howdy-birds.

2. Clark Rushing, telephone interview with the author, March 29, 2019.

3. Norman L. Christensen and William H. Schlesinger, "N.C. Forests Are Under Assault: Gov. Cooper Should Help," *Charlotte (NC) Observer*, November 14, 2017, https://www.charlotteobserver.com/opinion/op-ed/article184561713.html. Ironically, it seems that any renewable energy benefits from the pellets may be vitiated by the energy costs associated with transport of the pellets to Europe, where they are burned: "Biomass cannot be transported more than a short distance before the energy it contains is equivalent to the energy needed to haul it."

4. See Elizabeth Ouzts, "In North Carolina, Wood Pellet Foes See Opportunity in Cooper's Climate Order," Energy News Network, January 2, 2019, https://energynews.us/2019/01/02/southeast/in-north-carolina-wood-pellet-foes-see-opportunity-in-coopers-climate-order/.

5. Clark S. Rushing, Thomas B. Ryder, and Peter P. Marra, "Quantifying Drivers of Population Dynamics for a Migratory Bird throughout the Annual Cycle," *Proceedings*

of the Royal Society B: Biological Sciences 283, no. 1823 (January 27, 2016), https://doi .org/10.1098/rspb.2015.2846.

6. Anjali Mahendra and Karen C. Seto, "Upward and Outward Growth: Managing Urban Expansion for More Equitable Cities in the Global South," World Resources Institute Working Paper, 2019, https://wriorg.s3.amazonaws.com/s3fs-public/upward -outward-growth_2.pdf.

7. Bruno Oberle et al., "Summary for Policymakers: Global Resources Outlook 2019; Natural Resources for the Future We Want," International Resource Panel, United Nations Environment Programme, 2019, https://wedocs.unep.org/bitstream /handle/20.500.11822/27518/GRO_2019_SPM_EN.pdf?sequence=1&isAllowed=y.

8. From 88 billion metric tons in 2015 to 190 billion in 2019.

9. Jennifer Skene and Shelley Vinyard, "The Issue with Tissue: How Americans Are Flushing Forests Down the Toilet," Natural Resources Defense Council, February 2019, https://www.nrdc.org/sites/default/files/issue-tissue-how-americans-are -flushing-forests-down-toilet-report.pdf.

10. Scott Weidensaul, "Losing Ground: What's behind the Worldwide Decline of Shorebirds?," Cornell Lab of Ornithology, September 19, 2018, https://www.allabou tbirds.org/news/losing-ground-whats-behind-the-worldwide-decline-of-shorebirds/.

11. See David Hasemyer, "Plan for Fracking's Waste Pits Could Save Millions of Birds," InsideClimate News, June 15, 2015, https://insideclimatenews.org/news /09062015/fracking-gas-drilling-waste-pits-could-save-millions-birds-hydraulic -fracturing-audobon-society.

12. Elizabeth Shogren, "Killing Migratory Birds, Even Unintentionally, Has Been a Crime for Decades. Not Anymore," *Reveal*, April 8, 2019, https://www.revealnews.org /article/killing-migratory-birds-even-unintentionally-has-been-a-crime-for-d ecades-not-anymore/.

13. Liz Teitz, "Deemed an Aircraft Hazard, Egrets on San Antonio Urban Lake Will Be Asked to Leave," *San Antonio Express-News*, February 11, 2019, https://www .expressnews.com/news/local/article/Deemed-an-aircraft-hazard-egrets-on-San -Antonio-13602818.php#photo-14721529.

14. Nikki Belmonte, video interview at Piedmont Park, Atlanta, Georgia, April 10, 2019.

15. *Burrowing Owls: Building Habitat in Phoenix, AZ*, https://www.biophiliccities .org/burrowing-owls-film.

16. Cathy Wise, Audubon Arizona, interview with the author at the Rio Salado Habitat Restoration Area, Phoenix, Arizona, March 8, 2019.

17. And a recent experimental study shows they can take advantage of alarm calls of Southern Lapwings; see Matilde Cavalli et al., "Burrowing Owls Eavesdrop on Southern Lapwings' Alarm Calls to Enhance Their Antipredatory Behaviour," *Behavioural Processes* 157 (December 2018): 199–203, https://doi.org/10.1016/j.beproc.2018.10.002.

18. Greg Clark, interview with the author and site visit, Wild At Heart, Phoenix, Arizona, March 8, 2019.

19. Matthew P. Rowe, Richard G. Coss, and Donald H. Owings, "Rattlesnake Rattles and Burrowing Owl Hisses: A Case of Acoustic Batesian Mimicry," *Ethology* 72, no. 1 (January–December 1986): 53–71, https://doi.org/10.1111/j.1439-0310.1986 .tb00605.x.

20. Florida Fish and Wildlife Conservation Commission, "A Species Action Plan

for the Florida Burrowing Owl, *Athene cunicularia floridana*," Final Draft, November 1, 2013, https://myfwc.com/media/2113/burrowing-owl-species-action-plan-final-draft .pdf.

21. Florida Fish and Wildlife Conservation Commission, "Species Conservation Measures and Permitting Guidelines: Florida Burrowing Owl, *Athene cunicularia floridana*," 2018, https://myfwc.com/media/2028/floridaburrowingowlguidelines-2018.pdf.

Chapter 6: Vertical Bird City: Singapore, Hornbills, and Beyond

1. Rachel L. Carson, *The Sense of Wonder: A Celebration of Nature for Parents and Children* (New York: HarperCollins, 1956), 74.

2. Shayna Toh, "Visiting Pair of Hornbills Thrill Condo Residents," *Straits Times* (Singapore), August 25, 2017, https://www.straitstimes.com/singapore/environment /visiting-pair-of-hornbills-thrill-condo-residents.

3. Marc Cremades and Ng Soon Chye, *Hornbills in the City: A Conservation Approach to Hornbill Study in Singapore* (Singapore: National Parks Board, 2012), 85.

4. Cremades and Chye, *Hornbills in the City*, 205.

5. Neo Chai Chin, "The Big Read: Gynaecologist Goes from Observing Sea Life to Watching Birds," *Today* (Singapore), June 17, 2016, https://www.todayonline.com /singapore/big-read-gynaecologist-goes-observing-sea-life-then-skies.

6. Anuj Jain, "Final Report: OASIA Downtown Biodiversity and Social Audit," BioSEA, April 18, 2018.

7. Boeri Studio, Milan, "Vertical Forest," project description, accessed March 2019, https://www.stefanoboeriarchitetti.net/en/project/vertical-forest/.

8. Richard N. Belcher et al., "Birds Use of Vegetated and Non-vegetated High-Density Buildings—a Case Study of Milan," *Journal of Urban Ecology* 4, no. 1 (July 2018), https://doi.org/10.1093/jue/juy001.

9. For more detail about this project, see Tim Beatley, "Designers Walk: Toronto's New Forest in the Sky," *Biophilic Cities Journal* 3, no. 1 (November 2019): 23–25, https://static1.squarespace.com/static/5bbd32d6e66669016a6af7e2/t/5de9260c18cc940f eec96695/1575560721367/BCJ+V3+IS1_Designers+Walk.pdf.

10. Brian Brisbin, interview with the author, July 2019.

Chapter 7: Bird Appreciation: Changing Perceptions of Urban Birds

1. Katie Fallon, *Vulture: The Private Life of an Unloved Bird* (Lebanon, NH: ForeEdge, an imprint of University Press of New England, 2017), 1–2.

2. Daniel T. C. Cox and Kevin J. Gaston, "Urban Bird Feeding: Connecting People with Nature," *PLoS ONE* 11, no. 7 (2016): e0158717, https://doi.org/10.1371/journal .pone.0158717.

3. Chinmoy Sarkar, Chris Webster, and John Gallacher, "Residential Greenness and Prevalence of Major Depressive Disorders: A Cross-Sectional, Observational, Associational Study of 94,879 Adult UK Biobank Participants," *Lancet* 2, no. 4 (April 2018): E162–73, https://doi.org/10.1016/S2542-5196(18)30051-2.

4. Joe Harkness, *Bird Therapy* (London: Unbound, 2019).

5. Harkness, *Bird Therapy*, 247.

6. Severin Carrell, "Scottish GPs to Begin Prescribing Rambling and Birdwatching," *Guardian*, October 4, 2018, https://www.theguardian.com/uk-news/2018/oct/05 /scottish-gps-nhs-begin-prescribing-rambling-birdwatching.

7. Daniel T. C. Cox et al., "Doses of Neighborhood Nature: The Benefits for Mental Health of Living with Nature," *BioScience* 67, no. 2 (February 2017): 147–55, https://doi.org/10.1093/biosci/biw173.

8. Nikkie West, interview with the author, 2019.

9. Desirée L. Narango, Douglas W. Tallamy, and Peter P. Marra, "Nonnative Plants Reduce Population Growth of an Insectivorous Bird," *Proceedings of the National Academy of Sciences* 115, no. 45 (2018): 11549–54, https://doi.org/10.1073/pnas.1809259115.

10. For an excellent review of the history of the American lawn and the forces that helped to bring it about, see David Botti, "The Great American Lawn: How the Dream Was Manufactured," video, *New York Times*, August 9, 2019, https://www.nytimes.com/video/us/100000006542254/climate-change-lawns.html.

11. City of Vancouver, British Columbia, "Pacific Great Blue Herons Return to Stanley Park for 19th Year," March 20, 2019, https://vancouver.ca/news-calendar/pacific-great-blue-herons-return-to-stanley-park-for-19th-year.aspx.

12. Jim Bonner, interview with the author, April 22, 2019.

13. City of Moraine, Ohio, "The City of Moraine Historical Markers Map," n.d., http://ci.moraine.oh.us/pdf/Historical%20Markers%20Flyer.pdf.

14. Fallon, *Vulture.*

15. OhioTraveler.com, "Hinckley Buzzard Sunday," n.d., https://www.ohiotraveler.com/hinckley-buzzard-sunday/.

16. Hinckley Township, Medina County, Ohio, http://www.hinckleytwp.org/.

17. This interview and much of the content about the Lima Vultures was included in an "Ever Green" column in *Planning* magazine, November 2016.

18. The numbers of three Indian species of Vultures were reduced from an estimated 40 million in India in the 1990s to only tens of thousands by 2007. "In just over a decade, they were gone, their numbers plummeting to near extinction." Prerna Singh Bindra, "With India's Vulture Population at Death's Door, a Human Health Crisis May Not Be Far Off," Scroll.in, February 13, 2018.

19. Staff of Green Balkans, interview with the author, April 18, 2019.

20. Maureen Murray, "Anticoagulant Rodenticide Exposure and Toxicosis in Four Species of Birds of Prey in Massachusetts, USA, 2012–2016, in Relation to Use of Rodenticides by Pest Management Professionals," *Ecotoxicology* 26 (October 2017): 1041–50, https://doi.org/10.1007/s10646-017-1832-1.

21. GrrlScientist, "Rat Poison Is Killing San Francisco's Parrots of Telegraph Hill," *Forbes*, March 27, 2019, https://www.forbes.com/sites/grrlscientist/2019/03/27/rat-poison-is-killing-san-franciscos-parrots-of-telegraph-hill/#29116d8f48e6.

22. For example, see Laurel E. K. Serieys et al., "Widespread Anticoagulant Poison Exposure in Predators in a Rapidly Growing South African City," *Science of the Total Environment* 666 (May 20, 2019): 581–90, https://doi.org/10.1016/j.scitotenv.2019.02.122.

23. American Bird Conservancy, "New Study: Over Two-Thirds of Fatalities of Endangered California Condors Caused by Lead Poisoning," February 8, 2012, https://abcbirds.org/article/new-study-over-two-thirds-of-fatalities-of-endangered-california-condors-caused-by-lead-poisoning/.

24. Rumiyana Surcheva and Ivelin Ivanov, project manager for Bright Future for the Black Vulture, Green Balkans, interviews with the author, April 18, 2019.

25. Green Balkans, "Yet Another Egyptian Vulture Pair Have a Second Egg in the Green Balkans Wildlife Rehabilitation and Breeding Centre!," May 3, 2019, https://

greenbalkans.org/en/Yet_another_Egyptian_Vulture_pair_have_a_second_egg_in
_the_Green_Balkans_Wildlife_Rehabilitation_and_Breeding_Centre_-p7072-y2019.

26. See Michael Woodbridge and Scott Flaherty, "California Condors: A Recovery Success Story Faces New Challenges," US Fish and Wildlife Service Endangered Species Program, 2012, https://www.fws.gov/endangered/map/ESA_success_stories/CA/CA_story1/index.html; Reis Thebault, "The Largest Bird in North America Was Nearly Wiped Out. Here's How It Fought Its Way Back," *Washington Post*, July 22, 2019, https://www.washingtonpost.com/science/2019/07/23/california-condor-hatchlings-hit-conservation-milestone/.

27. Jeremy Bowen, "A Bulgarian Vulture's Odyssey into Yemeni War Zone," BBC News, April 18, 2019, https://www.bbc.com/news/world-middle-east-47974725.

28. Kate St. John, "Gifts from Crows," *Outside My Window* (blog), February 15, 2019, https://www.birdsoutsidemywindow.org/2019/02/15/gifts-from-crows/.

29. Katie Sewall, "The Girl Who Gets Gifts from Birds," BBC News, February 25, 2015, https://www.bbc.com/news/magazine-31604026.

30. John Marzluff and Tony Angell, *Gifts of the Crow: How Perception, Emotion, and Thought Allow Smart Birds to Behave Like Humans* (New York: Atria, 2012), 138.

31. Can Kabadayi and Mathias Osvath, "Ravens Parallel Great Apes in Flexible Planning for Tool-Use and Bartering," *Science* 357, no. 6347 (July 14, 2017): 202–4, https://doi.org/10.1126/science.aam8138.

32. Michael Roggenbuck et al., "The Microbiome of New World Vultures," *Nature Communications*, November 25, 2014, https://www.nature.com/articles/ncomms6498.

33. Pileated Woodpeckers are described as "keystone habitat modifiers" in Keith B. Aubrey and Catherine M. Raley, "The Pileated Woodpecker as a Keystone Habitat Modifier in the Pacific Northwest," 2002, USDA Forest Service General Technical Report PSW-GTR-181, https://www.fs.fed.us/psw/publications/documents/gtr-181/023_AubryRaley.pdf.

Chapter 8: Design for Safe Passage: Cities Such as San Francisco Lead the Way with Bird-Safe Buildings and Design

1. Terry Tempest Williams, *When Women Were Birds: Fifty-Four Variations on Voice* (New York: Picador, 2013), 225.

2. Bulgarian Society for the Protection of Birds, "Egyptian Vulture," http://bspb.org/en/threatened-species/egyptian-vulture.html.

3. Scott R. Loss et al., "Bird-Building Collisions in the United States: Estimates of Annual Mortality and Species Vulnerability," *Condor* 116, no. 1 (2014): 8–23, https://doi.org/10.1650/CONDOR-13-090.1.

4. Daniel Klem Jr., "Bird-Window Collisions: A Critical Animal Welfare and Conservation Issue," *Journal of Applied Animal Welfare Science* 18, no. sup1 (October 2015): S11–S17, http://dx.doi.org/10.1080/10888705.2015.1075832.

5. Daniel Klem, interview with the author, March 29, 2019.

6. Michael Mesure, telephone interview with the author, March 21, 2019.

7. Kathleen Clark and Ben Wurst, "Peregrine Falcon Research and Management Program in New Jersey, 2018," New Jersey Department of Environmental Protection, Division of Fish and Wildlife, https://www.nj.gov/dep/fgw/ensp/pdf/pefa18_report.pdf.

8. David Perlman, "Exploratorium Sets 'Net-Zero' Energy Goal," *San Francisco*

Chronicle, April 9, 2013, https://www.sfchronicle.com/science/article/Exploratorium
-sets-Net-Zero-energy-goal-4422432.php.

9. See San Francisco Planning Department, "Standards for Bird-Safe Buildings,"
adopted July 14, 2011, https://sfplanning.org/sites/default/files/documents/reports
/bird_safe_bldgs/Standards%20for%20Bird%20Safe%20Buildings%20-%2011-30-11
.pdf.

10. San Francisco Planning Department, "Standards for Bird-Safe Buildings," 32.

11. Moe Flannery, interview with the author, March 13, 2019.

12. Logan Q. Kahle, Maureen E. Flannery, and John P. Dumbacher, "Bird-Window
Collisions at a West-Coast Urban Park Museum: Analyses of Bird Biology and Window Attributes from Golden Gate Park, San Francisco," *PLoS ONE* 11, no. 1 (January
5, 2016): e0144600, https://doi.org/10.1371/journal.pone.0144600.

13. "Mira," https://studiogang.com/project/mira.

14. Sam Lubell, "Vikings Stadium: Reflector of Light, Murderer of Birds,"
Wired, March 10, 2017, https://www.wired.com/2017/03/vikings-stadium-reflector
-light-murderer-birds/.

15. American Bird Conservancy, "World's First Bird-Friendly Arena Opens," *Bird-
Watching*, January 8, 2019, https://www.birdwatchingdaily.com/news/conservation
/worlds-first-bird-friendly-arena-opens/.

16. Susan Bence, "The World's Dangerous for Birds—Fiserv Forum Makes It a Little Safer," WUWM, January 16, 2019, https://www.wuwm.com/post/worlds-dangerous
-birds-fiserv-forum-makes-it-little-safer#stream/0.

17. See Kyle G. Horton et al., "Bright Lights in the Big Cities: Migratory Birds'
Exposure to Artificial Light," *Frontiers in Ecology and the Environment* 17, no. 4 (May
2019): 209–14, https://doi.org/10.1002/fee.2029.

18. Lewis Lazare, "Flaws in Design of Apple Store in Chicago Might Make It
Tough to Sell," *Chicago Business Journal*, May 21, 2018, https://www.bizjournals.com
/chicago/news/2018/03/21/flaws-in-design-of-apple-store-in-chicago.html.

19. Blair Kamin, "New Apple Store to Dim Lights at Night after Group Says Birds
Are Flying into Its Glass," *Chicago Tribune*, October 30, 2017, https://www.chicagotri
bune.com/news/breaking/ct-met-apple-store-and-birds-1027-story.html.

20. Judy Pollock, president, Chicago Audubon Society, interview with the author,
April 2019.

21. See City of Chicago, "Chicago Sustainable Development Policy," updated January 2017, https://www.chicago.gov/city/en/depts/dcd/supp_info/sustainable_develop
ment/chicago-sustainable-development-policy-update.html.

22. It is not clear how the city will strengthen and give priority to birds in the existing Sustainable Development Policy. Judy Pollock told me she holds some hope that
they will be able to somehow make bird-safe design mandatory, but this all remains to
be seen. She is encouraged that the city has asked her group, Bird Friendly Chicago,
to help write the provisions that will be added to the policy.

23. Lisa W. Foderaro, "Renovation at Javits Center Alleviates Hazard for Manhattan's Birds," *New York Times*, September 4, 2015, https://www.nytimes.com/2015/09/05
/nyregion/making-the-javits-center-less-deadly-for-birds.html.

24. Caroline Spivack, "Bird-Friendly Buildings Bill Takes Flight in City Council,"
Curbed New York, December 10, 2019, https://ny.curbed.com/2019/12/10/21005140
/bird-friendly-buildings-bill-passes-city-council.

25. Chip DeGrace, interview with the author, site visit at Interface headquarters, Atlanta, Georgia, April 10, 2019.

26. Snøhetta, "Ryerson University Student Learning Centre," https://snohetta .com/project/250-ryerson-university-student-learning-centre.

27. Acopian BirdSavers, https://www.birdsavers.com/acopian-birdsavers-faq-fre quently-asked-questions.html.

28. J. K. Garrett, P. F. Donald, and K. J. Gaston, "Skyglow Extends into the World's Key Biodiversity Areas," *Animal Conservation* (July 2018): 153–59, https://doi .org/10.1111/acv.12480.

29. Adam Betuel, Atlanta Audubon, interview with the author, April 11, 2019.

30. Susan Elbin, interview with the author, January 31, 2019.

31. Kyle G. Horton et al., "Bright Lights in the Big Cities: Migratory Birds' Exposure to Artificial Light," *Frontiers in Ecology and the Environment* 17, no. 4 (May 2019): 209–14, https://doi.org/10.1002/fee.2029.

32. Benjamin M. Van Doren et al., "High-Intensity Urban Light Installation Dramatically Alters Nocturnal Bird Migration," *Proceedings of the National Academy of Sciences* 114, no. 42 (October 2, 2017): 11175–80, https://doi.org/10.1073/pnas.170857 4114.

33. Van Doren et al., "High-Intensity Urban Light."

34. Jesse Greenspan, "Making the 9/11 Memorial Lights Bird-Safe," National Audubon Society, September 11, 2015, https://www.audubon.org/news/making-911 -memorial-lights-bird-safe.

35. Javits Center, "A Year in Review: FY 2017–2018; Javits Center Annual Report," https://www.javitscenter.com/media/118901/8027_javits_annual_report_fy18_112718 _spreads-3.pdf.

36. Javits Center, "Year in Review."

37. Katie Zemtseff, "Urban Meadow Thrives on Rooftop," *(Spokane, WA) Spokesman-Review*, May 21, 2010, https://www.spokesman.com/stories/2010/may/21/urban -meadow-thrives-on-rooftop/.

38. PS 41, Greenwich Village School, "Greenroof Environmental Literacy Laboratory," https://www.ps41.org/apps/pages/index.jsp?uREC_ID=357954&type=d.

39. PS 41, "Greenroof."

40. Vicki Sando, PS 41, Manhattan, New York, interview with the author, March 5, 2019.

41. PS 41, "Greenroof."

42. PS 41, "Greenroof."

43. Dustin R. Partridge and J. Alan Clark, "Urban Green Roofs Provide Habitat for Migrating and Breeding Birds and Their Arthropod Prey," *PLoS ONE* 13, no. 8 (August 29, 2018): e0202298, https://doi.org/10.1371/journal.pone.0202298.

44. Partridge and Clark, "Urban Green Roofs."

45. Choose Chicago, "Chicago's Bird Sanctuaries," https://www.choosechicago .com/articles/parks-outdoors/chicagos-bird-sanctuaries/.

46. Scott R. Loss, Tom Will, and Peter P. Marra, "Estimation of Bird-Vehicle Collision Mortality on U.S. Roads," *Journal of Wildlife Management* 78, no. 5 (July 2014): 763–71, https://doi.org/10.1002/jwmg.721.

47. Loss, Will, and Marra, "Bird-Vehicle Collision Mortality," 769–70.

48. US Green Building Council, "Bird Collision Deterrence," https://www.usgbc.org

/credits/core-shell-existing-buildings-healthcare-new-construction-retail-nc
-schools/v2009/pc55.

Chapter 9: Birds in Ravine City: Toronto's Pioneering Work to Build Awareness and Design a Habitat City

1. Joe Harkness, *Bird Therapy* (London: Unbound, 2019).

2. Kyo Maclear, *Birds Art Life Death: The Art of Noticing the Small and Significant* (London: 4th Estate Books, 2017), 132.

3. Michael Mesure, webinar presentation to the Biophilic Cities Network, 2017.

4. Michael Mesure, interview with the author, April 2019.

5. Jenna McKnight, "Fritted Glass Creates Patterned Facade for Ryerson University Student Centre by Snøhetta," Dezeen, https://www.dezeen.com/2015/12/03/student-learning-centre-ryerson-university-toronto-snohetta-zeidler-partnership-architects-fritted-glass/.

6. Susan Krajnc, interview with the author, October 12, 2018.

7. BirdSafe, "Homes Safe for Birds," n.d., https://birdsafe.ca/homes-safe-for-birds/, produced by FLAP Canada, funded in part through LUSH Fresh Handmade Cosmetics Canada.

8. See https://birdmapper.org/.

9. City of Toronto, "Toronto's Ravine Strategy: Draft Principles and Actions" (Toronto, Ontario: City of Toronto, Parks and Environment Committee, June 2016), https://www.toronto.ca/legdocs/mmis/2016/pe/bgrd/backgroundfile-94435.pdf.

10. Toronto, "Ravine Strategy," 1.

11. Nina-Marie Lister and Cam Collyer, walking interview with the author at Evergreen Brick Works, October 11, 2018.

12. Francine Kopun, "How Toronto's Ravines Have Become Critically Ill—and How They Can Be Saved," *Toronto Star*, November 11, 2018, https://www.thestar.com/news/gta/2018/11/07/how-torontos-ravines-have-become-critically-ill-and-how-they-can-be-saved.html.

13. Joe Fiorito, "Trees Come Down on Bloor, and Condos Will Go Up," *Toronto Star*, June 19, 2013, https://www.thestar.com/news/gta/2013/06/19/trees_come_down_on_bloor_and_condos_will_go_up.html.

14. Emily Rondel, "High Park NighthawkWatch: (Not-So-Common) Common Nighthawks," High Park Nature, n.d., https://www.highparknature.org/wiki/wiki.php?n=Birds.NighthawkWatch.

15. Diana Beresford-Kroeger, *To Speak for the Trees: My Life's Journey from Ancient Celtic Wisdom to a Healing Vision of the Forest* (Toronto, Ontario: Random House Canada, 2019).

16. See https://themeadoway.ca.

17. Trevor Heywood, "Greenline: Expanding the Meadoway Treatment to Toronto's Hydro Transmission System," *Metroscapes*, May 2, 2019.

Chapter 10: Black Cockatoo Rising: The Struggle to Save Birds and Bush from a Proposed Highway

1. For the complete lyrics to Coldplay's "Fly On," see https://genius.com/Coldplay-fly-on-lyrics.

2. An earlier, shorter version of this account appeared as a blog post in *The Nature*

of Cities collective blog. Tim Beatley, "Black Cockatoo Rising: The Struggle to Save the Bushland in the City," *The Nature of Cities* (blog), August 9, 2017, https://www.th enatureofcities.com/2017/08/09/black-cockatoo-rising-struggle-save-bushland-city/.

3. Government of Western Australia, "EPA Technical Report: Carnaby's Cockatoo in Environmental Impact Assessment in the Perth and Peel Region," May 2019, https://www.epa.wa.gov.au/sites/default/files/Policies_and_Guidance/EPA%20 Technical%20Report%20Carnaby%27s%20Cockatoo%20May%202019.pdf.

4. Hugh C. Finn and Nahiid S. Stephens, "The Invisible Harm: Land Clearing Is an Issue of Animal Welfare," *Wildlife Research* 44, no. 5 (2017): 377–91, https://doi .org/10.1071/WR17018.

5. Peter Newman, email communication with the author, November 21, 2019.

6. See https://www.blackcockatoorecovery.com/.

7. Jo Manning, "500th Rehabilitated Black Cockatoo Released into the Wild," Murdoch University, April 23, 2018, https://phys.org/news/2018-04-500th-black -cockatoo-wild.html.

8. See Australian Fauna Care, "Kaarakin Black Cockatoo Rehabilitation Centre," https://www.fauna.org.au/kaarakin.html.

9. Claire Tyrrell, "Cockatoo on Song as a Dad After Being Shot," *West Australian*, December 20, 2018, https://thewest.com.au/news/animals/cockatoo-on-song-as-a -dad-after-being-shot-ng-b881055822z.

10. Trevor Paddenburg, "Endangered Red-tailed Black Cockatoos Seek Shelter in Perth," *PerthNow*, May 13, 2018, https://www.perthnow.com.au/news/wildlife/endan gered-red-tailed-black-cockatoos-seek-shelter-in-perth-ng-b88824116z. Veterinarian Simone Vitali noted that "vehicle strike is the main reason they're being injured around Perth, because the birds can be slow to take off and they tend to congregate at roadside puddles to drink."

11. Lucy Martin, "Prisoners Help Rehabilitate Black Cockatoos at Kaarakin Conservation Centre," ABC News (Australia), May 31, 2014, https://www.abc.net.au /news/2014-05-30/prison-inmates-looking-after-cockatoos/5486642.

12. And, as one prisoner noted, the visits to the center are so important to inmates that they have become a positive incentive for good behavior. Martin, "Prisoners Help."

Chapter 11: Birdicity: What Makes for a Deeply Bird-Friendly City, and How Do We Measure It?

1. The excerpt is from Emily Dickinson's poem "'Hope' is the thing with feathers."

> "Hope" is the thing with feathers—
> That perches in the soul—
> And sings the tune without the words—
> And never stops—at all—
>
> And sweetest—in the Gale—is heard—
> And sore must be the storm—
> That could abash the little Bird
> That kept so many warm—
>
> I've heard it in the chillest land—
> And on the strangest Sea—

Yet—never—in Extremity,
It asked a crumb—of me.

2. City of Vancouver, British Columbia, "Vancouver Bird Strategy," January 2015, iii, https://vancouver.ca/files/cov/vancouver-bird-strategy.pdf.

3. Alan Duncan, City of Vancouver, interview with the author, March 28, 2019.

4. City of Vancouver, British Columbia, "Words for Birds: A Creative Inquiry," https://vancouver.ca/parks-recreation-culture/words-for-birds.aspx.

5. Beth Boone, "Bird of Houston Press Release," Houston Audubon, September 24, 2019, https://houstonaudubon.org/newsroom.html/article/2019/09/24/bird-of -houston-press-release.

6. Nader Issa, "Designs Unveiled for World's First Floating 'Eco-Park' Planned for Chicago River," *Chicago Tribune*, February 7, 2019, https://chicago.suntimes.com /news/chicago-river-eco-park-floating-river-worlds-first/.

7. For more about the Wild Mile, see "Wild Mile Chicago," https://www.wildmile chicago.org/about-us.

8. "Controlled Burn of Prairie in Calvary Cemetery," *St. Louis Post-Dispatch*, December 10, 2018, https://www.stltoday.com/news/local/metro/controlled-burn-of -prairie-in-calvary-cemetery/youtube_b5561739-045d-5b38-ae47-87be62cec65b.html.

9. Laura Thompson, planner, Association of Bay Area Governments, interview with the author, July 17, 2019.

10. Melissa R. Marselle, Sara L. Warber, and Katherine N. Irvine, "Growing Resilience through Interaction with Nature: Can Group Walks in Nature Buffer the Effects of Stressful Life Events on Mental Health?," *International Journal of Environmental Research and Public Health* 16, no. 6 (March 2019): 986, https://dx.doi .org/10.3390%2Fijerph16060986.

11. One of the most important projects is the South Bay Salt Pond Restoration Project; see https://www.southbayrestoration.org/.

12. See the bill here: https://www.congress.gov/bill/116th-congress/house-bill/919 /text.

13. Designer Mitchell Joachim said, "It's essentially a vertical meadow for butterflies." See Adele Peters, "The Outside of This New Office Building Will Be a Giant Butterfly Sanctuary," Fast Company, May 16, 2019, https://www.fastcompany.com/90349805 /the-outside-of-this-new-office-building-will-be-a-giant-butterfly-sanctuary.

14. Jeff Mulhollem, "Native Forest Plants Rebound When Invasive Shrubs Are Removed," Penn State News, May 14, 2019, https://news.psu.edu/story/574315/2019/05/14 /research/native-forest-plants-rebound-when-invasive-shrubs-are-removed.

15. Jorge A. Tomasevic and John M. Marzluff, "Use of Suburban Landscapes by the Pileated Woodpecker (*Dryocopus pileatus*)," *Condor* 120, no. 4 (November 1, 2018): 727–38, https://doi.org/10.1650/CONDOR-17-171.1.

16. Doug Tallamy, interview with the author, March 13, 2020.

17. Audubon's Native Plants Database can be found here: https://www.audubon .org/native-plants.

18. For example, the city of Freiburg. See Timothy Beatley, ed., *Green Cities of Europe: Global Lessons on Green Urbanism* (Washington, DC: Island Press, 2012).

19. Kyle G. Horton et al., "Bright Lights in the Big Cities: Migratory Birds' Exposure to Artificial Light," *Frontiers in Ecology and the Environment* 17, no. 4 (May 2019): 209–14, https://doi.org/10.1002/fee.2029.

20. Texas Trees Foundation, "Urban Heat Island Management Study: Dallas 2017," https://www.texastrees.org/wp-content/uploads/2019/06/Urban-Heat-Island-Study -August-2017.pdf.

21. Carl Elefante, Colonnade Club, University of Virginia, interview with the author and Stella Tarnay, October 1, 2018.

22. Samir Shukla, "Birdsongs and Urban Planning," *Serendipityin* (blog), October 22, 2018, https://serendipityin.blog/2018/10/22/birdsongs-and-a-city/.

23. International Energy Agency, "The Future of Cooling," 2016.

24. Eleanor Ratcliffe, Birgitta Gatersleben, and Paul T. Sowden, "Bird Sounds and Their Contributions to Perceived Attention Restoration and Stress Recovery," *Journal of Environmental Psychology* 36 (December 2013): 221–28, https://doi.org/10.1016/j .jenvp.2013.08.004.

25. Disguise, "Fixed Install—2018: Flight Paths," https://www.disguise.one/en /showcases/fixed-install/flight-paths/.

26. Site visit and interviews at Aldea, New Mexico, July 6, 2019.

27. Daniel T. C. Cox and Kevin J. Gaston, "Urban Bird Feeding: Connecting People with Nature," *PLoS ONE* 11, no. 7 (2016): e0158717, 12–13, https://doi.org/10.1371/jour nal.pone.0158717.

28. For example, see National Audubon Society, "2019 Audubon Photography Awards," https://www.audubon.org/photoawards-entry.

29. See https://www.monticellobirdclub.org/bird-photography-contest/.

30. *New York Times* Editorial Board, "Public Art Takes Flight," *New York Times*, October 24, 2017, https://www.nytimes.com/2017/10/24/opinion/audubon-public-art -nyc.html.

31. "About Xavi Bou," *Ornitographies* (blog), n.d., http://www.xavibou.com/index .php/project/about navi bou/.

32. "About Xavi Bou." See also Laura Mallonee, "Mesmerizing Photos Capture the Flight Patterns of Birds," *Wired*, August 10, 2016, https://www.wired.com/2016/08 /xavi-bou-ornitographies/.

33. Miranda Brandon, "*Impact*," http://www.mirandabrandon.com/impact.html. See also Rene Ebersole, "Bird vs. Building: Portraits of Flight Gone Wrong; Minneapolis Artist Miranda Brandon Gives Victims of Bird Strikes New Life," *Audubon*, October 2015, https://www.audubon.org/magazine/september-october-2015 /bird-vs-building-portraits-flight-gone.

34. See, for instance, Bird Studies Canada, "Map-Guide to Common Birds of Vancouver," https://vancouver.ca/files/cov/map-guide-common-birds-of-vancouver.pdf.

35. Matthew Knittel, Cleveland Metroparks, interview with the author, April 17, 2019.

36. Peter Fisher, "Drones Killing Birds: What Can Be Done?," Independent Australia, May 19, 2019, https://independentaustralia.net/life/life-display/drones-killing -birds-what-can-be-done,12719.

37. Richard Louv, *Our Wild Calling: How Connecting with Animals Can Transform Our Lives—and Save Theirs* (Chapel Hill, NC: Algonquin Books, 2019), 40.

Chapter 12: Cultivating a Bird-Caring Citizenry

1. For the complete lyrics to "Make a Little Birdhouse in Your Soul," see https:// genius.com/They-might-be-giants-birdhouse-in-your-soul-lyrics.

2. Mary Elfner, interview with the author, May 10, 2019.

3. See the video *Richmond City School Students Saving the Wood Thrush*, https://vpm .org/articles/3689/join-richmond-city-school-students-in-saving-the-wood-thrush.

4. Richmond Audubon Society, "Team Warbler Project," http://www.richmond audubon.org/team-warbler-project/.

5. Atlanta Audubon also runs a teacher education program called Taking Wing, which assists teachers in using birds as a lens for teaching other subjects.

6. See International Living Future Institute, "Living Building Challenge," https:// living-future.org/lbc/.

7. eBird, "About eBird," https://ebird.org/about.

8. Richard Schuster et al., "Optimizing the Conservation of Migratory Species over Their Full Annual Cycle," *Nature Communications* 10, no. 1754 (2019), https://doi .org/10.1038/s41467-019-09723-8.

9. J. Drew Lanham, *The Home Place: Memoirs of a Colored Man's Love Affair with Nature* (Minneapolis, MN: Milkweed, 2016), 153.

10. Lanham, *Home Place*, 157.

11. Olivia Gentile, "A Feminist Revolution in Birding," Medium, April 13, 2019, https://medium.com/@oliviagentile/a-feminist-revolution-in-birding-95d81f4ab79b.

12. Karin Brulliard, "Sorry, Birdwatchers: People Think You're Creepy," *Washington Post*, April 13, 2016, https://www.washingtonpost.com/news/animalia/wp/2016/04/13 /sorry-birdwatchers-people-think-youre-creepy-according-to-this-study/.

13. Dana Fisher, Erika Svendsen, and James Connolly, *Urban Environmental Stewardship and Civic Engagement: How Planting Trees Strengthens the Roots of Democracy* (London: Routledge, 2016), 111.

14. Fisher, Svendsen, and Connolly, *Urban Environmental Stewardship*, 113.

15. Robert D. Putnam, *Bowling Alone: The Collapse and Revival of American Community* (New York: Simon and Schuster, 2001).

16. Fisher, Svendsen, and Connolly, *Urban Environmental Stewardship*, 59.

17. Margaret Renkl, "Surviving Despair in the Great Extinction," May 13, 2019, https://www.nytimes.com/2019/05/13/opinion/united-nations-extinction.html?action =click&module=Opinion&pgtype=Homepage.

18. Anna Lappé, "What the 'Insect Apocalypse' Has to Do with the Food We Eat," Civil Eats, April 17, 2019, https://civileats.com/2019/04/17/what-the-insect -apocalypse-has-to-do-with-the-food-we-eat/.

19. See Steffan Navedo-Perez, "New York City Takes 'Major Next Step' on Fossil Fuel Divestments," Chief Investment Officer, January 23, 2020, https://www.ai-cio .com/news/new-york-city-takes-major-next-step-fossil-fuel-divestments/undefined.

20. For example, see Half-Earth Project, https://www.half-earthproject.org/.

21. Wildlands Network, "Eastern Wildway," https://wildlandsnetwork.org/wild ways/eastern/.

22. Ron Sutherland, Wildlands Project, interview with the author, April 2019.

23. Antarctic and Southern Ocean Coalition, "Passing of Bob Hawke," May 16, 2019, https://www.asoc.org/explore/latest-news/1872-passing-of-bob-hawke.

24. Deborah Tabart, interview with the author, January 2018.

25. Australian Koala Foundation, "Petrie: Will He Act or Axe?," https://www.sa vethekoala.com/our-work/petrie.

26. See https://thelionssharefund.com/.

27. Mark Bittner, *The Wild Parrots of Telegraph Hill: A Love Story . . . with Wings* (New York: Broadway Books, 2005).

28. A recent study utilizing Christmas Bird Count data has concluded that there are twenty-five species of parrots breeding in twenty-three different US states. See grrlscientist, "Escaped Pet Parrots Are Now Naturalized in 23 U.S. States," *Forbes*, May 21, 2019, https://www.forbes.com/sites/grrlscientist/2019/05/21/escaped-pet-parrots -are-now-naturalized-in-23-u-s-states/#572c30b154cb.

29. From the short documentary film *Creating an 'Urban Ark' for Endangered Species in Los Angeles*, https://www.kcet.org/shows/earth-focus/creating-an-urban-ark -for-endangered-species-in-los-angeles.

30. *Urban Ark*.

31. Renkl, "Surviving Despair."

Bibliography

Ackerman, Jennifer. *The Genius of Birds*. New York: Penguin Books, 2016.

Audubon Society. "Native Plants Database," n.d. https://www.audubon.org/native -plants.

Beatley, Timothy. *Biophilic Cities: Integrating Nature into Urban Design and Planning*. Washington, DC: Island Press, 2011.

Beatley, Timothy. *Handbook of Biophilic City Planning and Design*. Washington, DC: Island Press, 2017.

Bittner, Mark. *The Wild Parrots of Telegraph Hill: A Love Story . . . with Wings*. New York: Broadway Books, 2015.

Carrell, Severin. "Scottish GPs to Begin Prescribing Rambling and Birdwatching." *Guardian*, October 4, 2018. https://www.theguardian.com/uk-news/2018/oct/05 /scottish-gps-nhs-begin-prescribing-rambling-birdwatching.

City of Toronto. "Toronto's Ravine Strategy: Draft Principles and Actions." Toronto, Ontario: City of Toronto, Parks and Environment Committee, June 16, 2016. https://www.toronto.ca/legdocs/mmis/2016/pe/bgrd/backgroundfile-94435.pdf.

Cremades, Marc, and Ng Soon Chye. *Hornbills in the City: A Conservation Approach to Hornbill Study in Singapore*. Singapore: National Parks Board, 2012.

Fallon, Katie. *Vulture: The Private Life of an Unloved Bird*. Lebanon, NH: ForeEdge, an imprint of University Press of New England, 2017.

Finn, Hugh C., and Nahiid S. Stephens. "The Invisible Harm: Land Clearing Is an Issue of Animal Welfare." *Wildlife Research* 44, no. 5 (2017): 377–91. https://doi .org/10.1071/WR17018.

Foderaro, Lisa W. "Researching Stop Signs in the Skies for Birds." *New York Times*, May 13, 2014. https://www.nytimes.com/2014/05/14/nyregion/researchers-hope -bird-friendly-glass-can-help-reduce-migration-deaths.html?emc=edit_th_20140 514&nl=todaysheadlines&nlid=66824535&_r=1.

Gunts, Edward, and James Russiello. "Richard Olcott/Ennead Architects Completes Bird-Friendly 'Integrated Science Commons' for Vassar College." *Architect's Newspaper*, May 20, 2016. https://archpaper.com/2016/05/richard-olcott-ennead-archi tects-vassar-college/#gallery-0-slide-0.

Harkness, Joe. *Bird Therapy*. London: Unbound, 2019.

Lanham, J. Drew. *The Home Place: Memoirs of a Colored Man's Love Affair with Nature*. Minneapolis, MN: Milkweed, 2016.

Lewis-Stempel, John. *Where Poppies Blow: The British Soldier, Nature, the Great War*. London: Weidenfeld & Nicolson, 2016.

Louv, Richard. *Our Wild Calling: How Connecting with Animals Can Transform Our Lives—and Save Theirs*. Chapel Hill, NC: Algonquin Books, 2019.

Marzluff, John. *Welcome to Subirdia: Sharing Our Neighborhoods with Wrens, Robins, Woodpeckers, and Other Wildlife*. New Haven, CT: Yale University Press, 2014.

Marzluff, John, and Tony Angell. *Gifts of the Crow: How Perception, Emotion, and Thought Allow Smart Birds to Behave Like Humans.* New York: Simon & Schuster, 2012.

Narango, Desirée L., Douglas W. Tallamy, and Peter P. Marra. "Nonnative Plants Reduce Population Growth of an Insectivorous Bird." *Proceedings of the National Academy of Sciences* 115, no. 45 (2018): 11549–54. https://doi.org/10.1073/pnas.1809259115.

Prum, Richard O. *The Evolution of Beauty: How Darwin's Forgotten Theory of Mate Choice Shapes the Animal World—and Us.* New York: Doubleday, 2017.

Strycker, Noah. *Birding without Borders: An Obsession, a Quest, and the Biggest Year in the World.* New York: Houghlin Mifflin Harcourt, 2017.

Strycker, Noah. *The Thing with Feathers: The Surprising Lives of Birds and What They Reveal about Being Human.* New York: Riverhead Books, 2014.

Tabb, Phillip James. *Serene Urbanism: A Biophilic Theory and Practice of Sustainable Placemaking.* London: Routledge, 2017.

Tallamy, Douglas W. *Nature's Best Hope: A New Approach to Conservation That Starts in Your Yard.* Portland, OR: Timber Press, 2019.

Viscount Grey of Fallodon. *The Charm of Birds.* New York: Frederick A. Stokes, 1927.

Wells, Jeffrey V. *Birder's Conservation Handbook: 100 North American Birds at Risk.* Princeton, NJ: Princeton University Press, 2007.

Wells, Jeffrey V. *Boreal Birds of North America: A Hemispheric View of Their Conservation Links and Significance.* Berkeley: University of California Press, 2011.